The Life and Death of
Leon Trotsky

The Life and Death of
LEON TROTSKY

VICTOR SERGE
AND
NATALIA SEDOVA TROTSKY

Translated by
ARNOLD J. POMERANS

Basic Books, Inc. Publishers

NEW YORK

THIS TRANSLATION FIRST PUBLISHED IN GREAT BRITAIN 1975
ORIGINALLY PUBLISHED IN FRANCE UNDER THE TITLE
Vie et mort de Leon Trotsky (AMIOT-DUMONT, 1951)
© 1973 BY ESTATE OF VICTOR SERGE
TRANSLATION © 1975 BY WILDWOOD HOUSE LTD, LONDON
PUBLISHED IN THE UNITED STATES BY BASIC BOOKS, INC.

LIBRARY OF CONGRESS CATALOG CARD NUMBER: 75-3759
ISBN: 0-465-03942-1

MANUFACTURED IN THE UNITED STATES OF AMERICA
75 76 77 78 79 10 9 8 7 6 5 4 3 2 1

CONTENTS

The Life and Death of
Leon Trotsky

INTRODUCTION TO THE 1973 EDITION

It was originally intended to publish this book as the *Memoirs of Natalia Ivanovna Sedova*. My father, Victor Serge, compiled it from notes taken during conversations and corrected each chapter as it was completed. The manuscript was revised by Leon Davidovich Trotsky's widow, as may be seen from her many annotations as well as the notes appended to the manuscript.

Victor Serge wanted the book to appear under Natalia Ivanovna's name, but when the manuscript was completed, a few days before his death, she insisted that it be published under his name, 'since the text makes it perfectly clear which are my own words'.

Their attitudes were dictated by both modesty and delicacy. Victor Serge felt that the book would carry more prestige and be more widely read under the signature of Trotsky's widow; Natalia Ivanovna, for her part, did not want to detract from Victor Serge's literary renown. Years later, Natalia expressed her regret to me and to those close to her that she had not put her name to the book. The work was finished in 1946. At that time, the real identity of Trotsky's assassin was not known, although the authors were not unfamiliar with the name of Ramón Mercader, as the first edition of Victor Serge's *Carnets*, published by Julliard, shows. They preferred to keep silent until his identity was fully established.

I understood from my father that had the book been entirely his own, he would have laid more stress on his own opinions, many of which did not entirely coincide with Natalia Ivanovna Sedova's.

As an example of Victor Serge's own style, I have, by way of a preface, included some lines he wrote shortly after his first visit to the house in Coyoacan in 1942.

VLADIMIR KIBALTCHICH

Mexico, 1971

1

THE OLD MAN*

To the memory of Leon Davidovich Trotsky

He was barely forty-five but we already called him the Old Man, just as we had Lenin at about the same age. 'Old Man', in popular Russian parlance, meant one grown wise in spirit, one meriting utter trust. The feeling he inspired in all those who approached him with sincerity was this: here is a man in whom thought, action and personal life are fused into one solid rock, without flaws or cracks, a man who will follow his chosen path without faltering, on whom one can rely absolutely at all times. He would not alter in essentials, he would not weaken in defeat, he would not shrink from responsibility or danger, he would not lose control even under torture. Master of circumstances, he had the self-assurance and inner pride of a simple and truly modest man. His pride stemmed from the realization that he was an instrument of history, one who did no more than was necessary for the sake of men's progress, be it from gaol, in exile, from an émigré's hotel room, on the battlefield or at the peak of power. Having proved himself early in life (he was Chairman of the first St Petersburg Soviet at the age of twenty-eight), he was self-assured enough to regard renown, government posts and the very heights of power quite dispassionately, to judge them by their fitness alone. He could be hard and implacable, like a surgeon performing a major operation. During the Civil War, he wrote that nothing was more humane in a revolution than the utmost ruthlessness. If I had to characterize him in a word, I would say that he was a doer, but one who brought to everything he did a lyrical touch. On the run in the Siberian countryside, he enthused about the snow; in the midst of the Revolution he reflected on the part played by the creative imagination in that exacting enterprise; surrounded by enemies in the

*Unpublished text by Victor Serge.

solitude of Coyoacan, he extolled those astonishing plants of Mexico, the cacti, as striking expressions of vital energy; assailed by stupidity and lies, he surprised the Dewey Commission with his theory about the birth of a new religion on the morrow of the coming revolutions, when mankind would have time to rest after the struggles which would have ushered in a new future. He was a non-believer but he was certain of the greatness of life, the nobility of man and the duty of service. He was even less capable of doubting these values than he was of believing in the old orthodoxies, those wretchedly inadequate antidotes to doubt.

His absolute conviction that he knew the truth made him impervious to argument towards the end and detracted from his scientific spirit. He was authoritarian, because in our time of barbaric struggles thought turned into action must of necessity become authoritarian. When power was within his reach in 1924 and 1925, he refused to sieze it because he felt that a socialist regime could not be run by decree. More fundamentally, no doubt, he also felt that if history demanded dirty jobs, they were best done by others, constitutionally more suited to them, and more willing to leave the verdict to posterity.

I have never known him greater, and I have never held him dearer, than I did in the shabby Leningrad and Moscow tenements where, on several occasions, I heard him speak for hours to win over a handful of factory workers, and this well after he had become one of the two unchallenged leaders of the victorious Revolution. He was still a member of the Politbureau but he knew he was about to fall from power and also, very likely, to lose his life. He thought the time had come to win hearts and consciences one by one – as had been done before, during the Tsar's rule. Thirty or forty poor people's faces would be turned towards him, listening, and I remember a woman sitting on the floor asking him questions and weighing up his answers. This was in 1927. We knew we stood a greater chance of losing than of winning. But, still, our struggle was worth-while: if we had not fought and gone under bravely, the defeat of the Revolution would have been a hundred times more disastrous.

His personality was exceptional only because he was the quintessence of the collective of which he was a part. He shared every facet of his character, spirit and outlook with the Russian revolutionary intelligentsia of the last half-century, with tens of thousands of militants, not excluding many of his opponents. Like Lenin's and many

of those whom circumstance had made less prominent or left in total
obscurity, his traits were those of several generations, developed to
a very high degree of individual perfection. These generations had
borne and formed him; they lived in him and in his own age, which –
being the product of the same historical circumstances – was indist-
inguishable from him, though everyone round him and behind him
seemed in some way his inferior. As I write this, I remember so many
names and see so many faces, and I am suddenly struck by the glaring
truth that his entire generation was destroyed because it set its sights
too high. It expected too much, and lost touch with the masses as
soon as they bartered greatness for peace and quiet.

The end of his life was played out in loneliness. He often paced
up and down in his study in Coyoacan talking to himself. (In this
he resembled Chernyshevsky, the first great thinker of the Russian
Revolution, who – on his return from the Yakutsk region after
twenty years of captivity – 'used to talk to himself while gazing at
the stars'.) A Peruvian poet brought him a poem called 'Solitude of
Solitudes' and Trotsky had it translated word for word because he
was so struck by the beauty of the title. All alone, he would engage
in discussions with Kamenev who had been shot long before; he was
often heard addressing him by name. Although he was still at the
height of his intellectual powers, what he wrote towards the end did
not approach his earlier work in quality. People often forget that
intelligence does not exist in a vacuum. What would Beethoven have
been had he been exiled among the deaf? A man's intelligence needs
to breathe. The 'Old Man's' intellectual greatness was a product of
his generation's. He needed direct contact with men of the same spiri-
tual stamp as himself, men who could understand his unspoken
thoughts and could argue on his own level. He needed a Bukharin,
a Pyatakov, a Preobrazhensky, a Rakovsky and an Ivan Smirnov;
he needed Lenin to be fully himself. Even among us, who were
younger but included such fine men as Eltsin, Solntsev, Yakovin,
Dingaelstadt and Pankratov (who can tell whether they are dead or
alive?), he could find no equal; they lacked the advantage of his ten
unique years of experience and thought. Some of his most fruitful
ideas were confined to his letters; these included nearly everything
with a bearing on his theory of the permanent revolution.

He was killed at the very moment when the world entered a new
phase of the permanent revolution by taking the senseless road of
war. He was murdered precisely because his possible return to the

land and the people of Russia, whom he loved with such extraordinary passion, posed too great a threat to its rulers. They had tried before to kill the legend of the man, an epic based wholly on truth.

Trotsky's own passion came to his murderer's aid: he allowed a stranger into his lonely study the better to speak his heart. But this man was all falsehood and perfidy. Obeying orders, he struck from behind while Leon Davidovich Trotsky was bent over a manuscript, and the ice-pick made a wound three inches deep in his skull.

Mexico   VICTOR SERGE
August 1st, 1942

PREFACE

In this book I have tried to paint the portrait of a man and to give an honest, although necessarily condensed, account of his life. If I have succeeded in this extremely difficult task, it is only because I have tried to keep to the known facts. For forty-four years – from 1896 to 1940 – Trotsky was at the centre of so many important events that much of his biography reads like a history of his time. Moreover, his intellectual energy was such that his collected works would fill something like fifty volumes. It has not been possible to enter into all the aspects or to relate all the episodes of the Russian Revolution in which he played a part; to do that, I would have had to write a complete history of fifteen years of titanic struggle. Instead, I have confined myself to Trotsky's main practical contributions and the wider pattern of his thought. I have deliberately omitted facts of minor importance and events in which his part was incidental.

This book is not meant as a critique of what Trotsky thought and accomplished, nor did I wish to sit in judgment on historical events. All I have tried to say is, 'Here is the man. This is how he was, how he thought, spoke and wrote. This is what he did. This is what happened to him.' My only concern has been historical accuracy.

I have, of course, consulted a vast number of documents, mostly in Russian, and, above all, the works of Leon Davidovich Trotsky. The unstinting help I received from Natalia Sedova-Trotsky was invaluable; her notes and recollections enabled me to fill in events of which I had no more than the most sketchy personal knowledge. Where her account reveals entirely new facts, I have reproduced it faithfully, and have distinguished it from my own text by setting it in quotation marks.

May I advise the reader anxious to obtain further information to consult the following works by Trotsky: *My Life*,[1] an autobiography completed in 1929; *The History of the Russian Revolution*,[2] which deals in minute detail with events during the decisive year 1917; *Stalin: An attempted appreciation of the man and his influence*,[3] and, finally, the *Bulletin Oppozitsii*, (*Opposition Bulletin*) published in Russian from 1929 to 1940.

Accounts of the last ten, particularly tragic, years of Trotsky's life have been fragmentary. I have therefore given an especially detailed picture of this period.

VICTOR SERGE

[1] Thornton Butterworth, London, 1930.
[2] Gollancz, London, 1932.
[3] Hollis & Carter, London, 1947.

One · Youth

I. *Childhood and family*

Leon Davidovich was born into a family of Jewish farmers, the Bronsteins, in the village of Yanovka, not far from Kherson in the Ukraine, near the Black Sea and the River Dneper. Their neighbours were German settlers; their home a low wooden house covered with thatch, a Ukrainian *khata*, enclosed by a fence covered with flowers and foliage in summer. In villages such as this, the houses are widely spaced, each in the middle of its yard, and the rhythm of life, bound to the soil and the animals, is governed strictly by the seasons. Here, the boy's days began at dawn and were filled with work until dusk and well after. The woods, the clouds, the river, the ploughing, the snow and the mud made a deep impression on him, too marked to inspire a poetic vision, but teaching him instead that rural life was harsh and inexorable.

His father, David Leontievich Bronstein, was an enterprising man and seemingly head and shoulders above his neighbours in intelligence and energy. By some thirty years of hard work, he had acquired lands, built himself a fine house, and managed to give his children a good education, but he did not become truly prosperous until the eve of the First World War and the Revolution, which was to sweep all away in its path.

When old David Leontievich had to travel to Germany to seek medical help for Anna, his wife, who was seriously ill, he happened to pass through Vienna just as his son was making his name as one of the leaders of the 1905 Revolution. The old man was tall, rather lean, determined, with a self-assured air, and immediately at home in all the Western cities he visited. Anna, who matched her husband's force of character and practical commonsense, read the papers to him, evidently pleased with her role as a woman of superior educa-

8

tion. They made a traditional and closely-knit married couple until her death in about 1912.

The Bronsteins had eight children, four of whom died in childhood. The four survivors grew up as a loving and hard-working family, the two oldest being born in time to absorb the provincial atmosphere of what seemed to be a stable Empire. Alexander Bronstein eventually became the owner of a brewery; he had nothing in common with his revolutionary younger brother and it is not known what happened to him during the Revolution. Elisabeth Bronstein married a doctor from Odessa and died in the early nineteen-twenties. Her younger sister, Olga, like Leon Davidovich, became involved with other young people who shared their progressive views. She was associated with the Social Democratic Party early on and married Leon Rosenfeld, who – under the name of Kamenev ('Man of Stone') – became one of the Bolshevik leaders. Olga never reached the political heights of her brother; she held various posts in the Soviet administrative hierarchy and for a time was in charge of the Society for Cultural Relations with Foreign Countries (V.O.K.S.). Although she did not belong to any opposition group and had been divorced from Kamenev, she perished, or lingered in captivity – no one knows where – after her brother's banishment and her former husband's execution. It is said that in 1939 she was seen in a Central Russian concentration camp for the wives and children of executed Communists. Here life or, rather, its slow destruction, proceeded under abominable conditions.

II. *Prison. Siberian exile. First marriage. Escape*

Leon Davidovich showed a passion for justice from earliest childhood. The customs of the village resulted in many minor wrongs which disgusted him so much that on one occasion they led to a quarrel with his father. When he was about ten, he was sent to a secondary school in Odessa, where he lived with the enlightened Spentzer family and made full use of their fine library. He completed his secondary studies at Nikolaev. There, at the age of nineteen, he founded the South Russian Workers' Union, together with several other young men. He had one serious clash with his own family, when he was arrested while carrying a suitcase full of subversive literature. His parents were furious, but his mother visited him at the filthy Nikolaev gaol and eventually there was a complete reconciliation.

Leon Davidovich spent some twenty months in various prisons. In 1900, he married a young member of his militant group, Alexandra Sokolovskaya, who – like him – had been sentenced to four years' exile in Siberia. The young couple were deported to Ust-Kut in Yakutia, where Alexandra had two little girls, Zenaida and Nina. During the great upsurge of the labour movement in 1902, Alexandra urged Leon Davidovich to escape to join the militant émigrés abroad. She herself could, of course, neither accompany him nor plan to join him later, because of her young children, one of whom was only four months old. Leon Davidovich accordingly fled by himself, but the deep affection and intellectual bond between him and Alexandra were to last to the end of their lives. In 1937, Alexandra, who was by then ageing and infirm but who had never concealed her unshakeable opposition to totalitarian rule, was reported to have been arrested and exiled to a lonely hamlet north of Enisey.

The years of his imprisonment and exile were years of study for Leon Davidovich and helped to mould and mature his personality. Neither gaol nor banishment was as terrible under the Tsars as it later became under Stalinist rule. Correspondence with foreign countries was both legal and simple. Publications and even clandestine literature arrived from all over the world. The exiles were reasonably free to move about and were able to engage in lively intellectual intercourse. Unlike future generations of exiles, they had no fears of being shot, and they enjoyed the active good will of a large section of the population. Finally, despite the desolation all around them, the arctic cold and the surveillance, they found it relatively easy to escape across the frontiers of Tsarist Russia with forged papers.

Leon Davidovich, from his icy village, contributed philosophical and literary articles to the Irkutsk liberal review, *Vostochnoe Obozrenie* (*Eastern Observer*), under the revealing *nom de guerre* of 'Antid Oto'. On looking through these articles, written when he was barely twenty-one, we can see that his style and outlook underwent few changes in future years. His style was ironic, his sentences succinct and devoid of embellishment. One of his articles illustrates the delight he took in playing with words. It was entitled 'Penitentialist ideas and humanist philo-prisonophy'. The young exile's reading included the Russian classics – Gogol, Herzen, Belinsky, Uspensky, Gorky, Andreev, Tolstoy – as well as Taine, Nietzsche, Ibsen, Arthur Schnitzler and Emile Zola. He found the 'dead conservatism' of Taine, 'that optimist of the past', odious, and contrasted it with the revolutionary's 'optimistic faith in the future – *"dum spiro, spero"'*. In Nietzsche's cult of pain, 'more obscure than profound', he saw the reflection of the sufferings of the lone voyager, 'a philosopher in poetry, a poet in philosophy'. To him, Nietzsche's morality was a worthless hangover from the past, and the *Übermensch* a lyrical product of a particular social system – capitalist Europe. Ibsen came in for little less censure: though he admittedly drew a convincing portrait of the stifling quality of bourgeois life, he built his hopes on an aristocracy of the spirit and, in so doing, mistook the true importance of science, showed his ignorance of sociology and advocated a sterile form of individualism. Only 'political parties, those immensely powerful forces of the present, can impel society in the right direction'. In Ibsen, 'the artist who denies holds sway over the symbolist and prophet.'

The Viennese playwright, Arthur Schnitzler, wrote, 'There is no cure for the fear of death.' Commenting on this epigram in the columns of the modest Irkutsk sheet, the young exile wrote: 'This is true only to the extent that man buries himself in the stifling dungeon of visceral and sexual emotions and sterile aestheticism. It is only by admitting fresh air, by contact with the minds of collective thinking, with the problems of the masses and with the social struggle, that the nightmare dread of death can be dispelled.' As for Leonid Andreev, who loved to dwell on the despair of the unconscious and was normally reduced to hopeless pessimism, 'Antid Oto' wrote that 'the earth has brought forth no greater happiness than that which comes from working and dying for the cause of mankind ...' 'This is no pessimism,' Leon Davidovich commented in an article written shortly before his escape from Siberia, 'this is the language of passionate faith and inspired courage.'

Passing through Irkutsk, he was given a forged passport in which he entered the first name that came into his head and which, as it happened, was also that of one of his gaolers – Trotsky. The name, which has a fine sound in Russian, may have been derived from the German *Trotz* – stubbornness, resistance, defiance.

III. *Meeting in Paris*

'It was during my adolescence', Natalia Sedova-Trotsky writes, 'that I became acquainted with "revolutionary ideas", ideas that, in Tsarist Russia, were often no more extreme than liberal ideas are in the West.

I was a boarder in the Kharkov grammar school. We used to organize student parties in the evenings and it was at these that I met young people involved in politics; they would bring us clandestine pamphlets denouncing the sufferings of the Russian people and proclaiming the eventual triumph of freedom ... When my secondary studies were over, I wanted, like so many others, to breathe the air of a free country, and so I went to Geneva to study science ... My special subject was botany, but I was more interested in the problems of society, especially after a student called Vetrova committed suicide in prison by burning herself to death, and inspired many young people at school. The great Marxist theorist, Plekhanov, led an influential circle in Geneva and I was happy to be introduced into it by a young militant in the *Iskra* [the *Spark*] group, of which Lenin was one of the moving spirits ... The Russian Social Democrats, who had not yet split up into Mensheviks [the minority] and Bolsheviks [the majority], ran enthusiastic study groups in Geneva, Paris, London and Brussels.

'In 1902, I was living in Paris. I used to take my meals in a flat in the rue Lalande, where we pooled our meagre resources to save money. Julius Martov used to come there; at the age of twenty-nine, he was already known as a founder of one of the earliest Russian social democratic groups and as a veteran of Turukhansk, the notorious Siberian place of exile. It was he who one day at table announced the arrival of a young fugitive from Siberia ... Leon Davidovich came to the rue Lalande on the same day he arrived in Paris. He was twenty-three and had just spent three years' exile in Eastern Siberia. His keen mind, his vitality and his capacity for hard work already set him apart as a forceful and mature figure. He was not greatly impressed by Paris at the time. He used to joke that Odessa was worth a lot more. Although he had come to Paris with the main object of making contact with the Russian émigré socialist movement, it just happened that one day the two of us were standing together looking at Baudelaire's tomb in the Montparnasse Cemetery ... and from that time on, our lives were inseparable. I had an allowance of about twenty roubles a month, say fifty francs, from my family, and Leon Davidovich earned about as much from his writing. We could only just make ends meet, but then we had Paris, the comradeship of the refugees, the constant thought of Russia and the great ideas to which we were devoting our lives ... '

IV. *The Russian intelligentsia in Paris and London*

Leon Davidovich had met determined and devoted men among the workers and students of Southern Russia when he was only eighteen. He had come to know even more in Siberia. In Zurich, Geneva, Vienna, Paris, London, Brussels and Liège, he came across large numbers of revolutionary émigrés, poor, idealistic, studious and eager, in short, he had found a congenial environment with thousands of young people like himself and a sprinkling of older men to look up to. He was part of a mass movement which was also a movement led by a revolutionary elite that could trace its origins back to the 1860s, through forty years of struggle. It included such great writers as Herzen, Chernyshevsky, Lavrov, Mikhailovsky and Kropotkin, and such now legendary heroes as Bakunin, Nechaev, Khalturin, Grinevitsky, Zhelyabov, Perovskaya and Kilbachich. The young Marxists among them were inspired by such great European socialists as Bebel in Germany, Victor Adler in Austria, and Jaurès, Guesde and Vaillant in France; their own acknowledged master was Plekhanov. Lenin, who was Trotsky's senior by nine years and who had also spent several years in Siberia, had become known through his remarkable writings. All these revolutionaries shared the deep conviction that the revolution which would free Russia was about to dawn.

We could quote the names of hundreds of men, most of whom have made their mark in history. Trotsky mentions many in *My Life*. In Siberia, around a bonfire, he had met the young Polish poet Dzerzhinsky, who was to become the head of the *Cheka*; during his escape, he became acquainted with the economist Krzhizhanovsky who later played an important part in Soviet economic planning.

In 1902, Trotsky rang Lenin's doorbell in London. Vladimir Ilyich and his companion, Nadezhda Krupskaya, received him so warmly that the friendship established between them then was, in spite of a number of disagreements, to last all their lives.

Trotsky's first circle of friends abroad included Martov, who became one of the socialist opponents of Bolshevism after the 1917 Revolution, Vera Zasulich and Leo Deutsch. In 1869, at the age of nineteen, Vera Zasulich had been involved in a conspiracy; at twenty-eight she had shot the Governor of St Petersburg who had ordered a student to be flogged. She had been acquitted and was now on the editorial staff of the Social Democrat *Iskra*, together with

Leo Deutsch, whose *Sixteen Years in Siberia*, translated into several languages, has a respected place in European socialist literature.

In 1877, when he was twenty-two years old, Leo Deutsch had tried to incite a peasant uprising in Chigirin by publishing a fake imperial rescript calling upon them to seize the land. Trotsky greatly prized the friendship of these two young people and of the old Marxist theorist, Paul Axelrod.

During the first few conferences he attended, Trotsky showed such outstanding oratorical gifts that he was sent on speaking tours to Belgium, Switzerland and Germany.

v. *The birth of Bolshevism. Trotsky discusses Lenin's ideas*

The Second Congress of the Russian Social Democratic Workers' Party met at the Maison du Peuple in Brussels in 1903, but in order to elude the Russian secret police, as well as Belgian surveillance, it was transferred to London. Trotsky represented the Siberian Union and was deeply distressed by the rift between the moderate minority and the intransigent majority, that is, between the Mensheviks and the Bolsheviks led respectively by Martov and Lenin. This breach was so painful to all participants that Lenin had what might almost be described as a nervous breakdown and Trotsky wrote quite desperate letters to his wife. Broadly speaking, it would be true to say that while the Mensheviks favoured collaboration with the liberal bourgeoisie against the *ancien régime*, the Bolsheviks adopted an approach that Lenin himself later defined as 'proletarian Jacobinism'. Lenin advocated a centralized party leadership that would ensure the 'hegemony of the proletariat' within the revolutionary movement. Trotsky opposed him in a pamphlet, which has since been lost but which created a considerable stir at the time. He showed the incompatibility of Jacobinism with socialism, and contended that any 'dictatorship of the proletariat' along such lines would soon degenerate into a 'dictatorship over the proletariat'. Lenin's authoritarianism appalled him. 'But that's dictatorship you're advocating,' he said to him one day. 'There is no other way,' Lenin replied.

vi. *The 1905 Russian Revolution. Trotsky, Chairman at twenty-six of the St Petersburg Soviet*

'The 1905 Revolution was to reconcile them but not to overcome their differences of outlook. The Revolution was the expected result of the Russian losses during the Russo-Japanese War. The revolutionary émigrés as a whole favoured a Russian defeat and opposed Russian colonial expansion; they hoped that military failure would shake the absolute monarchy. We were living in Geneva when the events of January 22nd, 1905, took place. Martov brought us the great news. A procession of working-class petitioners in St Petersburg, led by Father Gapon and carrying portraits of the Tsar at their head, were met at the Winter Palace with rifle fire and a cavalry charge; they left hundreds of dead and wounded in the snow. On hearing this Trotsky turned pale, became unsteady and nearly fainted ... Nervous tension tended to produce physical symptoms in him – as often happened before he spoke at meetings.'

He decided to return to Russia at once and did so carrying a passport issued in the name of Arbuzov. Natalia went ahead to look for secret lodgings, and found Petersburg at fever pitch. Workers' meetings were held in the woods. One at which Natalia was to speak was broken up by Cossacks and she was taken prisoner.

'I was well treated in gaol; I can still hear the wardress saying to me in ingratiating tones, "Your bath is ready, Madame Sedova." After some months, I was banished to Tver [Kalinin]. By then, Leon Davidovich was in hiding in Finland. An amnesty shortly afterwards helped to reunite us in Petersburg. We found a furnished room in a financier's house, where we lived under the name of Vikentiev. Leon Davidovich signed his articles "Leon Trotsky", but in the Soviet he was known as "Yanovsky". He hardly had an hour's rest. The whole of Russia seemed to be ablaze. The peasants were attacking the houses of the gentry, mutineers paralysed the fleet and the garrisons; a printers' strike in Moscow spread gradually to become the general strike of October 1905, which broke down the resistance of the Witte government. Up to that point, the Tsar, his ministers and the police had met popular demands with repression and anti-semitic pogroms. Now, the imperial manifesto of October 17th conceded democratic liberties under constitutional rule. But we remained sceptical about the heady "days of freedom". We believed that the autocracy was incapable of abdicating in any real sense.'

The idea of forming workers' assemblies, which were to exercise legislative and executive power, was in the air; Trotsky was one of those who fostered it. As a result, the first Workers' Council or Soviet of St Petersburg was formed, consisting of works and trade union delegates.

On the appointed day, hundreds of workers' delegates, guests and journalists assembled. The press reported the deliberations of this 'workers' parliament' in full, and the first chairman of the new assembly negotiated with the government in that capacity. When he was arrested, the leader of the Social Revolutionary Party, Victor Chernov, proposed that the Soviet should meet every act of repression by the government with terrorism. Trotsky opposed this view; the Soviet, he said, must concentrate its energies on paving the way for the insurrection of the workers. Yanovsky (Trotsky) was elected Chairman of the Soviet.

The Soviet demanded an eight-hour working day and proclaimed its solidarity with the Polish insurgents. Trotsky told a Polish delegation that 'proletarian solidarity knows no frontiers; it will abolish the autocracy and found a democratic republic.' When the revolutionary energy of the people of the capital began to ebb and the Soviet made plans to go underground, Trotsky proposed a direct appeal to the troops and published the now famous *Manifesto on the Finances of the Empire*. It began as follows:

> The government is on the verge of bankruptcy. It has turned the country into a desert sown with corpses ... We have decided to refuse to pay taxes or any other dues to the government, to demand that all wages be paid in gold or metal, to withdraw deposits from savings banks ... and to oppose the repayment of all loans made to the Tsar's government while it is openly waging war on the people.

In one month, this *Manifesto* was responsible for the withdrawal of ninety-four million roubles from state banks. On December 1st, 1905, Nicholas II received monarchist delegates in the palace of Tsarskoe Selo. The anti-Semitic leagues – the 'Unions of the Russian Peoples' – promised their monarch unconditional support. The eight newspapers of the capital which had published the *Manifesto on the Finances* were suspended. On December 3rd, troops, Cossacks, police and gendarmes surrounded the premises of the Free Economic Association, where the Soviet was in session, awaiting the arrest of all its members. The Executive Committee was meeting on the first floor with Trotsky in the chair. As the imperial guard sealed all exits, noisy protestations could be heard from the street. Trotsky stepped out on to the balcony and shouted, 'Comrades, do not offer any resistance.' He asked the revolutionaries to break the locks of their guns before surrendering them, then resumed his seat inside. Soldiers were crowding into the corridors and an officer stepped into the room. 'Kindly shut the door and do not interrupt our deliberations,' Trotsky told him. When the door remained open, one of the delegates started to harangue the troops. Gendarmes came in, their faces as grey as their uniforms and took up positions behind the chairs of the delegates. Trotsky declared the meeting of the Executive Committee closed.

At the end of December 1905, the Moscow insurrection was defeated following ten days of bitter street fighting. Years of black reaction followed, but the first Russian Revolution had stirred men's hearts, and not only in Russia. Trotsky, like Lenin, considered it a dress rehearsal for the 1917 Revolution. He also believed that it would have tremendous repercussions in the East: in the years that followed, popular movements surged up in Turkey, Persia and China.

VII. *Imprisonment, trial, escape and emigration*

'Trotsky was imprisoned in the fortress of Peter and Paul, on an island in the Neva right in the heart of Petersburg, and later in Kresty where he was reunited with his old friend, Leo Deutsch, now full of plans for a mass escape. Trotsky tolerated prison life extremely well. At Kresty the crowd of political detainees, including a fair number under sentence of death, maintained excellent morale; the revolutionaries destined for the scaffold took as lively a part in the discussions as the rest – and played leap-frog with them, as well. Trotsky's lawyer, Gruzenberg, passed on his letters and writings and a prison warder used to bring me personal messages.'

The trial of the fifty-one members of the Soviet was held in public – the fifty-second had been shot. At the first hearing, the accused, the counsel for the defence and the public stood in silent homage to their dead comrade, surrounded by guards with drawn swords. The revolutionaries formally accused the government of fomenting pogroms and of printing malicious anti-Semitic tracts. Trotsky spoke at length at the hearing on October 17th, 1906. He proclaimed that the masses had good cause for insurrection, denounced Nicholas II's 'constitutional' programme and showed that the only way of ushering in a new era in Russia was to convene a constitutional assembly.

'But we know the *ancien régime* too well to trust it for a single moment.' 'We are being prosecuted in the name of law and order ... If you call the pogroms, the assassinations, the arson and the violence "law and order", if you believe that there is no other way of governing the Russian Empire, then I plead guilty to the charge of armed rebellion against this regime!'

Like most of his co-defendants, Trotsky was stripped of all civil rights and sentenced to deportation for life. 'We had expected hard labour,' he said simply.

His letters to Natalia at the time contain lively descriptions of his journey into exile.

'We are very cheerful – and this after thirteen months in gaol. Although the carriage windows are barred, beyond them we can see freedom, life and movement ... The officer in command of our escort is obliging, and as for the men – nearly all of them have read accounts of our trial and show us marks of the greatest sympathy ... Up to the last minute, they did not know what kind of people they would be escorting, nor where. The strict security precautions surrounding our sudden departure from Moscow to Petersburg made them think we were about to be taken to Schlüsselburg for execution. I noticed in the hall of the prison that the men seemed very moved and quite exceptionally considerate, as if they felt slightly guilty. I didn't discover the reason until we boarded the train ... How happy the soldiers were when they found they were in the presence of "workers' deputies" who had been sentenced to no more than exile! ... The gendarmes seemed to keep a special watch on the escort; at least, that's what the latter think ...'

January 12th, 1906

'At every station, our carriage is surrounded by gendarmes and at larger stations they are reinforced by the mounted police. The gendarmes, their rifles slung, threaten anyone approaching, whether by accident or out of curiosity, with drawn revolvers. Only two kinds of people are guarded like this, "state criminals" and the most distinguished ministers ... On the one hand, there is this strict supervision, and on the other, tremendous courtesy within the limits prescribed. It all shows Stolypin's[1] constitutional genius ... We

[1] Prime Minister during the period of reaction following the 1905 Revolution.

are entitled to be proud of ourselves: they are afraid of the Soviet even after its death.'

January 16th

'Here we are in a village twenty versts from Tyumen. It's night in a peasant hut. The room is dirty and low. The floor is entirely covered by deputies of the Soviet and there is not a chink left free ... We chat and laugh ... We draw lots for a wide bench and fortune smiles on me. I'm always lucky ... When are we leaving? Where are we going? Nobody knows ... We need no less than forty sleighs. The ones in front are loaded with luggage and we, the "deputies", follow, two to a sleigh, guarded by soldiers. Only one horse pulls each sleigh. The rear is made up of troops. The officer and the superintendent head the convoy in a covered sleigh. The horses move at a walk ... On leaving Tyumen we were escorted by about thirty cavalry ... Such exceptional measures taken on orders from St Petersburg must mean that the authorities are determined to send us to the remotest corner of the country ...

'Everybody is asleep. The soldiers keep watch on us from the kitchen through the open door. Sentries pace up and down outside the window. The night is magnificent, moon-lit, the landscape all blue and covered with snow. What a strange picture, bodies stretched out on the floor fast asleep, and soldiers outside the windows and at the door! ... But as I am on my second journey of this kind, my impressions lack the old freshness ...

'Tyumen prison was crowded with political detainees; most of them had been deported by administrative decree. During their exercise period, they stopped beneath our windows and started to sing. They even waved a red banner inscribed with the words 'Long Live the Revolution!' They made quite a good choir; they had no doubt had time enough to learn how to harmonize their voices ... It was all very impressive and even moving ... We sent them a brief message of sympathy through the ventilators. The non-politicals sent us a very long petition, in prose and verse, asking us, "noble Petersburg revolutionaries" that we were, to help them in their ordeal ... '

January 26th   *Tobolsk prison*

'The doctor told us we are being sent to Obdorsk. We cover forty to fifty versts [twenty-five to thirty miles] a day. It is about twelve hundred versts from here to Obdorsk by the winter route ... Our

journey will take us a month, at least ... When we arrive, each of
us will be paid 1·80 roubles (just under one gold dollar) ... We are
told that between Berezov and Obdorsk, our sleighs will be drawn
by reindeer. Those who have brought their families were particularly
disturbed by the news ... Those wives who are accompanying their
husbands voluntarily, asked permission to look at the town during
our three days' stay at Tobolsk. The governor refused point blank
... A protest is being drawn up, but what's the good? The reply is
always the same: instructions from Petersburg.

'Nothing more is known here about Obdorsk ... All that is certain
is that it is somewhere north of the Arctic Circle ... Will there be
any chance of escape or will we be forced to wait for the revolution
somewhere between the North Pole and the Arctic Circle? ... Ah,
well, we'll see at Obdorsk. We shan't be idle there. Whatever else
you do, please send us newspapers and books, books and newspapers
... Who knows when our hopes will be fulfilled! Perhaps our
enforced stay at Obdorsk is a respite granted by history in which
we may complete our studies and forge our weapons ... '

VIII. *The making of an ideologist*

'One month later I received a garbled telegram. Leon Davidovich,
who had escaped, asked me to meet him at some obscure railway
station in the East, the name of which was not mentioned! Sending
the telegram seemed to me to be an act of madness. (I was living
at Terioki in Finland with our eldest son, Lyova, born during his
father's imprisonment, but the police were watching here, too ...)
He had mentioned a "railway crossing" ... I travelled in the direction
of Vyatka without really knowing where I was going ... The carriage
was full of rich people on their way to celebrate the carnival with
French wines, smoked fish and all sorts of expensive tit-bits. While
gorging themselves, they discussed what they were eating, gourmet-
fashion. I had never met people like this; I remember how astonished
I was to find that they existed when we could only think of life as
a ceaseless struggle for the future of Russia. All the same, I suddenly
became grateful to them because in discussing where they were going,
they happened to mention the village I was looking for: Samino.

'A small station surrounded by snow-covered forests and white
plains. Here Leon Davidovich was waiting for me, trembling with
joy at his escape ... He had slipped away at Berezov, half-way to

Obdorsk, on a reindeer-drawn sleigh driven by a drunken Zyrian. More than four hundred miles of white emptiness, in the icy desert, had filled him with exaltation ... He barely restrained me from marching to the telegraph office and speaking my mind to the idiot of a clerk who had failed to transmit the name of the station. When he got into the train, Leon Davidovich felt as if he would suffocate in the compartment; he leapt to the platform, and there, faced with the glittering steppe, let out a great shout of joy.

'He was only twenty-eight, well built, with thick and unmanageable brown hair and a small moustache. He had bold features, a rather bony face and extremely lively blue eyes ... He had worn glasses since his adolescence.

'We hid first in Petersburg and then in Finland, where Leon Davidovich resumed contact with Lenin and Martov. He wrote an account of his escape – *There and Back* – at one sitting ... The reactionary press received the news of his escape with a kind of helpless fury; the Chairman of the Soviet had managed to escape even before he had reached his destination! What were the police doing? They had had to keep watch on the whole of Russia, one huge prisoner in revolt, while terrorist attacks from one end of the country to the other, mostly organized by the Social Revolutionary Party, kept them busy ...

'*There and Back* brought in some money. Leon Davidovich travelled to Stockholm, and on to London where he attended the clandestine Congress of the Russian Social Democratic Workers' Party. There were no visa formalities ... He met a great number of people in the West: Maxim Gorky, Victor Adler, Bebel, Hilferding and Liebknecht, among others. I joined him and we settled in Vienna. The liberal and widely-read *Kievskaya Mysl* [*Kiev Thought*] regularly published despatches by Trotsky signed "Antid Oto" and paid him fairly well. All the same, life was full of hardships in Vienna. Leon Davidovich had to sell his books and at the end of each month we were always at our wits' end to find the rent. Quite often we had writs served on us. Our second son, Sergey, was born in Vienna in 1908. It was a time full of activity and filled with friendships. Trotsky made friends with Dr Adolf Joffe who was later to play an important part in Soviet diplomacy. A man of middle-class background, he, too, was familiar with Russian gaols. He was neurotic, in poor health, and had a fine intellect fired by his fervent idealism. He and Trotsky became co-editors of the Vienna *Pravda* [*The Truth*] and we were able to smuggle copies into Russia with the help of sailors and others.

'We had hardly any time off; though sometimes, on Sundays, we would explore the countryside round Vienna. We had already gone on a two-month walking tour of Southern Germany together with Parvus (Helphand), a most promising comrade from Russia. He was Trotsky's senior by ten years and one of the most remarkable of the Russian Marxists. He contributed to the Berlin *Vorwärts* [*Forward*] and would write his article every day at a wayside inn. Parvus had a scientific turn of mind, was thoroughly Westernized and a bold thinker. Together with Trotsky, he formulated the theory of the "permanent revolution" which, as it turned out, was to guide the entire first phase of the impending Russian Revolution. According to that theory, Russia could not stop at bourgeois revolution but would have to advance to socialism under the remorseless pressure of the proletariat, and hence act as a spur to the socialist revolution of Central and Western Europe.'

Later, during the First World War, Parvus showed a flair for commerce and made a good deal of money supplying arms to the Central Powers. In 1918, he asked Lenin for permission to return to Russia. Lenin refused, saying, 'You cannot make revolutions with dirty hands.' Parvus died in Germany in 1924.

Trotsky's circle of revolutionary friends grew. In Russia, he had met Leonid Krasin, who led the Bolsheviks' organization in the Caucasus. He also came to know Karl Radek, the caustic publicist of the German Social Democratic Party. Other acquaintances included Franz Mehring, Marx's biographer, Karl Kautsky and Rosa Luxemburg; the Austrian socialists, Otto Bauer and Alfred Adler as well as Victor and Fritz Adler, whom he used to meet on Saturday evenings in the Central Café in the narrow Herrengasse. He thought the Austrian Marxists had been tainted by middle-class values. He had known Ryazanov, Lunacharsky and Lenin's collaborators, Zinoviev and Kamenev for some time, and Kamenev came to see him in Vienna on Lenin's behalf.

Between 1906 and 1914, Russia suffered hard years of reaction, followed by the period of resurgence of the working-class movement. The same happened to the revolutionary émigrés. For them, the defeat of 1905 was followed by a wave of demoralization, internal bickering and bitterness; the ugly sore of police provocation within the parties suddenly opened up ... Many Russian writers took to mysticism; others wavered between despair and sexual abandon. The Social Democratic Party, papering over the deep cracks still dividing it, announced its newly found unity. One Marxist group wanted to turn its back on underground organizations. Trotsky, who was independent of both the Bolshevik and Menshevik factions, shared neither the moderate line of the one nor the illusions of the other, though he never fell prey to pessimism. He believed that economic developments in Russia would inevitably strengthen the working class and that, though a revival of the revolutionary movement was unlikely during the recession, it was bound to come about when the economy picked up again. In 1909, he wrote this prophetic message: 'Even today, through the black clouds of reaction, we can catch a glimpse of the first victorious rays of a new October.' (A reference to the successful general strike in October 1905.)

IX. *The Azev Affair*

The news of the Azev affair broke in 1909–10. Suddenly, the young Russian Revolution, until then confident of its integrity and purity, was faced with the most squalid kind of corruption in its own ranks.

The Social Revolutionary Party, unlike the Marxists, had always tended to rely on acts of individual heroism. According to incomplete figures, the S.R.P. organized fifty-eight assassinations in 1905, ninety-three in 1906 and seventy-four in 1907, all directed against leading figures of the regime and its most hated police officials. The Marxists, in general, condemned individual acts of terrorism on the grounds that they were no substitute for mass action and that they threatened to divert precious resources. Then came the bombshell revelation that Evno Azev, who was not only one of the heads of the S.R.P. but of all people the man in charge of the fighting arm, had been an agent of the secret police all along. The story seemed incredible, since even his own wife, the mother of his two children, had believed him to be a fearless revolutionary.

The affair proved all the more difficult to disentangle because the Central Committee of the S.R.P., having worked so closely with Azev for many years, refused steadfastly to believe in his guilt until his double game had been exposed beyond any shadow of doubt. Nor, it appeared, was he by any means the only police spy in the revolutionary movement, which was suddenly ravaged by suspicion and mutual recrimination.

Trotsky was one of the few who maintained his composure. While

others were moved to dwell on the abysmal depths of human degradation, he wrote, 'To keep up this callous game for seventeen years,
to deceive people without being discovered, one must be either a man
of exceptional genius or of the lowest intelligence, impervious to
others, determined to follow a line of action blindly, come what may
...' Azev was, in fact, a mediocre and unattractive man, whose lack
of education set him off from the rest of the revolutionary leaders,
some of whom were, however, impressed by his 'firmness' and his
'great practical qualities'. Trotsky regarded him as a man both uncouth and corrupt, whose very shortcomings had made him an
excellent police spy. He also stressed the importance of a passage
in the *Conclusions of the Committee of the Enquiry*: that terrorism
had led to 'the formation of a fighting arm set over and above the
Party and hence an easy prey for such as Azev; at the same time
it helped to produce in those around the successful terrorist – Azev –
a feeling of absolute trust and deference.' Azev relied on two bureaucratic machines, that of the Social Revolutionary Party and that of
the secret police – hence his strength.

It would be easy to see a parallel between Azev and another, much
more important, historical figure. The man who commands a disciplined and secret band of terrorists, supported by an influential party,
who has the right to order men to be killed, needs neither great moral
force nor great intelligence to reap the fruits of unchallenged power.
As for Azev, he bore out Trotsky's judgment to the full. After he was
unmasked and had been generously rewarded by the Ministry of the
Interior, he travelled round the Mediterranean for a time with a lady
of doubtful reputation, finally settling in Germany, where his principal occupation became playing the stock market.

x. *Vienna*

Vienna was the cradle of psychoanalysis, in which Trotsky was interested though never deeply involved. There was complete harmony
between his inner life and his overt behaviour. He lacked the time
for a serious study of psychology, but he attached enormous importance to the character, mentality and preoccupations of men. His
psychological insight no doubt helped him to establish close contact
with the masses and to sway large crowds. He contributed articles
on literature, painting and poetry to *Kievskaya Mysl* – always, it
goes without saying, as a committed Marxist.

He admired Jaurès. 'He is not a doctrinaire partisan of political compromise, though his passion, his talents and his iron resolve are all devoted to it. But he does not make a fetish of compromise, and when the time comes he will muster all his strength ...' (1909) Jaurès's enthusiasm was 'ingenuous to the point of genius'. Trotsky considered Jaurès and Clemenceau the two dominant figures of French political life.

He admired Tolstoy but completely rejected his contempt for science.

Mystical moralist and enemy of the revolution, Leon Tolstoy ... feeds the revolutionary spirit of the believers ... Rejecting capitalist culture ... he is well received by the bourgeoisie abroad ... Conservative anarchist ... who at eighty has become the symbol of liberation ... History has defeated but not broken him. In the evening of his days he has kept his precious gift of moral indignation intact ... telling the autocracy, 'I cannot keep silent'. He denies us his sympathy ... but we shall always appreciate his powerful genius which will live on as long as art and inflexible moral courage survive. (1908)

Trotsky approached the human condition with tenacious optimism, without denying its complexity. 'The reactionaries believe that thought is a destructive factor and hence cry: *Écrasez l'infâme!* Nothing could be further from the truth. The psyche is the most conservative of elementary forces: because it is lazy, it becomes "hypnotized by routine".' He was a champion of intelligence and the imagination and quoted this passage from Dostoevsky: 'Realism that goes no further than the end of one's nose is more dangerous than the most unbridled fantasy, because it is blind ...' He attacked Renan for depreciating humanity by saying that 'great men only take part in practical affairs because of their faults or their mediocre qualities.' 'Culture,' he retorted, 'if not animated and inspired by scientific thought, becomes mere creature-comfort.' (1911) He inveighed against the 'facile mystical alchemy of Berdyaev and Merezhkovsky'. The latter had written that 'the early Christians would not have accepted martyrdom, had some glimpse of the future history of the Church been vouchsafed them.' Trotsky asked him, 'And what about you? What is your attitude to the history of primitive religion?' He discussed suicide and defended those revolutionaries who had killed

themselves in gaol. Suicide was 'a social, not a biological, phenomenon'. Of child suicide, he said that 'the extreme sensitivity which
drives a child to take this step might, in different and more favourable
circumstances, have led him to develop a personality rich in promise.'
(1912) Elsewhere he wrote that 'rationalism can only be powerful
when it is fused with the consciousness of the masses.' (1914)

He always regarded himself as a dilettante in the arts, but his
comments on Viennese art, on Frank Wedekind, Arno Holz and on
the satirical paper, *Simplicissimus*, abound in philosophical insights.
'The soul which is dazzled by paths that lead nowhere is a stranger
to passion and vigour. To make amends, it may long for valour and
simple human integrity ... but its picture of passion lacks passion
and its picture of vigour lacks vigour ... ' Rodin 'subordinates the
flesh to movement, but to an inner movement, to the soul incarnate
in the flesh .... Constantin Meunier has discovered the worth of
labour ... Something greater than art dwells in the very depths of
society, enabling art to return from exile, enriched by the drama of
labour and embattled humanity, and itself enriching labour and the
human struggle.' (1911) 'Scratch a haughty individualist and all you
will find is a vulgar cynic.' 'Painting is rendered insipid by the contrast between the modernity of its form and the cold archaism of
its content.' 'Man is a complex psychological entity and, if he is true
to himself, will look to art for an aesthetic interpretation of what
moves him as a social and moral being ... Men do not live, have
never lived nor will they ever live, as passive onlookers.' (1913)

The Balkan wars began in 1912. Trotsky travelled to Serbia, Bulgaria and Rumania as correspondent of *Kievskaya Mysl*. He
denounced the atrocities committed by the Bulgars against the
Turks. His interest in the war was that of the revolutionary observer,
not of the military commentator. At the same time he drew a pitiless
portrait of Tsar Nicholas II, guilty of massacring the workers, of anti-
Semitic pogroms, of the oppression of Finland, and of the Russo-
Japanese War – on the eve of which the Tsar had announced, 'There
will be no war; I wish my reign to be a peaceful one ... ' In this
connection we can do no better than offer the following quotation
by Trotsky (1908): 'We do not create events; at most, we can foresee
them ... Immense and terrible events are taking shape, amid enormous tensions, in the heart of what is called civilized mankind ...
and those who try to predict them are treated like insane prophets
of doom'.

XI. *Paris during World War I*. Nashe Slovo. *Trotsky expelled from France. Spain*

'On August 2nd, 1914, the first day of World War I, Trotsky wandered through the avenues of Vienna, which were thronged with excited and patriotic crowds shouting, "Death to the Serbs!" He wondered what was going on in their heads. Our little six-year-old Sergey came home with two black eyes for having shouted, "Long live the Serbs!" "Every moron and halfwit is out in the streets today," Victor Adler said sadly. The chief of the Vienna police asked Trotsky to leave the capital that very day. The interview took place at about two o'clock, and at six we were on the train to Zurich.

'At the end of 1914, we found ourselves in Paris once more. The Germans were at Compiègne and their bombers kept dropping their small loads on Paris, the most threatened city in the world, the capital of the country which had shed more blood than any other, and was now plunged into the gloom of its first black-out. We lived in the rue Oudry, near the Place d'Italie, in a densely populated district. Walks through Paris were our only amusement. There was so much mourning that black had become the latest fashion; even the street-walkers wore black. The housewives I knew seemed to live in the shadow of their absent men. The wife of a soldier who had been home on leave said to me, "Since he has been and gone, things are worse than ever". Perhaps anxiety for somebody you love, with its hopes and fears, is harder to bear than the certainty of irreparable loss. In a tram, I heard a soldier enthuse about the quality of a bottle of wine; that done, he switched to showing off his lice ... Paris experienced the terrible war in all the fibres of its being, in its very stones and in all the shadows of its nights ...

'Trotsky went on sending his despatches to Kiev, but he devoted most of his energies to the Paris Russian socialist daily, *Nashe Slovo* [*Our World*]. Two hundred and thirteen editions appeared from January 1915 onwards. Our group had two objectives: to work for the Russian Revolution, now inevitable because, as we saw it, the war was crippling the autocracy, and to restore socialist internationalism, which had been shattered on the outbreak of hostilities. Nothing was more galling to us than the thought that workers, until quite recently brothers in the International, should now be drawn up against one another to shed each others' blood for the sake of conquests all of them should have abhorred.

'*Nashe Slovo* was run on the devotion of a few militants who contributed their labour as well as what little money they could spare. Paying for paper and printing was a daily worry. Trotsky would write until three in the morning and deliver his manuscript to the printers when he took Sergey to school. The French censor, answerable to the Russian Embassy, mutilated his articles ... A number of Bolsheviks in Paris had yielded to the intoxication of patriotic fervour and had joined the Foreign Legion; several had got themselves killed. Lenin and Zinoviev were in Switzerland, Kamenev and Sverdlov in Siberia; Bukharin was in the United States. In Paris, we renewed our acquaintance with the Menshevik Martov, intelligent, passionate, and irresolute as ever. He finally left the editorial board of *Nashe Slovo* after interminable arguments with Trotsky. Another comrade, Antonov-Ovseenko, gave himself unstintingly to the cause. He was of small to medium build and thin, his pale face, topped by a chestnut mane, was lined through overwork, and his pince-nez were always askew. He had led an unhappy home life because his wife, worn out by the demands of their child, would not forgive him their poverty. "He had a wealthy childhood," she said, "but I never had anything but herrings to eat ... "

'Antonov-Ovseenko, the son of a senior officer, and himself a regular soldier, had taken part in a military mutiny in Poland in 1905 and had organized a military rising in Sebastopol in 1906. He was sentenced to death, but his sentence was commuted to hard labour for life. He escaped, played an important part in the Revolution and was finally shot in 1937.'

Antonov-Ovseenko and Trotsky made contact with the small group of French internationalist syndicalists connected with *La Vie Ouvrière*: Pierre Monatte, Alfred Rosmer, the teacher Fernand Loriot and the poet Marcel Martinet. They were approached by other trade unionists: by Merrheim of the Metalworkers' Federation, by Dumoulin, and by Bourdon of the miners. By contrast, *Nashe Slovo* had hardly any dealings with the French Socialist Party.

In September 1915, Trotsky went to Switzerland to attend a conference of socialist internationalists called by the Italians. The delegates assembled in Zimmerwald, a small mountain village near Berne. Lenin and Zinoviev represented the Bolsheviks, Axelrod and Martov the Mensheviks; Trotsky came as the delegate of *Nashe Slovo* and Nathanson and Chernov represented the Social Revolutionaries. Ledebour and Hoffman were members of the German delegation, while Kolarov and Rakovsky represented the Balkan Socialist Federation. Also present were Modigliani, Morgari, Lazzari, Serrati (Italy), Henriette Roland-Holst (Holland), Karl Radek (Poland), Merrheim and Bourderon (the left-wing minority of the French General Federation of Labour), a delegate from the Polish Jewish Bund, as well as some Swiss and Swedish delegates. Two lines emerged during the discussion of the draft manifesto proposed by Trotsky. One was in favour of the restoration of the Socialist International, the other demanded a complete break with all the old parties playing war politics and the formation of a new Socialist International, the Third. The question was never settled but in the end Lenin voted in favour of Trotsky's text. An International Socialist Commission was elected. It would sit in Berne and would consist of Robert Grimm, Morgari, Charles Naine and Angelica Balabanov.

In Marseilles there was a mutiny aboard the *Askold*, a Russian warship carrying troops to France. A police spy claimed that the whole thing had been stirred up by *Nashe Slovo*, which was neither true nor even probable, but the Russian Embassy at once called for Trotsky's deportation from France. Malvy, the Minister of Interior, signed the warrant, ignoring the protests of Jean Longuet and of Briand, Leygues and Painlevé, who pointed out that everything published in *Nashe Slovo* had been passed by the French censor. However, there was a little phrase which served as an excuse for everything – '*C'est la guerre!*' Trotsky wrote later in *My Life*: 'Had the lies of war been explosives, there would have been enough of them to blow up the entire planet.' England, Italy and Switzerland refused to admit him. The polite inspectors who accompanied him to Irun, just beyond the Pyrenees, advised him not to draw attention to himself.

Trotsky did not speak a word of Spanish. In Madrid, he spent his time in the Prado. Meanwhile a French police commissar, Bidet – nicknamed Faux-Pas Bidet – reported him to the Spanish authorities as a 'dangerous anarchist'. He was arrested and the authorities proposed deporting him to Havana, but eventually relented and allowed him, with severe restrictions of movement, to wait for a boat to New York. When news of his arrest leaked out, the Spanish republicans defended him, but, knowing nothing about his views, they thought he had been victimized for his 'pacifism'. The reactionaries regarded him with sympathy because they thought him to be 'pro-

German', but could not understand why he was described as an anarchist. The secret police took a great interest in him. Natalia joined him in Barcelona with the two boys, and together they boarded the Spanish steamer *Montserrat* and sailed for New York. The sea was rough and the company worse.

XII. *New York. Internment in Canada*

They arrived in New York at the beginning of January 1917, in a downpour of sleet. 'New York is the fullest expression of our modern age,' Trotsky wrote in *My Life*.

'Bukharin greeted us with a bear-hug. He is twenty-nine, vivacity itself, has an open, smiling face, is affectionate and a lively conversationalist with a touch of humour. He is full of ideas; a serious economist, a scholarly but rigid Marxist, a somewhat undisciplined disciple of Lenin. We had known him in Vienna, and had hardly got off the boat when he told us enthusiastically about a public library which stayed open late at night and which he proposed to show us at once. At about nine o'clock in the evening we had to make the long journey to admire his great discovery – on the way back we got to know the exhausted faces of the New Yorkers.

'From the next day on, Trotsky worked with Bukharin, Chudnovsky and Melnichansky on *Novy Mir* [*New World*]. We lived in a working-class district in the Bronx.

'On March 8th, 1917, we read the long-awaited but still sensational news of the fall of Nicholas II and the beginning of the Russian Revolution ... Bukharin left for Russia almost immediately by way of San Francisco, Tokyo and Siberia ... On March 25th, Trotsky received his first genuine passport from the Russian consulate representing the Provisional Government. On the 27th, "in a deluge of flowers and speeches" [*My Life*], we embarked again, this time as citizens of an infant republic ...

'But the more or less secret agents of the Tsar were still about. There were six of us revolutionary exiles on board, Melnichansky, Chudnovsky, Trotsky, myself and two others. The imperial police denounced us to the British, probably as being "pro-German". In Halifax, Nova Scotia, the military authorities, who understood nothing of events in Russia and who had nothing to say except the inevitable "There's a war on", put us all under arrest, despite our protests, and though our papers were in order ... Trotsky and the comrades were thrown into the P.O.W. camp at Amherst; the two children and I were boarded out with a police inspector, a naturalized Russian who lived in utter squalor. Though he was not a really bad man, he was so stupid as to verge on the comical. Having been ordered to keep a discreet watch over me, he nevertheless boasted to me of his many disguises ...

'Trotsky kept speaking to the interned workers and sailors about the significance of the Russian Revolution. The prisoners took to him at once, which led to continuous conflict with the British officers. "If only I had this agitator in an African colony", one of them was heard to say. The Foreign Minister of the Russian Provisional Government, Miliukov, who used to have sharp disagreements with Trotsky, finally yielded to the demands of the revolutionary parties and in April requested that the ex-Chairman of the first St Petersburg Soviet and his travelling companions be released.

'We embarked again, this time on a small boat which was pounded mercilessly by the Atlantic waves. Chudnovsky paid court to a little Russian dancer ... He was an overgrown boy with a bad complexion and somewhat curly hair, a student who was perhaps too talkative for our taste and quick to flare up. "Will he be steadfast? Will he stay the course?" Trotsky used to wonder. In the event, Chudnovsky did not waver. His energy was all-consuming and, as soon as we seized power, he became inseparable from his insurgent's rifle. He was wounded in the defence of Petrograd and killed in the Ukraine in 1918. Our other travelling companion, Melnichansky, was a stout watchmaker, red-faced and thoughtful, who had been a member of the American Socialist Party. He took part in the Moscow rising, became one of the leaders of the Soviet trade union movement, struck up a friendship with Tomsky – and was made to pay for it. He died, presumably shot, in 1937.'

Two · Revolution

I. Return to Russia. The Soviets and the Provisional Government

'We returned to Russia after ten years of exile, in the midst of a triumphant revolution, but to a country impoverished and bled white by the war. The first contact we had with the Russian authorities, at Tornio on the Finno–Swedish border, was chilly in the extreme – and this had nothing to do with the weather. All Trotsky's papers were retained for examination with a promise that they would be sent on to the Presidium of the Petrograd Soviet, the only address we could give them. An officer insisted on being told what journals "Mr Trotsky" would be writing for. "We would be extremely interested to know," he said. L.D. replied courteously "For any that I please, of course." Not very welcoming, this new regime!

'At the Russian border, we drew into a station amid the snow-clad forests. It was decorated with red banners, and a small, happy crowd was there to greet us enthusiastically. Karakhan, Uritsky and Fedorov were among them – of those three who came to welcome us so hopefully, not one has survived. Moyse Uritsky was assassinated by a counter-revolutionary student in 1918; Fedorov disappeared into a concentration camp in 1935; Karakhan was shot in 1937.

'In Petrograd, we enjoyed the hospitality of Serebrovsky. During the revolutionary struggles of 1905 we had known him as the metalworker, Loginov; in those days he had been at pains to conceal his middle-class origins and had distinguished himself in the street fighting. By now, he was a qualified engineer, director of the Nobel works and comfortably settled. He belonged to the moderate majority of the socialist movement. His wife apparently felt that her husband began to treat her coolly as soon as the "exalted revolutionary" moved in ... And so we found another room. Needless to say, we were penniless.

32

'The Empire had crumbled within a few days in the face of spontaneous strikes and of workers' demonstrations in the streets of Petrograd. Women's cries for bread outside the bakers' shops had heralded the end of an autocracy that had lasted for three hundred years. The small revolutionary groups were so bewildered that the Bolsheviks recommended a return to work just as the garrison began to fraternize with the demonstrators. This fraternization on the part of hundreds of unknown heroes proved to be the turning point. The Tsar's government was probably alone in not being taken by surprise, as appeared later from the various reports of top officials who daily described an even more desperate situation. In the event, police and Cossack reprisals caused some bloodshed: 1,382 dead were picked up in the streets of the capital.

'On February 27th, militants together with factory and battalion delegates had gone into session in the Tauride Palace, in a wing normally occupied by the Duma – that Tsarist pseudo-parliament, which lacked rights or powers, enjoyed neither prestige nor popularity, and was led by a liberal majority which, confused by events, increasingly resorted to holding quite pointless secret meetings. But once the militant workers and soldiers, renewing the tradition of 1905, had established the Executive Committee of the Soviet [Council] of Workers' Deputies, that body became the only true seat of power, a sort of parliament of the masses. The official party leaders were either in exile abroad, in Siberia or in gaol. A few little-known socialists, most of them moderates who had never dreamt of playing a decisive part, were content to recognize the Provisional Government of the Duma liberals. In fact, there were two executives – the Provisional Government which ran the country in theory, and the Soviet which ran it in practice. The former attempted to put a brake on the movement of the masses and to save the dynasty; the latter controlled and prodded the former, forcing it to democratize the army and to arrest the Tsar. The leader of the Labour group, Kerensky, had joined the Provisional Government as a representative of the Soviet without the latter's authority, and had thus presented it with a *fait accompli*. All Russia had greeted the new regime with enthusiasm.

'In New York, Trotsky had pointed out in *Novy Mir* that the formation of the Provisional Government would create immense social problems. In fact, power had fallen into the hands of the upper-middle classes, accustomed to the mildest kind of parliamentary opposition, and hence anything but Russian democrats. Prince Lvov, a very colourless figure, was Prime Minister; the leader of the Constitutional Democratic Party, Miliukov, was Minister of Foreign Affairs. He was a highly intelligent historian and liberal politician, determined to protect the middle classes at any price – as later events were to show. The important Ministry of War was entrusted to Guchkov, an extreme right-wing liberal who had played an influential part in the reactionary regime that had followed the 1905 revolution . . . Neither agrarian reform nor the establishment of a republic based on universal suffrage could be expected from such men, for they realized only too well that any constituent assembly, no matter what its complexion, would surely drive them out. Kerensky, a Social Revolutionary lawyer and a member of the Soviet, first joined the Cabinet as "Minister of the Revolution", and then informed the Soviet of the step he had taken, covering himself with a smoke screen of eloquent verbiage. The position of the reactionary Guchkov became untenable. When his efforts to maintain discipline in an exhausted army which loathed its command merely hastened the complete break-down of discipline, Kerensky, who knew how to address the troops in the kind of inspirational language they liked to hear, was appointed Minister of War.

'"The more dangerous a party was to the old regime, the more cruelly beheaded it appeared at the moment of the revolution," Trotsky wrote in his *History of the Revolution*. Victor Chernov, the leader of the Social Revolutionaries who looked upon themselves as the party of the peasants, was abroad, and so were the Social Democratic Internationalist Martov, the Mensheviks Tseretelli and Dan, and the Bolsheviks Kamenev, Sverdlov, Rykov and Stalin. Dzerzhinsky was in gaol. Lenin and Zinoviev did not return from Switzerland until April 3rd, 1917, after passing through Germany together with thirty-two other political refugees in the famous "sealed train" – which, incidentally, was not sealed at all but closely guarded by the German police. The British authorities having refused to help Russian political refugees to return from Switzerland to Russia, the Swiss socialist, Fritz Platten, approached the German Embassy in Berne and secured the right of passage for one railway carriage, which was to enjoy extra-territorial rights. Ten European socialists signed a public declaration approving this arrangement (Paul Levy from Germany; Henri Guilbeaux and Fernand Loriot from France; Bronsky from Poland; Fritz Platten from Switzerland;

Lindhausen, the mayor of Stockholm; Stroem, Türe Nerman, Chilboom and Hansen from Sweden and Norway). In his farewell letter to the Swiss workers, Lenin wrote: "It has fallen to the lot of the Russian proletariat to begin the series of revolutions whose objective necessity was created by the imperialist world war ... We know well that the Russian proletariat is less organized and intellectually less prepared for the task than the working class of other countries ... Russia is an agricultural country, one of the most backward in Europe ... But the peasant character of the country may lead to the development of a democratic-capitalist revolution in Russia and make that a prologue to the world-wide Socialist revolution ... "'

It was the third year of World War I. Clemenceau in France was bracing himself for a supreme war effort. The Germans were shelling Paris and had unleashed a vicious submarine war against England. There was fighting in Mesopotamia, Palestine, Macedonia and in the African bush. The Austrians and Germans had broken through the Italian front at Caporetto. The United States entered the war on April 6th, 1917. The Russian Empire had spared neither its blood nor its resources for more than two years, so much so that the country was utterly exhausted and the war detested by both the working masses in the towns and also by the peasantry, from whom the bulk of the army was drawn. In Galicia and Bukovina, the Russian offensives had petered out for lack of ammunition. The army's medical services were undoubtedly the worst organized in the world. The Petrograd garrison, one hundred and fifty thousand peasants in uniform, opted for the Revolution because they held the old regime responsible for a war which they felt was odious.

Three forces were at work in Russia now. First there was the Provisional Government, which represented the liberal bourgeoisie and was attached to the dynasty. This group, in fact, spoke for a tiny minority only – but a minority wielding great fortunes and enjoying the fruits of Empire. Another force was the Soviet, consisting of Social Revolutionaries and Mensheviks who were inclined to compromise with the bourgeoisie because they feared the responsibility of power, and who came to be known collectively as the 'Compromisers'. Finally, there were the masses who looked to the Revolution not for a change of ministry but for an end to the war, an end to semi-feudal misrule and for the creation of a just society and democracy.

When Kerensky, the Minister of War, mounted an offensive in

Galicia on April 18th, 1917, which resulted in the deaths of thousands of young people and quickly turned into defeat, four hundred thousand workers massed in the streets with placards demanding, 'All power to the Soviets!' This was a genuine and spontaneous expression of the popular will, because the Bolsheviks were still in a small minority. Lenin had only just arrived in Russia on April 3rd, and the hundreds of thousands of demonstrators were not voicing agreement with him – it was he who agreed with them. Thus, not so long afterwards, a Bolshevik leaflet addressed to the troops proclaimed: 'Full powers to the workers' and soldiers' Soviets! Immediate peace without annexations or indemnities ... ' But it also called on the soldiers not to dissipate their energies by mutinies against a government supported by the majority of the people, and this at a time when that government was in a state of permanent crisis and its unpopularity was growing!

Petrograd was a large city and the most modern in Russia. It was built in the eighteenth century with long, straight thoroughfares, intersected by canals, and its centre held a host of beautifully proportioned palaces in the baroque or empire style. The River Neva, flanked by embankments of pink granite, divided the city in two – the working-class suburbs had none of this imperial grandeur. They were dingy, with miserable streets and small wooden shacks, but what vigour, thought and devotion the city produced during this anxious yet promising period undoubtedly came from there. The city of the civil servants, of the military, of the upper-middle class, of the Court, of elegance and of commerce, was suddenly filled with army greatcoats, sailors' caps, and throngs of workers on their way to meetings and demonstrations. It seemed that after a long winter sleep everyone was determined to think for himself and to hammer out a new destiny.

'We lived as modestly as we had done in Paris and the Bronx. Each day brought joyful or grave political news together with the constant problem of finding something to eat ... Trotsky was perhaps the most popular speaker in Petrograd; he was pressed day and night by delegations to address naval crews, regiments, factories and trade unions; he often had to speak several times a day. He tried not to overstrain his voice, and to get enough sleep, but it was not always possible. In the Cirque Moderne he had his own platform; it was comparable to a Jacobin Club of the French Revolution, though much more crowded. In the large ring, he would talk to people pouring in from the streets; they made an enthusiastic and intelligent audience, following his every gesture with glowing eyes.'

The day after his arrival in Petrograd, in a speech to the Soviet, he had formulated his three 'commandments': '1. Distrust of the bourgeoisie. 2. Control of our own leaders. 3. Confidence in our own revolutionary forces.' He expressed his 'categorical' lack of confidence in the Provisional Government. Twenty days later, the Soviet of the Kronstadt sailors clashed with the Provisional Government whose orders the Soviet refused to obey. Though the ministers passed repressive measures, Trotsky counselled moderation: 'We must ensure that local authorities are set up and that the ultra-reactionary commissars, who might become the executioners of the revolution, are eliminated ... ' He persuaded the sailors to agree to an amicable resolution and drew up their manifesto of loyalty to the Russian people. This document predicted that one day soon power would pass into the hands of the Soviets. (May 31st, 1917) Trotsky stressed the irreconcilable differences between the aims of the Provisional Government and those of the Petrograd Soviet. 'The impotence both of the government and of the Soviet is leading us into a situation of inconceivable gravity.' (June 2nd, 1917) He drafted a 'peace programme' for the international socialist conference in Stockholm; in it he defended the rights of small nationalities, and the right to national self-determination, called for plebiscites in such disputed cases as Alsace-Lorraine, and advocated a United States of Europe without standing armies or secret diplomacy. 'The United States of Europe is the only conceivable form of the European dictatorship of the proletariat.' At the first All-Russian Congress of Soviets he said, amid interruptions and hostile demonstrations, 'There are no guarantees that we shall not be crushed, that our revolution will not be stifled by a coalition of world capital and that we shall not be nailed to the cross of world imperialism ... ' He saw no salvation except through a European, and especially a German, revolution. 'And if Germany does not rise, or if she rises too feebly, we shall move our troops, united by bonds of revolutionary discipline, not in the cause of national defence but of the revolutionary offensive ... ' (June 9th)

These views brought Trotsky into conflict with the majority of the Soviets. His main opponents were the Minister of the Interior, Tseretelli, and Fedor Dan, both ardent Menshevik supporters of the coalition cabinet, and as such anxious to contain the Revolution by parliamentary rule. Trotsky considered their policy completely mistaken: by denying the popular revolution they were merely paving the way for the necessarily bloody triumph of counter-revolution.

II. *July 1917*

'Trotsky became extremely unpopular with his opponents. A woman friend repeated to me some very unpleasant, indeed threatening, remarks she had overheard in the queue outside the baker's. The other people in our house turned against us. Happily, we made a new friend, a sailor called Markin, whom the boys, then aged twelve and ten, had met at the Smolny Institute. They were quite grown up for their age and passionately interested in politics; Lyova and Sergey were terribly proud of their father. Markin, a large, rather taciturn fellow, with a lofty brow, searching eyes and a ready smile, grew very fond of the children. He told them about his private life, which had been wrecked by a woman's infidelity ... When Markin found out who we were, he spoke up for us discreetly but no doubt very firmly to the other tenants in our house. As revolutionary sailors were highly respected, icy stares made way for friendly greetings almost overnight. Markin later became a valued colleague and a brave comrade-in-arms.'

A real, spontaneous revolution broke out on July 2nd, 1917, and again on the 4th and 5th. The initiative came not from the revolutionary party, which was against it, but from army and works committees, swept forward by the masses. Anarchists played some part in the birth of the new movement. Followed by lorries bristling with machine-guns, massive columns of soldiers and armed workers, many comprising the entire labour-forces of factories, invaded the centre of the capital and marched towards the Tauride Palace, the seat of the Petrograd Soviet, in perfect order, sometimes led by military bands and sometimes with their rifles at the ready. The cry was, 'Down with the capitalist ministers! All power to the Soviets!' The sailors from Kronstadt arrived in formation. Only three regiments stayed loyal to the Provisional Government; when they had superior strength, Cossacks and cadets from the military academies occasionally attacked the demonstrators. But these bloody skirmishes did nothing to stem the human tide. The Bolshevik Central Committee, whom this popular uprising had taken completely by surprise, called first of all on the demonstrators to disperse peacefully; only when this proved of no avail did they make common cause with the masses and try to prevent violence. From the balcony of a small hotel on the right bank of the Neva, which had belonged to a ballerina, Sverdlov and Lenin addressed the determined crowd across a sea of bayonets, and counselled moderation. Zinoviev and Trotsky took the same line, and attempted to check the violence of the masses who were preparing to arrest the Provisional Government and the Executive Committee of the Soviet. Trotsky was on the pavement outside the Tauride Palace when he first saw the extraordinary spectacle of a great mass of humanity surging forward with seemingly irresistible force. Soldiers, sailors and workers carrying red banners advanced in columns of twenty, disciplined and completely controlled, and filled the street from end to end. A Menshevik, who happened to be standing next to Trotsky, turned to him in distress, and reproached him bitterly, 'Now, what do you say?' 'I say we should go and have a look,' Trotsky replied, trying to restrain his enthusiasm, but also alarmed because he shared Lenin's fears that the moment for the seizure of power had not yet come and that there might be unnecessary bloodshed. He knew that, in Petrograd, the battle had been won before it had even been joined. But what of the rest of Russia? Or the soldiers at the front? It was a time to temporize, to urge the masses to go home. Trotsky was standing at the entrance of the Tauride Palace when an angry mob surrounded the 'Peasants' Minister', Victor Chernov, and forced him into a car. Chernov was the grand old man of the Social Revolutionaries and, as such, one of the chief advocates of collaboration with the bourgeoisie. Raskolnikov, a young naval officer and a Bolshevik, tried to release him. Then Trotsky climbed on to the bonnet of the car in which Chernov was being held. He was recognized and a bugle-call ordered silence for him. He shouted, 'All those in favour of violence to Citizen Chernov raise their hands!' When not one hand was raised, Trotsky declared, 'Citizen Chernov is free.'

Thirty thousand workers from the Putilov works were encamped in the courtyard of the Tauride, braving the rain. Armed demonstrators went in and out of the Palace as they pleased. A worker in a blue shirt, with no belt and a rifle in his hand, was heard shouting at Chernov, 'Why don't you take power, you son of a bitch, when they're handing it to you on a plate?' But rain, fatigue and the appeals of the revolutionaries all combined to make the armed demonstrators withdraw on July 5th. At once the Provisional Government and reactionary elements seized the initiative. Pogroms began again to cries of, 'Drown the Jews and Bolsheviks!' The *Pravda* printing works were ransacked. A Minister made a sensational disclosure to the officers of the loyal regiments: irrefutable proof had just come to hand that Lenin and his accomplices were German agents.

III. *Slander campaign. Trotsky in Kresty gaol*

By a tradition as old as political folly and dishonesty, revolutionaries in wartime are said to 'play the enemy's game', even though an incompetent or corrupt government plays into the enemy's hands much more obviously. It is a small step from this accusation to the claim that the opposition is in the pay of the enemy, and to support that claim with a plentiful supply of documents specially forged by the secret services. One could write the most hair-raising stories about the quality of the Tsarist counter-espionage agents, whom the Provisional Government had inherited, and still fail to plumb the depths of their schemes of intrigue. Diplomats and ministers had no sources of information other than offices staffed with double agents, die-hard reactionaries and adventurers in search of easy money. They unleashed a storm of slanders against the Bolsheviks, and particularly against Lenin 'who had come from Germany in a sealed train'. Thousands of socialists had learned to trust Lenin's probity during the past twenty-five years, and found the very idea that a revolutionary of his stamp could have made common cause with the general staff of any army completely ludicrous. However, the voices of these socialists were drowned by those of the masses who knew nothing about the life of underground parties. No wonder, then, that they paid heed not only to the calumnies of the Provisional Government, but also to the wilder accusations of those reactionary forces who claimed that the liberal ministers, the moderate socialists, and even 'that Yid, Kerensky', were in the pay of foreigners. 'Compromisers' of all shades of opinion declared that they did not believe the slanderous story and even tried to do a little, without much enthusiasm to be sure, to defend their revolutionary opponents against the rising tide of filth.

Lenin and Zinoviev escaped to Finland where they lived for some time in a lakeside cabin. On the evening of July 5th, Lenin had said to Trotsky, 'Now they are going to shoot the lot of us.' 'Perhaps not,' Trotsky had replied.

Such liberal statesmen as Miliukov and Nabokov maintained that 'German gold had played a big part in the Russian Revolution.' These leaders of the rich did not know, and probably could not conceive of, the strength of the poor. So many senseless accusations were bruited about that Victor Chernov resigned his ministry – a former Tsarist police chief had described him as a German spy. Officially he was only accused of defeatism, for had he not participated in the Zimmerwald conference of September 1915? On July 20th, Trotsky spoke out in defence of his adversary from the tribune of the Soviet of Workers', Soldiers' and Peasants' Deputies. 'Everybody thinks they can stab Lenin in the back ... Whoever accuses Lenin of being a German agent is a scoundrel. Lenin's good name is as precious to us as Chernov's is to you ... And we will also protect Chernov.' Chernov, he explained next day, was being hounded because he had tried to pass an agrarian law with which the bourgeois ministers did not agree. Chernov withdrew his resignation a few days later. As for the Bolsheviks, the historian Sukhanov, who witnessed the whole affair, said that 'the absurd slander against them blew away like a cloud of smoke.' For a detailed analysis of these events, the reader is referred to Trotsky's *History of the Russian Revolution* and *My Life*. General Ludendorff had this to say in his *Memoirs*: 'I could not suppose that [the Russian Revolution] would become the tomb of our might ...'

'Trotsky, though not himself included in the official slander campaign, expressed his solidarity with Lenin in an open letter to the Provisional Government, published in Maxim Gorky's diary. "You cannot," he wrote, "have any logical grounds for excluding me from the decree on the basis of which you saw fit to issue a warrant for the arrest of Comrades Lenin, Zinoviev and Kamenev ... As you can have no reason to doubt, I am no less determined an opponent of the Provisional Government's general policy than these Comrades ... " During the night of July 24th, 1917, while a Kerensky Cabinet was being formed, Trotsky came home at about two in the morning after attending a number of meetings. He went to bed and fell into a deep sleep. I myself slept very fitfully, as if sensing danger. When I heard the thud of boots in the courtyard of the building, I woke up at once and drew back the curtains: the courtyard was full of soldiers. The soft darkness showed the first light of dawn. I shook Trotsky. "They've come," I said. He got dressed. I told Larin, with whom we were staying. He was in no hurry to open up. An officer appeared. He began by asking for Lunacharsky, but in spite of the telephone calls we made, ended up by taking Trotsky away.

'He was held in the Kresty gaol, as in 1905. Raskolnikov, Kamenev and Lunacharsky were there, too ... I tried to get permission to visit him but the examining magistrate, a man called Aleksandrov, made excuses not to see me. I slipped a porter a rouble to make an appointment for me. When I eventually got to see him he was quite friendly, but I refused to shake hands with him ... I was allowed to speak to Trotsky through a metal grille. "You did right," Trotsky said. "You don't shake hands with people like that ... " The charges against Trotsky were even more inept than they were far-fetched. They tried to question him about his alleged journey through Germany with Lenin; they quite obviously mixed him up with Martov, who did return to Russia in the "sealed carriage". Next, they wanted to know whether he had not brought ten thousand dollars of German gold from New York. In fact, Russian, Latvian, Lithuanian, Finnish and German socialists in New York had given him the proceeds of a collection, which amounted to $310 and which he used to defray the travelling expenses of five political exiles ... The prosecutor's master-stroke was the testimony of an N.C.O. called Ermolenko, a double agent who had been paid by the Germans to establish contact with the Ukrainian nationalists and who had heard some German officers say, "Lenin is working in the same direction ... " Trotsky threw the papers in the magistrate's face, declaring that he thought it degrading to cooperate further in an investigation of that type.

'The British Ambassador, who some months earlier had tried to justify the Russians' detention in Canada on the grounds that they were pro-German, now took good care not to repeat the charge.

'Our children had been sent to Terioki, in Finland, near the Russian frontier. I used to go and see them now and then and found them happy, sunburnt and mad about swimming and fishing. One day, I discovered them crouched in a corner, furious and hurt. Some people in the boarding-house had apparently said that Lenin and Trotsky were German spies. The two lads had thrown themselves at the slanderers, one armed with a knife and the other with a chair ... All day, while waiting for me, they had eaten nothing. I took them back to Petrograd.

'Most of the people Trotsky met in the prison exercise yards were young workers, soldiers and sailors, all of them embittered and indignant. They had believed in freedom and the revolution; they had never imagined that all it boiled down to was political chicanery. The Cossacks were roaming the streets again; examining magistrates of the old regime were instituting all sorts of proceedings; the Tsar's rabble had a free hand; prices were rising and the indiscriminate printing of paper money turned wages into a practical joke, and there was no prospect of improvement. Leon Davidovich told the prisoners that the true revolution would not come until the exploited classes themselves seized power. He felt sure that the prisoners' indignation was matched by that felt in the workers' suburbs and that the coalition of "Compromisers", who claimed to stand for "revolutionary democracy", with the liberal bourgeoisie and their reactionary allies, could not last for long. And he was right.

'At the preliminary trial, he was the only one to adopt a fiercely aggressive stand, accusing the magistrate of being in league with forgers and slanderers.

'Whenever I saw him, he was in good spirits. Lyova and Sergey used to bring him food. Since the trams were always crowded, they used to ride on the buffers.'

IV. *Kornilov's insurrection*

The danger was mounting. The failure of the July uprising had strengthened the forces of reaction. The propertied classes, driven by fear, rejoiced at the thought that the monster of Bolshevism had at last been decapitated. 'Revolutionary democracy', that is, the Social Revolutionaries and the Mensheviks, had lost a good deal of ground and was now shivering in the cold wind of unpopularity. True, the new Kerensky cabinet had a majority of socialist ministers and the Ministry of Agriculture had even gone to the Social Revolutionary, Chernov, whom the Press had accused of inciting the peasantry, but, in fact, the socialist ministers were more impotent now than when they had been in a minority. Kerensky strutted about as 'the leader of the nation' but the 'Compromisers' in the Soviets merely tolerated him for want of a more credible figure, and the Constitutional Democratic Party (the so-called Cadets), representing the liberal bourgeoisie, distrusted him and preferred to place their faith in the generals of the old regime. The situation was manifestly unstable, and Miliukov agreed with Lenin and Trotsky that a strong and stable government was needed. The only point at issue was by whom and for whom. In his *History of the Revolution*, a lucid bourgeois account, Miliukov says that August 1917 was the year of secret conclaves and intrigues aiming at a dictatorship. Kerensky wanted dictatorial powers to bolster up his self-appointed role of arbiter between the classes; the League of Officers, openly supported by the industrialists, merchants, financiers and landowners, preferred General Kornilov, 'hero and leader of the Russian people'.

Kerensky then called a State Conference in Moscow, far away – as he thought – from the revolutionary atmosphere of the capital. Here all Russia's 'social forces' would be represented, with Soviet delegates nicely balanced by the bourgeoisie and the army command. Kerensky was careful not to raise the question of a republic; he spoke as the chairman of the Council of Ministers of the 'Russian State'. General Kornilov turned up with a guard of honour of Tekke Cossacks in red cloaks, sabres drawn. He played on the danger to the nation, saying that the Germans were on the point of taking Riga, and demanding full powers. The Right applauded enthusiastically, their obvious delight only marred by the knowledge that the workers of Moscow had called a one-day protest strike, which was so complete that the assembled notables could not even ride on a tram or be served with a drink. A secret strike committee of two Mensheviks, two Social Revolutionaries and two Bolsheviks was in constant session, ready to call out the workers and the garrison in case of a Rightist coup d'état. Inside the assembly, there were several clashes between the Right and the Left. In particular, when a young Cossack officer rose to disassociate his men from an extremely reactionary speech by General Kaledin, *Hetman* of the Don army, the Left rose in a body, shouting, 'Glory to the revolutionary Cossacks!', while the Right protested indignantly. One of the officers shouted 'German marks!' whereupon there was uproar and the Left immediately closed ranks. Civil war was in the air.

Miliukov, who had a confidential interview with Kornilov in order to draft or conclude an agreement between the Liberal Party and the generals, described him as 'short but solidly built, with Mongolian features, small black and piercing eyes that would light up mischievously'. The reactionaries' candidate for the job of dictator was, in fact, a defeated war lord – he had foolishly lost his division, been captured and later escaped from Austria. He was known as a man of great physical courage, but his colleagues, Generals Alexeiev, Brusilov, Denikin and Ruszky, thought little of his wider ability. Low intelligence but high personal courage, inflexibility to the point of cruelty, lack of scruple, arrogance – such were the qualities that made the reactionaries look upon him as an ideal leader. The corner-stone of his entire programme was the reintroduction of the death penalty in the army, both at the front and also behind the lines, so as to purge the soul of the nation with the help of the firing squad. Kerensky had just appointed him commander-in-chief of the Russian Army.

On August 21st, the Germans captured Riga. Though all eye-witnesses were agreed that the Latvian soldiers, who had gone over to the Bolsheviks, fought bravely in the defence of their capital and withdrew in exemplary order, and that the general staff had once again proved its incompetence, the press blamed the defeat on 'workers who would not work and soldiers who would not fight'. The story was picked up by all the major newspapers of Europe. On August 26th and 27th, Kornilov sent the so-called 'Savage Divi-sion' consisting of Caucasian cavalrymen and commanded by General Krymov, not against the Germans but against Petrograd. The socialist 'Compromisers' who had a majority in the Soviets, real-ized at once that their policy had failed and that Kornilov was about to unleash a campaign of terror against the working classes. The Menshevik minister, Tseretelli, who had spent the day before disarm-ing the Kronstadt sailors, was now calling them back to arms.

The atmosphere in Petrograd had changed so much that, far from believing the false charges against him, sailors came to Kresty Prison to seek Trotsky's advice, offering to release him and the other pri-soners by force or even to arrest the Provisional Government. 'No,' Trotsky told them, 'don't shoulder the responsibility of a mutiny at this critical moment ... Our hour is coming.' But the situa-tion remained tense and it was feared that the 'Savage Division' would take Petrograd by surprise and massacre all the political prisoners.

One day, Trotsky was walking in the prison yard with sub-lieutenant Raskolnikov, a determined lad with strong features, who was extremely popular with the Kronstadt sailors. 'What cowards they are,' Trotsky said of the government. 'They ought to declare Kornilov an outlaw, so that any soldier might know that he had the right to shoot him down.'

Petrograd remained calm. On August 27th, Savinkov, the ex-terrorist Social Revolutionary and now Minister of War and of the

Navy, announced that General Kornilov enjoyed the complete confidence of the Provisional Government. That same day, Kerensky relieved Kornilov of his supreme command. In fact, there was no longer any government, since the Liberal ministers – the Constitutional Democrats – had resigned the day before, lest they would have to support or oppose Kornilov openly. In any case, it no longer mattered. Kornilov, the 'dictator-hero', replied to a summons by Kerensky with a manifesto in which he declared that 'the Provisional Government, having yielded to the pressure of the Bolshevik majority in the Soviets, is now working hand-in-glove with the German General Staff.' He would outlaw all Bolsheviks, moderate socialists and even Kerensky himself. Miliukov, the leader of the Liberals, advised Kerensky to resign because power was obviously on Kornilov's side, and offered his services as a mediator. The British Ambassador, Buchanan, made a similar offer. Kornilov's victory seemed imminent.

At this point, the Petrograd Soviet set up a Committee of Revolutionary Defence. Red Guards were hurriedly formed in all working-class districts and within a very short time forty thousand men had joined their ranks. The Putilov works issued them with about a hundred field-guns; the railwaymen disrupted the communications of the seditious army; the printing workers made sure that papers of the Left continued to appear. Kronstadt offered to fight. The soldiers and sailors heard that firing squads were being brought in by Kornilov and, at Vyborg, they shot their superior officers for concealing the news from them. Kerensky appealed to the Bolsheviks 'to come to the defence of the Revolution'.

The Commander of the 'Savage Division' was unable to move his men because the railwaymen had blocked the track by tearing the rails up. Kornilov's Cossacks were holding meetings, some of which were addressed by speakers from the Soviet. The soldiers raised a banner with the inscription 'Land and Liberty' over the staff car of the 'Savage Division'. Delegations from various Petrograd regiments went out to meet Kornilov's troops, not to fight but to talk. In the end Kornilov was left with no more than eight badly armed Cossack squadrons, and these disintegrated so quickly that the would-be dictator found himself isolated. General Krymov, having been summoned to Petrograd by Kerensky, listened to the Prime Minister's remonstrations and then blew his brains out. The 'Savage Division' ceased to exist, but the Red Guards in the workers' districts

remained. Kornilov was arrested a few days later and replaced as
Commander-in-Chief by General Alexeiev.

Kornilov was treated by the authorities with the utmost consideration, being kept under purely nominal arrest from which, with the
connivance of the High Command, he later escaped, to start the Civil
War in Southern Russia. He was killed at Ekaterinodar in 1918.

'On September 4th, Trotsky was granted bail of three thousand
roubles and released. I went to fetch him from the gaol, but he had
gone straight to a meeting of the Soviet Executive Committee. The
emotions generated by the insurrection had not yet subsided. People
wondered how the High Command would react and murmured
about Kerensky's and Savinkov's collusion with the seditious
general. Yesterday's persecutors and their victims were unexpectedly
reunited by the common danger. A few days later the Petrograd
Soviet had its first Bolshevik majority. Tseretelli, handing over to
Trotsky, said, "May you last as long as three months!"'

(v) *Between two dictatorships. Trotsky as President of the Petrograd
Soviet*

The pitiful attempt of the reactionaries to set up a dictatorship had
utterly discredited and divided the Provisional Government. The
view of Miliukov, who most accurately mirrored the feelings of the
upper-middle class, the generals, the aristocracy and the employers,
was that Kerensky had betrayed Kornilov after first encouraging
him; the Socialists, and even those 'Compromisers' among them who
still supported Kerensky for want of anyone better, regarded him
as being suspect of complicity, to say the least, with Kornilov. As
for his colleague, Savinkov, the former terrorist turned Minister of
War, their suspicion quickly turned into certainty; he was dismissed
from the government and expelled from the Social Revolutionary
Party. Miliukov concluded that Russia, now 'divided into two irreconcilable halves' had only two choices – Kornilov or Lenin. It goes
without saying that Miliukov, the liberal statesman, did not state
this conclusion publicly at the time; it was Miliukov, the historian,
who did so much later, in his *History of the Russian Revolution*. He
had had a confidential interview with Kornilov and he had known
the date of the attempted insurrection well in advance. An article
by Miliukov, written for the Liberal daily *Rech* (the *Word*) on August
29th, the day that Kornilov's insurrection collapsed, and scrapped

at the very last moment so that the paper appeared with blank spaces, was handed to Ryazanov by the printing workers and eventually published. It contained the following sentence: 'We are not afraid to say that General Kornilov has pursued the very path we ourselves believe is needed for the salvation of the Fatherland.' Apparently the Liberals who were 'not afraid to say' such things on the morning of August 29th had developed cold feet by the evening of the same day. Industrialists locked up their factories, declaring a state of famine at the same time. The bread ration in Petrograd was one pound of black bread per day; in Moscow it was just under two pounds a week. Workers demonstrated in the textile factory districts with placards saying simply 'We are hungry'.

The Bolsheviks were making headway. As the Russian Social Democratic Workers' Party they had held their semi-clandestine Fifth Congress in August. In the absence of Lenin and Zinoviev, who had fled the country, and of Trotsky, who was in prison, the main reports were submitted by Bukharin and Stalin. It was decided to combine forces with the 'United Social Democrats', better known as the *Mezhraiontsy*, whose leaders included Lunacharsky, Joffe, Ryazanov, Uritsky, Karakhan, Trotsky and Manuilsky. As a result four thousand militants were brought into the fold.

The new Central Committee consisted of Lenin, Zinoviev, Trotsky, Kamenev, Nogin, Alexandra Kollontai (who was in prison), Stalin, Sverdlov, Rykov, Bukharin, Artem, Joffe, Uritsky, Miliutin and Lomov. The party now had a hundred and seventy-six thousand members. Lenin recommended a compromise with the moderate socialists. 'All power to the Soviets – a government made up of Social Revolutionaries and Mensheviks and responsible to the Soviets ... At this moment, but only at this moment ... this kind of government can take power by peaceful means ... ' However, the Social Revolutionaries (led by Chernov) and the Mensheviks (led by Tseretelli and Dan) bluntly refused to take office without the bourgeoisie and in opposition to it. Lenin then wrote that by seizing power 'the Soviets could still – and this is probably their last chance – ensure the peaceful progress of the revolution ... ' If not, 'the force of circumstances is such as to make a bloody civil war inevitable ... ' (Articles written on September 3rd and 26th, 1917.)

A democratic conference called by the 'Compromisers' was held from September 14th to 22nd in the Aleksandrinsky Theatre. Its object was to establish a so-called Pre-Parliament intended to support, check, inspire and direct the Provisional Government. It was composed of representatives of all popular democratic organizations, but in such a way that the 'extremists' would be in a minority. The conference gave Kerensky a mixed reception: there was strong heckling as well as applause from his supporters. Trotsky spoke sharply amid stormy interruptions but clearly had the support of the Left. When Kerensky, questioned about the reintroduction of the death penalty, replied, 'Why don't you wait till I have signed my first death sentence?', Trotsky said, 'If the death penalty was necessary in the first place, then how dare Kerensky say that he will not make use of it? And if he considers it possible to promise ... not to apply the death penalty then ... its restoration becomes an act of foolishness transcending the limits of criminality.' Trotsky then rounded on the 'Compromisers' with, 'You are turning that man into a lynchpin of Russian Bonapartism.' (Uproar and shouts of 'Liar! Demagogue!') The vote showed that the government benches were in sad disarray. After the coalition had gained a scant majority out of the 1,492 votes, an amendment excluding the Cadets was passed, thus making a coalition quite unworkable. Kerensky, for one, refused to take any part in an exclusively socialist government.

He accordingly formed a new cabinet with the Cadets. It included Konovalov, considered to be a left-winger by his fellow Liberals; Tretiakov, President of the Moscow Stock Exchange Committee; Smirnov, President of the Moscow Military Industrial Committee; and Tereshchenko, a leading sugar manufacturer, who was made Foreign Minister. On the same day, the Bolsheviks won a majority on the Executive Committee of the Petrograd Soviet. There were now thirteen Bolsheviks, six Social Revolutionaries and three Mensheviks, with Trotsky as President. The new majority reflected a shift in working-class opinion, which had, at last, placed real power in the hands of the most uncompromising revolutionary party. During the 'democratic conference', Lenin had sent the Bolshevik leaders a number of hastily written notes from his hiding-place, all calling for immediate action, and particularly for an end to the farce in the Aleksandrinsky Theatre. The Bolsheviks decided that he had failed to appreciate the real situation in the capital. Later, the Central Committee considered destroying these notes; Lenin opposed the step on the ground that he did not want them to create around him a legend of infallibility.

Should the Bolsheviks take part in the Pre-Parliament, recognize its usefulness and sanction its activities by their presence? The Central Committee was divided on this point. Trotsky, Stalin and Sverdlov were against taking part, but Rykov, Kamenev and Nogin voted for participation and obtained a majority at a meeting of some hundred and thirty militants. Lenin came down strongly in favour of Trotsky's stand. On about September 20th, 1917, Trotsky appeared before the Pre-Parliament and read a declaration of his party's programme. The Bolsheviks then walked out. The declaration included the following points:

'(1) Expropriation without compensation of landed estates ... (2) Workers' control of production and distribution and of the banks; nationalization of the most important industries ... (3) Abrogation of secret treaties ... an immediate offer of a democratic peace to all the peoples at war ... (4) The right of national self-determination; the ending of repression in Finland and the Ukraine ...' In addition, there were a number of more immediate demands, including: '(1) An end to repressive measures against the working class; abolition of the death penalty in the army ... the removal of all counter-revolutionary elements from army cadres ... (2) The election of local authorities ... (3) Arming of the working class and formation of Red Guards. (4) Dissolution of the Council of State and the Imperial Duma. Immediate convocation of a Constitutional Assembly. (5) Abolition of the privileges of the nobility and equal rights for all citizens. (6) An eight-hour working day and social security.'

From mid-September, Lenin sent message after message to the Central Committee from Finland, all peremptory in tone, calling for the immediate seizure of power, if need be by insurrection. As the Bolsheviks were in the majority in the Moscow and Petrograd Soviets, Lenin had no doubts about their easy victory.

The Kerensky cabinet announced that it would 'not shrink from the most energetic measures' to maintain order. It declared the Committee of Baltic sailors dissolved, but immediately revoked the order. It sent troops to occupy the city of Tashkent in Turkestan, where the Soviet, largely Social Revolutionary in composition, had seized power. The troops were met with a general strike, and the situation remained unchanged. There were growing fears of yet another Rightist insurrection.

VI. *Portrait of Trotsky*

This is the story of a man and not a history of the Russian Revolution, but at this point in our account the man was so closely linked with history that he became an integral part of it. He seemed to be its spokesman and its conscious and willing instrument. He was undoubtedly a leader of the masses, but only because he understood them well enough to translate their aspirations and will into ideas and actions. He stood out from his peers because of his personal ability, which he had scorned to use for selfish ends ever since he had been an adolescent. His name appeared daily in the columns of the world press, and many journalists to whom the mentality of the Russian revolutionaries was a complete mystery described him as ambitious. If he sought power, it was for the workers, soldiers and peasants, not for its rewards or for his own glorification. To him, power was – and would become so increasingly – nothing but a source of heavy responsibility, danger and worry. If he was prepared to exercise power, it was only in order to serve.

In his speeches he often invoked history. 'History has condemned these parties ... the scrap-heap of history awaits him ... the logic of history ... history teaches... ' He was not conjuring up a myth but invoking a discipline that would serve him as a guide to action, and was hence unlike those dry academic discussions for which he had no time. He would often refer to the French Revolution; he believed, and said, that if the Russian proletariat lacked intelligence and resolution, it would suffer the fate of the Paris Commune. Trotsky's powerful personality was matched by his remarkable and sincere self-effacement. Thus he delivered brilliant speeches on behalf of the Kronstadt sailors (and it was not known until much later that he was the author of their manifesto), on behalf of the Soviets and of the Party, but only after long discussions during which he would listen, make suggestions, yield ground and never lay down the law unless basic principles were at stake. It would be absurd to call him ambitious but less than frank to call him modest. He was well aware of his worth, and clearly considered himself superior to many. This was obvious from his sardonic smile when he listened to some of their arguments. He was not afraid to dismiss some great man of the moment as an 'incurable poseur', 'a narcissistic braggard', or a 'tireless phrase-monger', during private discussions that turned out to be not particularly private after all. While granting that someone had an excellent brain, he might add that he was paralysed by timidity and lack of resolution. But as soon as it came to his comrades-in-arms, the sardonic smile and the snap judgments were gone; instead, there was a brotherly concern to praise and foster whatever strength, talent and devotion there was in them. He thought of himself as no more than one of the first in a massive push forward. This attitude was by no means peculiar to Trotsky: it was shared to a greater or lesser extent by an entire revolutionary generation, inspired by an unselfish ambition to achieve the Revolution and to start the transformation of the world. This spirit was born during the 1860s; it was fathered by the Nihilists, who had rejected the old values and defended rational thought and social duty in Chernyshevsky's day. The Marxists had enriched this mixture with socialist objectivity, minimizing the role of the lone individual in history and stressing that of the individual working alongside the masses. This generation did not die out until 1936–7 – when those who had survived were killed in the dungeons of the Lubianka.

'During the last two months before the Bolsheviks seized power, we were living with comrades in the strictly middle-class district near the Tauride Palace. We had just one room. People of means had begun to "speculate", buying food on the black market, but we lived off our rations and the occasional windfall. Leon Davidovich took no rest or recreation. We had no time to pay visits or to receive visitors. Personal relations went entirely by the board and were replaced by contacts with militants. Leon Davidovich went to work very early in the morning. As President of the Soviet he had been assigned a large, square, sparsely furnished room in the Smolny Institute where he received hundreds of delegates from various organizations every day ... The staircases were strewn with sunflower seeds. There were posters and hand-written notices all along the walls. Crowds of people in peaked caps and dark green tunics moved along the corridors. Telephones shrilled non-stop. You had to develop a special skill to sort out the facts from the rumours ... Leon Davidovich did his best to husband his energies without sparing himself. He tried hard to avoid overwork and to discipline himself so as to achieve "optimum output". The fashion was for casual clothes – he never followed it. He was indifferent to fashion and could not understand people who bothered about the precise shade of a necktie, but he had an innate fastidiousness and a horror – particularly for himself as President – of slovenliness in dress, as in all other matters. He took his meals in the canteen, a large hall containing wooden tables and benches. There he would eat indifferent cabbage or fish soup, *kasha* [buckwheat porridge], stewed fruit and tea. He did not smoke. He was slightly above average height, well built but not overweight. His complexion was pale, set off by his thick dark hair, small moustache and a little beard at the point of his chin. His pince-nez accentuated his penetrating look. He was to be thirty-eight on November 7th, 1917, the day of the victorious rising.

'In all this feverish activity, he hardly had time to see his children. He often spotted his older daughters, Zina and Nina, two big girls with shining eyes, among the crowds at public meetings, at the end of which he was invariably surrounded by so many people that he could not exchange more than a look and a smile with his children. Our two boys were at high school; they sometimes went to the Soviet after their lessons. I was working for the Cabinet-Makers' Union and was given permission to have the boys in for lunch with me.'

VII. *Trotsky is made President of the Military Revolutionary Committee of the Petrograd Soviet*

Ever since the fall of Riga, the Army High Command, in agreement with the Provisional Government, had wanted to send the Petrograd garrison to the front, ostensibly for the defence of the capital. Could those who had failed to defend Riga, only to use its fall as a pretext for a coup d'état, be trusted? Was their object not simply to disarm the workers, to bleed the revolutionary troops, rather than to deploy them to the best effect? Would their despatch to the front not be the final sacrifice of the Revolution on the altar of a pointless war, run by the Tsar's old generals? The soldiers' section of the Soviet, no less than the workers' section and the Bolshevik Party, decided to oppose the posting of any member of the garrison outside the city. Petrograd could, after all, be defended on the spot and the Revolution must not, whatever happened, be left to the mercy of the generals. From the tribune of the Soviet, Trotsky quoted the right-wing liberal, Mikhail Rodzianko, who had been President of the Duma during the March days and had issued this extraordinarily cynical and inept statement to *Utro Rossii* (*Russia's Morning*): 'Petrograd is in danger ... Let Petrograd fare as it may ... They say that if it should fall, the central institutions may go under as well ... My answer is that

I should be very happy to see them go under; they have done Russia nothing but harm ... ' There could have been no clearer or more authoritative statement of right-wing defeatism. Rodzianko went on: 'After the surrender of Riga, law and order returned to the city; it was safer than ever before. All that was needed for complete security was to shoot a handful of agitators and bring back the police ... ' When he was reminded that the fall of Petrograd would involve the loss of the Baltic fleet, Rodzianko replied that some crews were completely demoralized already. At which Trotsky commented, 'So the bourgeoisie intends to deliver up Petrograd and the fleet to the Kaiser!'

The Soviet decided to set up a Military Revolutionary Committee charged with establishing contact with the fleet, the Finnish garrison and the front lines, as well as with supervising all measures connected with the defence of the capital. The 'Compromisers' vainly opposed this initiative, which they had good reason to denounce as a preparation for the seizure of power by the Bolsheviks.

At that moment, the strands of power in Russia were tenuously interwoven. Kerensky pretended to govern and believed he was governing in fact, but the only real authority behind him was the General Staff in Mogiliev. The Bolsheviks had a majority in such important Soviets as those of Petrograd, Moscow and Tsaritsyn, but the socialist 'Compromisers' still had a majority in the executive committees of these Soviets. The peasants, who had increasingly taken to seizing estates, and burning the 'nests' of the aristocracy and of the gentry, were still almost entirely under the influence of their traditional party, the Social Revolutionaries, led by Chernov, Gotz and Avksentiev. They were, however, becoming more and more disillusioned by Government delays in passing the agrarian law and in summoning the Constituent Assembly which was to settle the agrarian problem. The Constituent Assembly was scheduled to meet on November 29th – but would it not be postponed again? Would a reactionary coup not prevent its convocation? From over ninety per cent of the agricultural districts that made up the immensity of Russia came reports of clashes and bloodshed.

Trotsky addressed the Congress of Northern Soviets on October 12th. It was decided to convoke the Second All-Russian Congress of Soviets on October 20th, a proposal to which the Central Executive of the Soviets agreed with ill grace. In Petrograd, tension mounted by the day. There was talk of nothing but the imminent uprising; the newspapers even gave dates – this week, next week. While the Petrograd Soviet issued denials, the Cossacks announced a patriotic demonstration. Both sides were keeping their powder dry. Trotsky thundered at a vast crowd: 'Let this be your oath – to defend with all your might, at whatever cost, this Soviet which has shouldered the glorious task of leading the Revolution to victory, and to give the people land, bread and peace.' The crowd, their hands raised, solemnly repeated the oath in rhythmic unison.

When a delegation of workers from Sestroretsk arsenal came to offer him weapons, Trotsky signed an order for five thousand rifles to be issued to the Red Guards. He had no right to do so as the arsenal belonged to the state, and was pleasantly surprised when the arms were actually delivered. He did not treat his responsibilities to the Soviet lightly. One rainy night, on leaving the Smolny Institute after an extended sitting, he burst out laughing at the sight of the two cars placed at the disposal of the entire Soviet, turned up his collar and strode off alone through the puddles. Sverdlov took the tram.

At the Garrison Conference held on October 21st, Trotsky moved a number of brief resolutions which were passed. The third of them called on the Congress of Soviets to seize power.

The Military Revolutionary Committee, with Trotsky as its President, broke officially with the garrison staff, and declared that none of its orders need be obeyed unless they were endorsed by the Committee. The staff begged to disagree with this decision.

The Soviet called a series of meetings for October 22nd, which was a day both of feverish exultation and of the rallying of workers, soldiers and enthusiastic ordinary people. In the Maison du Peuple, beneath its great metal dome, Trotsky called on the masses and on the garrison to defend the coming Congress of Soviets and to impose its will. In his *Russian Revolution* Sukhanov wrote:

Around me there was a mood very near to ecstasy. The crowd looked as if, at any moment and without a word or signal, it might break into a fervent hymn ... Trotsky had formulated some brief and very general resolution, something like, 'We shall defend the cause of the workers and peasants to the last drop of blood. Those in favour?' – and thousands raised their hands as one man. I looked at the lifted hands and burning eyes of the men, women, boys, workers, soldiers, peasants, and of the typically petit bourgeois characters, too ... Trotsky continued to speak, and the packed crowd kept their hands raised high ...'

The Peter and Paul fortress, built on an island on the Neva in the centre of Petrograd, bristling with arms and containing an arsenal of a hundred thousand rifles, was held by troops hostile to the Military Revolutionary Committee, and hence promised to be a good strategic base for the Provisional Government. Trotsky proposed to take it from within, by persuasion. He went there accompanied only by the Bolshevik N.C.O., Lashevich. At the Smolny, the result of this mission was anxiously awaited. Inside the fortress walls, Trotsky and Lashevich were virtually powerless in the hands of their enemies. Anti-Bolshevik speeches were being made as they arrived, but the men decided to give them a hearing as well, with the result that the garrison decided to place itself under the command of the Military Revolutionary Committee (October 23rd).

VIII. *Trotsky organizes and directs the rising of November 7th, 1917*

Lenin, the champion of an immediate uprising, returned from Finland to Petrograd so as to be present during crucial meetings of the Bolshevik Central Committee. Needless to say, he was in disguise, so the meetings were held with a minimum of security precautions. On October 10th the Committee assembled in the flat of the Menshevik historian, Sukhanov. Sukhanov himself was not told, but his wife was a Bolshevik. Lenin came in wig and spectacles, and had shaved off his beard. The twelve present (out of the twenty-one-man Central Committee) had tea and sandwiches of black bread and sausage during their closed discussion. Sverdlov spoke of 'a conspiracy by the High Command'. Kamenev and Zinoviev, Lenin's two most faithful supporters, spoke against the proposed uprising. Trotsky's old friends, Joffe, Uritsky and Sokolnikov, as well as Trotsky himself, supported Lenin. A Committee of Seven was elected to deal with the political direction of the movement, consisting of Lenin, Zinoviev, Kamenev, Trotsky, Stalin, Sokolnikov and Bubnov. However, this Committee never met.

On October 16th, members of the Central Committee met members of the Petrograd party committee and others in the suburbs. A vote in favour of an insurrection was carried by twenty votes to two (Zinoviev and Kamenev). This majority did not exactly mirror the state of mind of a number of militants who would have preferred a postponement and greater circumspection. Rykov, Tomsky, Nogin, Manuilsky, Frunze, Kalinin, Chudnovsky, Volodarsky, Miliutin and Stalin, in their different ways, all sympathized with Kamenev and Zinoviev. Their chief argument was that 'we have no right to stake everything on the card of armed insurrection'; that the Provisional Government was strong enough to inflict a bloody defeat on the masses; and that it would be wiser to establish an influential opposition in the republican institutions of the future, particularly in the Constituent Assembly. That opposition would, in due course, take power peaceably or, if necessary, by revolution.

Trotsky agreed with Lenin that the propitious situation would not last indefinitely; that the disillusioned masses would soon sink back into indifference; that the revolutionary party, weakened as a result, would be defeated or driven back by the counter-revolution; and, finally, that the bourgeoisie would make a separate peace with Germany and that Russia would remain 'a semi-imperialist and semi-colonial capitalist country'. However, Trotsky, unlike Lenin, believed that the uprising must have a defensive character and he was against intervention by the Red Guards except in defence of the Soviet Congress. 'But won't *they* forestall us?' Lenin asked suspiciously. He favoured an initiative and was convinced that the counter-revolution would strike at any moment. 'They'll take us by surprise,' he said.

The debate grew acrimonious. 'Lenin has gone mad,' some of his comrades were saying. On October 17th, Zinoviev and Kamenev wrote to Maxim Gorky's paper *New Life*, attacking the decision adopted the night before. Lenin demanded their expulsion from the party, but this request was turned down. 'Are you for or against the insurrection?' people would ask one another as soon as they met. When Trotsky's sister, Olga Kameneva, put the same question to me on the stairs in the Smolny, and I replied 'For, of course,' she walked away with a disapproving toss of her head.

Kerensky, meanwhile, reassured the High Command that the Provisional Government was in full control of the situation. Addressing his ministers in the Winter Palace, he was brimming over with confidence and even declared that the new move gave him the happy chance to 'finish off the Bolsheviks once and for all'. If they went into action, 'they will be crushed completely; I have more men than

I need.' *Rech*, the Cadet newspaper, said much the same thing in its edition of October 21st, and it was widely believed that the Bolsheviks' impending defeat would reduce their influence in the Constituent Assembly altogether. The 'Compromisers' continued to compromise; in particular, they advised Kerensky not to place the Military Revolutionary Committee under arrest, a feat that would, in any case, have been difficult to accomplish.

In the decisive days of October 23rd, 24th and 25th, 1917, the Provisional Government gradually collapsed under popular pressure. It was as if a phantom, once regarded by others no less than by itself as a creature of flesh and blood, had been unmasked. Kerensky's Cabinet took decisions and ordered up troops from the front, but the troops scarcely moved; it ordered the bridges over the Neva to be raised, but the insurgents promptly lowered them again and traffic went on as usual; the Minister of Justice, Maliantovich, who had been Trotsky's defending counsel during the St Petersburg trial of the Soviet deputies in 1906, ordered the arrest of the ring-leaders and above all of 'Bronstein-Trotsky', but a colonel, accompanied by a handful of men, who had ventured into a working-class district in search of Lenin, was himself arrested. Kerensky was still addressing the Pre-Parliament assembled in the Mariinsky Palace. 'We are faced with an insurrection,' he said, 'and this just at the moment when the Provisional Government is taking up the question of transferring the land to the peasant committees and of measures to bring the war to an end.' Not before time! He went on to say that the 'rabble' would be routed. 'Those groups and parties who have dared to lift their hands against the state are liable to immediate, decisive and permanent liquidation.' Vain rhetoric! Kerensky, the applause of the Right still ringing in his ears, was not even given a vote of confidence by the socialist 'Compromisers' – Dan and Matov declared that he shared responsibility for the situation with the Bolsheviks.

On October 25th, the day on which the control of the capital passed into the hands of the Military Revolutionary Committee, Kerensky scuttled backwards and forwards between the Winter Palace, the seat of government, and his headquarters, a hundred yards away across the square. Anxious ministers, who no longer had any ministries, staff or cars, arrived one by one, having been allowed through by insurgent patrols. At headquarters, senior officers became desperate; the great white staircases were deserted; General Alexeiev withdrew discreetly; through the windows the square was seen to be empty. Kerensky then placed the engineer Palchinsky in charge, promised him strong reinforcements from the front, climbed into a car which somebody had discovered and which flew the American flag, and made off at full speed.

IX. *The seizure of power*

The city lay perfectly calm. Only the working class, the garrison and the phantom government took the slightest interest in what was happening: the middle classes were quite happy, for they were firmly convinced that the tide was turning and that there would be vigorous reprisals against the Bolsheviks. The main streets displayed their customary air of affluence; public offices, schools and theatres carried on as usual, the shops were open and the black marketeers as busy as ever; the night clubs entertained their usual clientele of officers, and people enjoyed themselves. It rained steadily.

The Smolny Institute was well over a mile away from the city centre, with its Winter Palace, Army Headquarters, grand-ducal palaces and smart restaurants. The two were worlds apart. The Institute was a large building in the bleak Empire style; by its side stood a baroque monastery with pretty blue domes, surrounded by gardens. The Smolny backed on to the black and swollen Neva. Across the river lay the working-class districts of Okhta and Vyborg, now heavily fortified. The streets near the Institute were straight, unpretentious, even shabby. Men with peaked caps, who had marched en masse from their factories, and detachments of troops gathered in them solemnly, braving the cold, autumnal rain. Formerly, the Smolny had been occupied by young ladies of the nobility. The old signs above the doors in the corridors still proclaimed 'Staff Room', or 'Form Mistress', but pieces of cardboard saying 'Anarchist Committee', 'Military Section', 'Social Democratic Party', had now been stuck over them. The whole building seemed to be in chaos, although, appearances to the contrary, the work done was systematic enough. Maxim guns were posted. Arms were brought in and distributed. Typewriters churned out warrants, orders, car licences, urgent messages. The staircases were filthy. Exhausted men, their rifles beside them, slept under the chandeliers in the white, pillared halls.

As delegates to the Second All-Russian Congress of Soviets arrived, they were greeted by Sverdlov, a small man with a black goatee. Overworked but tireless, he asked them questions and told them about the latest events. Kamenev, the opponent of the insurrection, now spared no effort to make it a success. He was thirty-four, with a broad, slightly fleshy, intellectual face, and a short, very thick, fair beard; he wore pince-nez and was dressed in a crumpled suit. Dzerzhinsky, a slight man, his profile lengthened by a sparse beard – he had been a prisoner until the beginning of the year – hurried out on some mission with a set expression. Antonov-Ovseenko had a lined face; his pince-nez were askew and his great mane was dishevelled. Chudnovsky and Podvoisky studied a map of the city in preparation for the surrounding of the Winter Palace. Trotsky was receiving delegations, consulting hastily on the stairs and in one doorway after another – he was engaged in several conferences at once and rushed from room to room, all the time issuing orders. There was a constant exchange of messages: the Red Guards Conference reported an estimated strength of between twenty and forty thousand men, but a shortage of arms; the Soviet of Vyborg had requisitioned motor cars; factory committees were forming ambulance units staffed by working women; the troops at Krasnoe Selo, Novy Peterhof, and Gdov were joining the movement, as well as the garrison of thirty thousand at Luga. The Soviets in Schlüsselburg and Kronstadt had the situation well in hand; the garrison of Revel (Tallinn) had been won over; at Helsingfors, the Finnish fleet and army were ready and preparing to bring their ships up the Neva.

On October 24th, Trotsky proposed that the Bolshevik Central Committee place at the disposal of the Military Revolutionary Committee two members for the purpose of establishing contacts with the postal and telegraph workers and the railwaymen; that a third member keep the Provisional Government under constant watch and that reserve headquarters be established in the Peter and Paul fortress. It was resolved to detail Dzerzhinsky to the postal and telegraph workers, and Bubnov to the railwaymen. Miliutin was appointed to organize the supply of food.

Trotsky left the Smolny for the Cirque Moderne where he addressed the motorcycle battalion, which was still loyal to the Provisional Government. Though the meeting was stormy, Trotsky won over a large majority. He then returned to the Smolny Institute to address the Bolshevik delegates to the impending Congress of Soviets. 'We are on the defensive ... If Kerensky refuses to bow to the will of the Congress, he will be facing us with a police – not a political – problem ...' He went on to speak to the Petrograd Soviet.

'If it is the Provisional Government's intention to stab the revolution in the back, we shall return blow for blow and answer iron with steel ...' Meanwhile, the Provisional Government had sealed the doors of a Bolshevik printing press, and Trotsky, informed of this by a working man and woman who approached him on the staircase, sent a detachment of sappers to the spot with orders to blow off the seals. He also issued orders on behalf of the Military Revolutionary Committee that the presses be restarted. The orders were carried out as if by magic. Lenin was astounded and delighted when he heard the news.

In the city, around the railway stations, at the approaches to bridges and in the telephone exchange, there were scuffles between the Junkers (Officer Cadets), Red Guards and troops, but no bloodshed – they invariably ended with the Junkers being arrested or retreating. Insurgents, enthusiastically welcomed by the printing workers, proceeded to seize a number of right-wing presses.

The Central Executive Committee of the Soviets held an all-night session in the Smolny Institute, most of it devoted to mutual recriminations. When Dan shouted at the Bolsheviks, 'The counter-revolution will sweep you away!' Trotsky replied, 'There will be no civil war, for the enemy will surrender and you, Comrades, will be masters of Russian soil!' The meeting broke up at about four o'clock in the morning. Trotsky, in a state of nervous exhaustion and almost at the end of his tether, dropped fully dressed on to a sofa, and slept for a few hours.

Outside, in the damp night, insurgents with cartridge belts slung round their greatcoats warmed themselves at braziers while keeping watch.

x. *Seizure of the Winter Palace*

On October 25th, troops moved up in good order to the Winter Palace. The soldiers and sailors bore themselves well and there were no breaches of discipline. The Military Revolutionary Committee had made sure there would be no hitches. A quick check of the credentials of the deputies to the Second Congress, though carried out in an atmosphere of some confusion, had revealed that 390 deputies out of 650 were pro-Bolshevik, that 505 Soviets had voted in favour of the seizure of power and that 86 had voted for 'democracy'. At the First All-Russian Congress of Soviets held in June 1917, the

'Compromisers' had been very much in the majority, but now their number had not only been cut drastically but they were also divided among themselves. The Social Revolutionary Party had split and its left wing, by far the stronger faction, held separate deliberations. At 2.35 a.m., Trotsky told the Petrograd Soviet that the Provisional Government had ceased to exist, and that the Winter Palace was about to be occupied. But he was wrong on this point.

The Second All-Russian Congress of Soviets had assembled in the Institute's columned hall, lit by chandeliers. A plebeian crowd, many of them in shabby army greatcoats, jostled in the elegant white chamber, filling it with coarse tobacco smoke. At 10.40 p.m. the Menshevik Fedor Dan opened the session on behalf of the Executive. A presidium was elected by proportional representation: fourteen Bolsheviks, seven Social Revolutionaries, three Mensheviks, and one Internationalist. Some Bolshevik opponents of the insurrection were among those elected, but Lenin headed the list. At one point, Dan and another Menshevik inadvertently walked into a room where a private discussion was taking place, and, seeing a bespectacled man with his cheek bandaged, immediately identified him as Lenin.

It was a tiring night. Straw mattresses and blankets were put out in the small room in which Lenin was waiting impatiently. Trotsky came and stretched out beside Lenin, hoping to snatch some sleep between speeches, but the telephones and messengers gave them no peace. Suddenly Trotsky felt faint. He asked Kamenev for a cigarette, murmured, 'That's all I needed,' and passed out for a moment or two. When he came to, he saw Kamenev leaning over him anxiously. 'Shall I call a doctor?' he asked. 'No, just get me something to eat instead.' Trotsky could not remember when he had eaten his last meal.

Kamenev presided over the Congress. Under the cloud of tobacco smoke which now obscured the chandeliers in the crowded hall, and in an overheated atmosphere reeking of stale breath and sweat, the debate between the 'Compromisers' and the revolutionaries raged fiercely. Dan, Martov, Lozovsky and other Mensheviks in turn implored Congress to put their trust in peaceful methods. 'A civil war brings the threat of counter-revolution... We must have a power recognized by the whole of democracy.' The guns of the Peter and Paul fortress and of the cruiser *Aurora*, which was thought to be shelling the Winter Palace, could be heard clearly. The Mensheviks pro-

tested against what they called 'this Bolshevik conspiracy' and withdrew. Others followed to harsh shouts of 'Good riddance!
Deserters!' Martov, who was on the left of the Menshevik party,
stepped on to the platform. He and Lenin had been friends as young
men and at one time it would not have taken much to win him over
to Bolshevism. He was a sickly person, with a lofty forehead and
fine features, highly strung, extremely intelligent, eager and honest.
Trotsky always thought him singularly indecisive. On the platform
in the noisy, smoke-filled hall, Martov and Trotsky confronted each
other before the feverishly excited audience. Martov demanded a
compromise. 'Stop the bloodshed! The guns are roaring...' Trotsky
hammered out his answer. 'A conspiracy? No, an insurrection! The
uprising of the popular masses needs no justification. We have steeled
the revolutionary energy of the workers and soldiers ... We have
forged the will of the masses for a rising ... We have won, and now
you are asking us to renounce our victory and to make a compromise. With whom? Who is there to compromise with?' Martov
walked out of the hall, angry and desperate. A few Social Revolutionaries announced their intention of going to the Winter Palace
'to bury ourselves in the ruins'. A large sailor with a black beard
took the floor to tell the would-be martyrs that the *Aurora* was
merely firing blanks. The left-wing Social Revolutionaries now declared their reserved support for the insurrection. Among them was
the slender figure and tortured face of Maria Spiridonova, a former
terrorist who had served long years of hard labour. To prevent last-
minute changes of heart, Trotsky now moved an act of indictment
against the 'Compromisers' who had prepared the ruinous offensive
of June 18th, had supported a government which had betrayed
the people's cause, had been accessories to the agrarian reform
swindle, had prolonged the war, and had been accomplices of the
bourgeoisie.

'Who feels disturbed by the sound of gunfire?' he asked. 'Not we.
On the contrary, we work all the better for it.'

Lenin was cursing in his little room. 'Why hasn't the Winter Palace
been taken? Do something! You all deserve to be shot!' Round the
Palace, the insurgent troops were becoming impatient as well. 'The
Bolsheviks haven't taken to diplomacy this late in the day, have
they?' someone was heard to mutter. The attack could have flushed
out the Provisional Government quite easily, but Antonovo-
Ovseenko, Chudnovsky and Podvoisky were anxious to avoid

bloodshed and to keep the damage down. The ministers were in permanent session, first of all in the Malachite Chamber which overlooked the Neva and then in a large room in the interior of the Palace, round a table illuminated by only one lamp, shaded with newspaper. Palchinsky urged the defenders to resist; the reinforcements promised by Kerensky would be there at any moment, he said. Meanwhile the Palace was being held by a few dozen Knights of St George, some Ural Cossacks, shock troops and the Women's Battalion. Footmen in imperial livery moved from room to room, officers were getting drunk at the bar, and little knots of people met in the corridors, in corners and on the staircases to discuss whether it was best to resist, to give in, or to seek death. Groups of cadet officers surrendered, and so did the Ural Cossacks. The lights in the windows went out, and the Palace fell into an oppressive darkness. Chudnovsky delivered an ultimatum: surrender or we start shelling, and while those to whom it was addressed were still debating whether he should be shot, the *Aurora* boomed out a thunderous blank. On the embankment the people looked on calmly and the trams ran normally in nearby streets. There was an exchange of rifle fire between the square and the Palace. Suddenly, it became apparent that the Palace had sprung back to life. In some of the courtyards men faced one another, hand grenades at the ready. Antonov-Ovseenko, followed by a detachment of insurgents, raced up the great staircase. 'Where is the Provisional Government?' He was shown a room, guarded by Officer-Cadets with fixed bayonets. Antonov-Ovseenko, a slight man dressed in an overcoat and wearing a black felt hat, pushed the bayonets aside and went in. The pale-faced ministers received him with due solemnity at the half-lit conference table. Antonov-Ovseenko told them they were under arrest. The only resistance he encountered was from the crowd in the square outside who wanted to lynch his charges. It was with some difficulty that he eventually had them escorted to the dungeons of the Peter and Paul fortress, so familiar to the revolutionaries, from which they were released very soon afterwards.

The capture of the Winter Palace had produced few casualties. According to rumour, the members of the Women's Battalion were molested by the insurgents, but that rumour had very little, if any, substance; excesses were extremely rare. The looting of the Palace stopped with the defeat of its defenders; the insurgents took immediate steps to put an end to it and searched everyone coming out.

At about 3 a.m. on October 26th, Kamenev informed the Congress of Soviets that the Provisional Government had been placed under arrest. The hall was overjoyed. At 5.17 a.m., Krylenko, 'reeling with exhaustion', announced that the Twelfth Army had joined the insurgents. There were tears of joy, and the delegates hugged one another. Then, amid stormy applause, the meeting was declared closed at 6 a.m.

'I remember those days and nights as a sort of lucid delirium. So many things happened that it is impossible to sort out the jumbled sequence of events, to tell in retrospect who was where and who played what part. A great many details are still being debated by the historians. On October 26th, the course of events did not stop, though nobody had had more than the odd snatch of nervous sleep, ready to wake at the slightest sound. I returned to the Smolny Institute. I saw only unshaven faces, distorted by fatigue, and heavily ringed, puffy eyes. Leon Davidovich's features were drawn; he was pale, exhausted and over-excited. But there was a sense of contained happiness, and we felt there was not a moment to spare for anything but the task in hand. We slept only just enough to prevent ourselves collapsing from fatigue. The hours and days were filled with concerted and single-minded action, though we were often swept along by events and had to improvise as we went along. At the high school, our children were attacked but managed to hold their own; after the seizure of power, the liberal teachers and the middle-class children made their lives so miserable that we were forced to transfer them to an elementary school.'

xi. *The First Soviet of People's Commissars. Trotsky becomes Commissar for Foreign Affairs*

On October 26th, the Central Committee of the Bolshevik Party discussed the formation of a Soviet government. 'My head is still spinning,' Lenin said with a laugh. Victory was intoxicating. Trotsky suggested that the bourgeois and discredited term 'Minister' be replaced by 'People's Commissar'. There was some bad news: Kerensky, whose arrest had been ordered, was rallying troops, and General Kornilov and his accomplices, comfortable in exile at Bykhov where they were guarded by their own Cossacks, had left for the south, no doubt to organize a civil war with the help of the High Command. The liberal newspapers wrote that the pockets of the Red

Guards were lined with German marks, and so on, while the armed workers, living on short rations of black bread, rested and shivered round the braziers. It was decided to ban the most slanderous papers.

The Second All-Russian Congress of Soviets resumed its sitting at nine in the evening with the indefatigable Kamenev in the chair. The atmosphere was similar to that of the day before: the delegates were fired with enthusiasm. Kamenev at once gave the floor to Lenin, whom very few of those present knew by sight, but about whom they had been told the most vicious lies for years. They now saw a 'stocky, short and upright man with a remarkable head, plain features, prominent cheek-bones, clean-shaven, small, slightly Mongolian eyes and a penetrating gaze'. This was Trotsky's description of Lenin, written later; I should like to add that he struck me chiefly by his simplicity, his Volga Russian looks, ruddy complexion and smooth, high forehead, his vigorous bearing, his evident good humour and his irony, his thoughtful and decisive personality. He never strove for effect or used oratorical tricks. At the time, he was forty-seven years old.

Gripping the edges of the reading stand, Vladimir Ilyich surveyed the crowd and waited for the ovation to subside. Then he said, 'Comrades, we shall now proceed to construct the Socialist order.' Trotsky points out that this sentence, quoted by John Reed, cannot be found in the minutes of the Congress, because the stenographers had walked out along with the right-wing Socialists, but that the words were quite in character with Lenin's way of thinking and style. Lenin then went on to read the draft of a declaration in which the Congress proposed to open immediate negotiations for a just, democratic peace, without annexations or indemnities, to all warring peoples and their governments, but added that it was fully prepared to examine any other peace suggestions. It undertook to annul all secret treaties signed by the old regime. The declaration was adopted unanimously, whereupon the entire hall burst loudly into the 'Internationale', followed, the delegates' eyes dimmed with tears, by the 'Funeral March'. Lenin and the presidium joined in.

Next, the delegates voted on Lenin's land reform decree. It ran to some thirty lines and provided for the expropriation without compensation of large, privately owned estates, and those belonging to the Crown and the Church, all of which were handed over to peasant committees; smallholders were allowed to retain their land. This brief document, ushering in the agrarian revolution, was amplified by regulations enforcing the 242 demands of the peasants which had been collated by the Social Revolutionaries and published in August. Lenin felt they would help to ensure the survival of the new regime by rallying the peasants to it at a crucial moment. About a quarter of the land under cultivation was in the hands of 134,000 landlords; of these, 30,000 aristocrats held more than 5,000 acres each. Peasant holdings, previously burdened with taxes, mortgages and debts, were freed at a stroke.

It was not until these major proposals had been adopted that a list of members of the Council of People's Commissars was submitted to the Congress and approved by acclamation. Governmental power was to be concentrated in the hands of the Council of People's Commissars, responsible to the Congress of Soviets and its Central Executive Committee. The original Council (there were many subsequent changes) consisted of: Head of the Government – Lenin. Interior – Alexis Rykov, a thirty-six-year-old 'veteran' revolutionary and member of the 1905 St Petersburg Soviet, four years in prison, eight years' deportation, of peasant origins. Agriculture – Vladimir Miliutin, thirty-three, an economist, arrested eight times, five years in prison, two years' deportation. Commerce and Industry – Victor Nogin, thirty-nine, textile worker, influential member of the Moscow Soviet, with a similar life-history to Rykov's and Miliutin's. Foreign Affairs – Trotsky. Justice – Georgy Lomov, twenty-nine, lawyer, organizer of the Moscow Metalworkers' Union, various prisons. Nationalities – Joseph Stalin, thirty-eight. Education – Anatol Lunacharsky, forty-two, writer. Provisions – Ivan Teodorovich, forty-one, an intellectual of noble origins, sentenced to penal servitude. Labour – Alexander Shliapnikov, thirty-three, metal worker, participated in the 1905 uprising and in the March 1917 revolution, President of the Metalworkers' Union. Posts, Telegraphs and Telephones – Glebov-Avilov. The economist Skvortsov-Stepanov was proposed for the position of People's Commissar of Finance but no decision was taken. The nomination of a Commissar for Railways, too, was deferred because of a conflict with the Railwayworkers' Union; and military and naval affairs were allocated to a committee consisting of Antonov-Ovseenko, Dybenko, a sailor, and Krylenko, a non-commissioned officer.

Zinoviev was appointed editor of *Izvestia*, the official organ of the Soviets, and Kamenev was selected for President of the new All-Russian Congress of Soviets.

All members of the government were Bolsheviks. The Congress put up no alternative candidates; moreover, the left-wing Social Revolutionaries refused to participate in government. The moderate wing of the Bolsheviks, which had opposed the insurrection until the day before, was represented by Zinoviev, Kamenev, Rykov and Nogin, in important posts. The name of Joseph Djugashvili (Stalin) became publicly known for the first time. The son of a Georgian cobbler, Stalin had grown up in the Caucasus, had experienced imprisonment and deportation to Siberia and had been co-editor of the official Bolshevik journal. During the uprising, he had made brief appearances in the Smolny Institute, though there are no records of his activities there; presumably he was working on his newspaper. In 1907–8 he had rendered his Party important services through a series of daring bank raids in the Caucasus. It was probably Lenin's idea to offer Stalin a government post.

When a right-wing Socialist spoke up at the Congress and advocated reconciliation with 'revolutionary democracy', that is, with the parties that had supported Kerensky, Trotsky replied at length. He rejected collaboration with anyone themselves favouring collaboration with the reactionaries. 'We rest all our hope on the possibility that our revolution will unleash the European revolution. If the insurrectionary peoples of Europe do not crush imperialism, then we shall be crushed – that is indubitable. Either the Russian revolution will raise the whirlwind of struggle in the West, or the capitalists of all countries will crush our revolution.' Trotsky nevertheless left the door open to a peace treaty with bourgeois governments and stressed that no time limit had been set.

The October Revolution has often been reproached for overthrowing a democratic regime. However, historians – even of the Right – admit that, at the time, Russia had no democratic institutions of any influence, except for the Soviets and the parties represented in them. The army, commanded by the old generals, the administrations and ministries, run by the old officials, the press, by now a dismal spectre in the hands of the old rulers, the monarchist bourgeoisie and the even more reactionary nobility, posed a continual threat. The Right did not conceal its intention of establishing a 'strong government', that is, a dictatorship that could only hope to subdue the peasants, the working class and the Left by terror. Russia, without stable institutions, was threatened by Fascism before that word had been invented, and in this sense the Soviet uprising was a genuine defensive measure.

Throughout the territory of the old Russian Empire, power passed into the hands of the local and regional Soviets, not without conflict with the right-wing Socialists, but without armed clashes. At Kazan, the Soviet, supported by forty thousand members of the armed forces, had actually seized power before the fall of the Winter Palace in Petrograd.

In Moscow, by contrast, blood was spilled for an entire week. Here, one of Trotsky's friends played what may have been a decisive part in the fighting: the good-natured giant Muralov, with his impressive moustaches. A brave man of sound common sense, he had been an agricultural expert, an officer, and a fighter for the Revolution ever since 1905.

Some terrible episodes occurred during the clashes in Moscow. Whereas in Petrograd the Bolsheviks merely disarmed their opponents and set them free as soon as they promised not to bear arms against the Revolution, in Moscow the Whites rarely scrupled about the lives of their prisoners. When the Bolsheviks in the Kremlin had surrendered, the garrison having been promised that their lives would be spared by the Committee of Public Safety, the cadet officers wasted no time in lining up the arsenal workers and mowing them down with machine-guns. This was the first mass execution during a Revolution that, despite all the tumult and clashes, had endeavoured to avoid bloodshed – with it began the White Terror. But such was the spirit of the people that, even after victory, they allowed the guilty to go unpunished, and simply disarmed the military academies. For the rest, the Military Revolutionary Committee declared that all Muscovites were 'free and inviolable citizens'.

Three · Power

1. *Problems, strains and dangers. Trotsky and Muraviev victorious at Pulkovo*

The seizure of power exacerbated rather than solved problems in the days that followed. By their strike, the civil servants and technicians paralysed part of the public services; in particular, the suspension of the telegraph service gave free rein, in the absence of accurate news, to malicious rumour. Kerensky was advancing at the head of an army on Petrograd, hoping, no doubt, that its citizens would share the fate of the Paris Commune. Confused reports, pressing difficulties, rumoured dangers, political arguments and clashes, and improvised solutions, swept the capital like leaves in an autumn storm. The Smolny Institute continued to be the seat of insurrection, packed with men in dirty uniforms and with exhausted faces; little groups were constantly holding private discussions, and the telephones shrilled continuously. People slept on sofas, gulped inadequate meals and talked endlessly in clouds of tobacco smoke; Lenin and Trotsky were left with the task of creating order out of the chaos that surrounded them everywhere.

Trotsky at first felt a let-down after the extreme nervous tension of the rising, and considered becoming a publicist or press officer rather than accepting a post in the new government. He not only had a writer's temperament and a philosopher's love of ideas, but he also believed that, as a Jew, he should not play too prominent a part in public life. However, Lenin brushed aside his objections and asked him to become Chairman of the Council of People's Commissars. Every hour brought new demands, and since no socialist movement had ever before been able to consolidate its victory, the press gave the Bolsheviks anything from two weeks to two months.

70

Trotsky now saw to the defence of Petrograd: he ordered trenches to be dug, barricades to be built and mobilized the workers. On October 29th, cannon-fire could be heard in the heart of the city. A Committee for the Safety of the Fatherland, run by Social Revolutionaries, had incited the Junkers, who then seized a number of buildings. As the death toll mounted, Trotsky appealed to the Red Guards to hold their fire: 'The living are worth more to us than the dead! Prisoners can be used for exchanges ... '

He rallied the people against Kerensky. Though nobody knew how strong the enemy was, it was decided to take the offensive. A small number of officers gave their services to the Revolution, quite a few of them not because of revolutionary sentiments but because of their inveterate hatred of Kerensky, the spokesman of 'revolutionary democracy'; others because they hoped that the struggle between the Soviets and the Provisional Government would result in the victory of the counter-revolution. One of them, Colonel Muraviev, a Social Revolutionary, displayed considerable energy. During the freezing night of October 30th, he and Trotsky drove to the front lines, with no idea of what to expect, and were greeted with the immensely cheering sight of their orders being carried out. The efforts of the workers made up for everything. Convoys advanced through the night and men in cloth caps stood guard at all the cross-roads. An old colonel called Walden deployed his artillery on the Pulkovo Heights, some thirty miles from Petrograd, and the Cossacks' half-hearted offensive was stopped dead. Trotsky sent his first victorious communiqué to the Smolny. Next morning, with soldiers, sailors and the Red Guard, he entered the imperial palace of Gatchina without meeting any resistance, although the palace was surrounded by Cossacks and armoured cars. The Cossacks had obviously had enough, and their commander, General Krasnov, awaited arrest in a sumptuous panelled hall. He claimed that he had implored Kerensky to surrender to the Soviets and had even provided him with an escort to Petrograd but that Kerensky, eluding his vigilance, had escaped once again. Krasnov, an old monarchist and a notorious reactionary, was released on parole. He immediately proceeded to the Don, where, with German support, he became one of the most redoubtable leaders of the counter-revolution. Yet it was Krasnov who was to appeal to all Cossacks to deliver Russia from the 'benighted mob who sold themselves to the Kaiser'!

As People's Commissar for Foreign Affairs, Trotsky had few

illusions about his job. 'I shall publish the secret treaties and then shut up shop.' He realized that no government would recognize the Soviets until they were firmly in the saddle. He found the Ministry empty and the doormen fearful, and had to order the arrest of Prince Tatishchev before the safes were opened. Trotsky then put the sailor, Markin, in charge of the building, and ordered the dismissal of thirty-three senior civil servants who had deserted their posts and of twenty-eight diplomats accredited to countries ranging from the Great Powers to Paraguay.

Next, he ordered General Dukhonin, Kerensky's last Chief of Staff, to propose an immediate ceasefire to the enemy. When Dukhonin demurred, the People's Commissars had him replaced by the ensign Krylenko, who marched into Army Headquarters at Moghilev accompanied by a detachment of Petrograd troops and routed the officer corps. Dukhonin was lynched by his own troops.

Meanwhile, a crisis had developed inside the Soviet government, where several Bolsheviks objected to Lenin's and Trotsky's measures against the bourgeois press. 'The capitalists must be deprived of the means of manufacturing public opinion at their whim,' Trotsky told them peremptorily. Had not one of these newspapers just repeated the slander that German generals were in the Soviet government? Again, when the moderate Bolsheviks (Kamenev, Zinoviev, Rykov, Miliutin and Nogin) advocated a socialist government comprising all parties represented in the Soviet, and when Lenin and Trotsky successfully opposed them, the moderates resigned from the Central Committee and from the Council of People's Commissars. They changed their minds a few days later when they discovered that an alliance with the right-wing socialists was impossible.

The civil servants' and technicians' strike aggravated the situation. Trotsky told the saboteurs that they were playing with fire. 'The country and the army are facing starvation ... We shall requisition stocks and confiscate goods ... ' His solutions were always drastic and uncompromising. When the Whites opened a campaign in the Don region under Hetman Kaledin and in the Urals under Hetman Dutov, Trotsky refused to negotiate with them. They had placed themselves outside the law and had to be crushed.

Hardly had the crisis in the Central Committee blown over, when mobs began to raid the cellars of the palaces, getting drunk on rare wines and spirits and reeling through the streets. Trotsky ordered hand-picked Red Guards to throw grenades into the cellars; they faced the anger of the drunken mob from behind a protective screen of machine-guns. The sailor Markin had to leave his People's Commissariat for Foreign Affairs to help in these operations.

'It was about this time that Lenin asked Leon Davidovich privately, "What if the two of us are shot by the Whites? Do you think Sverdlov and Bukharin will manage?" Leon Davidovich burst out laughing. "We can only hope they don't shoot us," he said. "The devil only knows what the Whites can do," laughed Lenin in return.

'We were moved from our small lodgings in Tauride Street to the Smolny Institute for greater security and convenience. We were assigned two square rooms with high ceilings and lit by large windows. I remember that since I could not find any material to make tunics for our two boys, I used the gaily coloured velvet covers from the tables there. Lyova and Sergey did not approve of my makeshift solution and hated wearing their multi-coloured tunics. One day Lenin, who shared rooms off the same corridor with his wife and sister, looked in and saw the children. He paused in front of them, stood them side by side, stepped back to admire the effect and then said, "That looks very nice ... " I was struck by this unexpected remark and delighted that Lenin should take an interest in such trifles. From that day on, the children put on their tunics without protest ... Everywhere round us committees were in session, while the building continued to bristle with machine-guns.'

In Russia and abroad people had begun talking of 'Lenin and Trotsky's dictatorship'. They were profoundly mistaken. The Central Committee, and the various Soviet and local committees, deliberated freely and passionately and often expressed vehement differences of opinion. Every decision was placed before party assemblies, before the Soviets, Congresses and Executive Committees. There was, if anything, too much talk and complete freedom for all shades of socialist opinion. Anarchists, right-wing Social Revolutionaries (who were openly linked with the counter-revolution) left-wing Social Revolutionaries (who were soon afterwards to join the government and to receive five portfolios) and various groups of Menshevik Socialists, all had their clubs, their press and their elected bodies. Maxim Gorky's paper *Novaya Zhizn* (*New Life*) was still publishing such comments as, 'Lenin, Trotsky and their followers have drunk of the poison of power ... These blind fanatics and unscrupulous adventurers are, it seems, hurling themselves headfirst into what they call "social revolution", but what is in fact anarchy and certain shipwreck for the proletariat and the revolution ...' The Central Executive Committee of the Railwaymen, dominated by right-wing socialists, remained a powerful force, and monolithic party control was neither a fact nor was it even an objective. On the contrary, the 'dictatorship of the proletariat' aimed at the broadest possible democracy for the workers. The entire policy of the Bolshevik leaders was based on constant appeals to the masses, and relied on their support and their initiative, as everyday life showed only too palpably. Lenin's and Trotsky's personal authority had no foundation other than their prestige among the masses. Lenin's direst threat, whenever he was in a minority on some issue, was his resignation. Even the most heated discussion in the party resulted in nothing worse than such threats, which were never implemented because the comradeship of men who had known each other for many years unfailingly prevailed in the end.

Trotsky always believed that he shared in the collective responsibility of the Central Committee and the Council of People's Commissars, even when his work took him to the front and did not allow him to take part in the formulation of some of the most important measures. No account of his life can there' ᵔ ᵔ complete without some reference to the legislative wor¹

II. *Dissolution of the Constituent A*

Trotsky fully agreed with the majori   Central Committee about ordering the dissolution of the C.   uent Assembly. At the elections, which were held at the end of November, the right-wing socialists had scored a resounding victory with 22,600,000 votes (Social Revolutionaries: 20,900,000 votes; Mensheviks: 1,700,000 votes) as against a little over nine million for the Bolsheviks, and 4,600,000 for the middle-class Constitutional Democrats. The opening of the Constituent Assembly on January 18th, 1918 (New Style) was preceded by stormy demonstrations. The Assembly elected Victor Chernov, the former Minister of Agriculture, as its President. After a short oratorical clash, the young Raskolnikov read the final declaration of the Bolshevik deputies (one hundred and sixty-one members out of the total of five hundred and twenty): 'As we are not prepared to gloss over the crimes committed by the enemies of the people, we prefer to withdraw, and leave it to the Soviets to deal with the counter-revolutionary elements in this assembly ... ' A sailor, the anarchist Zheleznyak, asked the President, Chernov, to adjourn the session on the grounds that 'the stewards are tired'. At the same time, the tribunes roared out: 'Enough is enough!' Chernov could feel the sharp breath of mutiny, and withdrew. A Social Revolutionary group had planned to kidnap Lenin and Trotsky, but the Central Committee of the Social Revolutionary Party had ordered them to desist from attacks on these and equally popular public figures. Some days earlier, two Social Revolutionaries had fired at Lenin's car. They were arrested soon afterwards and my recollection is that they eventually joined the Bolshevik Party.

Trotsky justified the dissolution of the Constituent Assembly by pointing out that the peasants had voted for 'land and freedom' without really understanding what was happening in Petrograd and Moscow, and that, as a result, they had supported an electoral list comprising Kerensky and his friends, on the one hand, and his vehement opponents, the left-wing Social Revolutionaries, on the other.

The Constituent Assembly had restored power to the very men whom the Soviet rising had separated from it, and who were now driven by such a desire for revenge that they were ready to make common cause with the generals. 'We should have had to mount a new insurrection in a few weeks' time,' Trotsky wrote. The dissolution of the Constituent Assembly produced no immediate reaction, but the Social Revolutionaries decided to prepare for an armed confrontation.

III. *The negotiations at Brest-Litovsk. Trotsky leads the Russian delegation*

The army neither would nor could continue the fight. During some thirty months, from 1914–16, Russia had sustained greater losses than any other power involved in World War I. In Galicia and Turkey, Russians were still occupying enemy territory. The incompetence of the imperial government in the matter of provisioning, in military supplies and medical services, the brutal treatment of the men by their officers, and the unpopularity of a long war for which the masses could see no justification – all these had resulted in the collapse of Tsarism. Ever since, the number of peasant-soldiers who 'planted their bayonets in the soil' and simply returned to their villages had grown from week to week. Soon they would fight tooth and nail to seize and hold on to the land, and they had no wish to fight for a Provisional Government that refused to grant their demands, let alone for the conquest of the Dardanelles. They realized, too, that the Bolsheviks and their allies were alone in the struggle for a people's peace and against the 'imperialist design to carve up the world'.

The Central Powers, that is Germany, Austro-Hungary, Bulgaria and Turkey, were quick to respond to the Soviet offer of peace, and in mid-December 1917, signed a twenty-eight-day ceasefire. The first Soviet delegation, headed by Joffe, and assisted by Kamenev and Karakhan, went to Brest-Litovsk, where they were met by Prince Leopold of Bavaria and General Hoffmann. The Austrians and Germans pretended to agree to the principle of 'peace without annexations or indemnities', and formally undertook not to transfer their troops from Russia to the Western front, an undertaking they had no intention of honouring. Both sides were playing for time, the revolutionaries for propaganda purposes and the Germans and Austrians for strategic reasons no less than in order to learn how to cope with an unprecedented situation. According to Trotsky, they had expected to meet the usual kind of politician, full of rhetoric for public consumption but venal at heart and ready to engage in 'realistic' horse-trading. In fact, they were confronted with quite a different species who forced them to put their cards on the table – although they were able to disguise their demands for what was, in effect, the annexation of Poland and the Baltic Countries as a sincere concern for the self-determination of nations.

The Soviet delegation then proposed that the negotiations be transferred to neutral Stockholm, but were met with a refusal amounting to an ultimatum. After a short break in the negotiations, Trotsky himself set out for Brest-Litovsk, accompanied by Joffe, Kamenev, Karakhan and a team of experts. Karl Radek took part in the second phase of the negotiations which began on February 1st, 1918.

The talks were held in a town that was in a state of near-complete destruction, at a military headquarters ringed round with barbed wire. The members of the first Soviet delegation had taken their meals together with their opposite numbers, and had exchanged conventional courtesies, but as soon as Trotsky arrived he put an end to this, and private conversations and civilities ceased. The resulting drop in temperature was not something Trotsky had intended; he felt genuinely ill at ease, sometimes indignant with, and sometimes contemptuous of, the bourgeois diplomats whom he regarded as rogues and hardened reactionaries. He was particularly suspicious of the fat General Hoffmann, whose sound knowledge of Russian suggested that he had had perhaps more experience of spying than of politics. It soon became clear to both parties that no genuine agreement would be reached, that the negotiations would be drawn-out and fruitless. Trotsky spoke as plainly as he could, but his remarks were addressed more to the outside world, and particularly to European socialists, than to his German counterparts. Every day brought a host of irritating incidents, and the German Foreign Minister, Richard von Kühlmann, the Austrian Foreign Minister, Count Czernin and the German Supreme Commander on the Russian front, General Hoffmann, did not hide their exasperation. Undaunted, Trotsky continued to pursue his ideological and legal arguments with cool audacity. He fully endorsed Joffe's formula: 'No expression of the will of the people can be authentic unless it is the result of a completely free vote, cast in the absence of foreign troops.'

When Hoffman objected to the Russian propaganda speeches, Trotsky replied, 'As revolutionaries we reserve the right to propagate our republican and revolutionary convictions ... ' He went on to declare 'our solidarity' with the working masses of Germany and with those of all warring countries, and announced that Russia's new policy was completely independent of that of the Allies. 'Our policy is not conducted from behind the scenes; our revolution has got rid of the backcloth and the wings.' When he was told that the Russian delegation spoke the language of the victor, which was totally inappropriate in the circumstances, Trotsky replied fiercely, 'We do not deny that the policies of the old ruling classes have undermined our country ... However, a forward-looking policy must be based on a country's potential and inner forces, which – once called into play – will sooner or later prove all-powerful.' The Germans and Austrians exclaimed, 'Unerhört! What impertinence!' from time to time, and General Hoffmann concluded the discussion with 'Genug! Enough!'

Trotsky declared that Russia granted the Ukraine and Armenia, two former provinces, the right to self-determination. And this is what he had to say about Poland, then occupied by German troops but recently declared 'independent' by the Central Powers:

We have not the slightest wish to deny Poland's right to independence, but what we have here is the creation of a government on a principle that would be rejected by the most conservative politicians of any country you care to mention. We recognize the right of the Polish people to decide their own destiny and we would be the first to agree that amends should be made for the historical wrongs inflicted upon them, but we cannot accept that the territorial hybrid devised by a Polish minister ... truly expresses the will of the Polish people ...

This was a reference to the schemes of the pro-Austrian Polish puppet government headed by Kuczarcewski. By contrast, the Council of People's Commissars had just recognized the independence of Finland without any conditions (December 31st, 1917).

Long diplomatic wrangles brought Trotsky into headlong clashes with von Kühlmann, Czernin and Hoffmann from which nothing was gained but time. Thus while the Germans were at great pains to show that the reactionary puppet government they had set up in the occupied territories expressed the will of the people, Trotsky pressed them relentlessly for a withdrawal followed by popular referenda. 'But you, too, govern by force,' a German spokesman said. 'To be sure,' Trotsky replied, 'all governments rest on force, but whereas you use violence against the strikers, we use it against the capitalists ... We are revolutionaries but we are also realists. We prefer to call annexation by its proper name.'

At the end of January, the Rumanian Army, led by a Russian general, occupied Bessarabia and threatened the Russian Black Sea coast. Trotsky immediately expelled the Rumanian mission from Russia and confiscated the Rumanian gold deposits in Moscow. The Soviets promised to take care of these funds until they could be handed back to the Rumanian workers.

Among Russia's old allies, the Brest-Litovsk negotiations brought forth repeated accusations of treason, and allegations that the Bolsheviks were in the pay of Germany. In Germany, they produced concern as well – and almost the same insults. Thus the Berlin *Tägliche Rundschau* proclaimed that 'neither Lenin nor Trotsky really wants peace which ... would spell the gallows or gaol for them. Hence they are doing all they can to stir up trouble throughout the world, and particularly in the Central States.' The German Social Democratic press wrote in much the same vein, and Russia's own right-wing Socialists, and her counter-revolutionaries, ceaselessly denounced 'the shameful peace'.

IV. *'Neither war nor peace.' The Treaty of Brest-Litovsk*

The distressing negotiating game could not go on for ever, and when Trotsky returned to Petrograd he put forward his plan. The Bolsheviks and the left-wing Social Revolutionaries gave it a tumultuous reception. Among the Bolsheviks, Zinoviev favoured the immediate signing of a peace treaty, for though it might weaken the German revolutionary movement, it would give their Russian comrades a breathing space. Lenin wanted the negotiations to continue until the enemy presented an ultimatum, and then sign the treaty under protest. 'If necessary,' he said, 'we must sacrifice ourselves for the German revolution which comes well before our own.' But when would it come? A strong Bolshevik faction, including Bukharin, Pyatakov, Karl Radek, Béla Kun, Uritsky, Unschlicht and Vladimir Smirnov, opposed any dealings with imperialism and advocated revolutionary war. At a party conference, held on January 21st, this left-wing group obtained thirty-two votes, as against fifteen for Lenin and sixteen for Trotsky. In the Bolshevik Central Committee a majority supported Trotsky.

On February 10th, Trotsky addressed the Brest-Litovsk peace conference. He had with him the text of his speech, written, with few corrections, in his small, neat hand.

The peoples ask when this self-destruction of mankind, provoked by the greed and lust for power of the ruling classes, is going to end ... We no longer want to take part in this purely imperialist war in which the claims of the possessing classes are settled in human blood ... We are withdrawing our people and our army from the war. Let our soldier-labourer return to his fields and in peace till the land that the revolution has taken from the landlords and given to the peasants ... We are demobilizing our army. We refuse to sign an annexationist peace treaty. We declare that the war between the Central Powers and Russia has ended.

At this, the Russian delegation withdrew, leaving the rest of the conference speechless. At a special meeting of the delegates of the Central Powers, von Kühlmann and the Austrians opposed the resumption of hostilities against Russia, but the view of Ludendorff, who favoured it, prevailed in the end. The Germans needed the

Ukraine, with its vast store of grain, and were determined to crush Bolshevism before launching their great offensive in France.

Trotsky and several left-wing Social Revolutionaries were in Lenin's room at the Smolny Institute when a telegram was delivered which made Lenin turn pale. A German offensive had started and was meeting no resistance – the Russian trenches were abandoned, the command did not exist, and the Germans were advancing along the railway lines capturing town after town. 'This beast knows how to pounce,' Lenin said over and over again. The Central Committee met twice on February 18th. In the morning Lenin was out-voted. In the afternoon, he shouted in exasperation that the revolutionary phase was over and made his most effective threat – he would resign unless the peace treaty was signed. Messengers from the front kept bringing in news of fresh disasters, and when Lenin presented his motion once again, it was carried with Trotsky, Sverdlov, Sokolnikov, Stalin, Vladimir Smirnov and Zinoviev voting in favour, and Uritsky, Lomov, Bukharin, Joffe, Krestinsky and Dzerzhinsky voting against.

On March 3rd, 1918, Sokolnikov, accompanied by Chicherin, Joffe and Karakhan, crossed the lines and signed the treaty, or the German *Diktat*, without bothering to read it or to enter into any discussions, thus making it abundantly clear that Russia was acting under duress. An emergency Congress of the Soviets ratified the treaty on March 16th and the Reichstag did so a few days later.

During the anxious days that had gone before, Trotsky had drafted a proclamation entitled 'The Socialist Fatherland in Peril' for the Council of People's Commissars. It contained the following draconian instructions:

> What cannot be removed must be destroyed. All grain must be removed or buried. All machinery, whether operational or dismantled, is to be evacuated. All metal must be buried. Railway engines and trucks are to be evacuated. Pull up the rails and blow up the bridges; burn the forests and crops behind the enemy's lines ... Fight with firearms and side-arms. Protect the rear. Shoot all spies, *agents provocateurs* and counter-revolutionary traitors ... In defending its liberty and its life, the Soviet Republic urges workers in every country to struggle against exploiters and brigands.

Trotsky received offers of support from the British and French military missions. In this connection, Lenin sent the Central Committee the following hasty note: 'Please include my vote among those in favour of accepting aid and arms from the Anglo-French imperialist bandits. Lenin.' Lenin spoke to Trotsky about a possible withdrawal to the Urals, of taking up a defensive position in Siberia, and even of a last-ditch stand on Kamchatka. In a corridor of the Smolny Institute, Bukharin, deeply upset, embraced Trotsky with tears in his eyes and implored him to declare himself in favour of a revolutionary war.

The Treaty of Brest-Litovsk deprived Russia of the Baltic countries and sanctioned the subjection of Poland to Germany. It imposed 'independence' on the Ukraine, through which German columns were advancing upon the Don and the Caucasus. It enforced the withdrawal of Russian garrisons from Finland, which entailed the sacrifice of the peaceful Finnish revolution which had just triumphed. It imposed indemnities to the tune of 3,000 million gold roubles, or 1,500 million dollars.

Trotsky admitted that, had he signed the peace treaty sooner, the Soviet Republic might have obtained less disastrous terms. In that case, however, German imperialism would not have been completely unmasked, nor would the legend of Bolshevik connivance with it have been so totally discredited. He did not regret exploiting the propaganda potential of the negotiations to the full, feeling the pulse of German socialism and convincing the working class in the west of the Bolsheviks' total opposition to Austro-German imperialism. Later he would consistently maintain that the Brest-Litovsk negotiations had played a decisive part in the inner collapse of the Central Powers.

v. *Life in the Kremlin. Visit by Trotsky's father*

The von der Goltz division landed in Finland, and the Council of People's Commissars moved from Petrograd to Moscow. As a result, Petrograd became a less tempting objective for the Germans and counter-revolutionary Finland. Trotsky gave up the Commissariat of Foreign Affairs and, at Lenin's request, became Commissar of War and of the Navy.

'Up to then, all he had known of Moscow was the inside of the Butyrki gaol. The old capital, built in concentric circles round the tall crenellated walls and gilded onion-domes of the Kremlin, still had the colourful look of an ancient, commercial city, Christian and feudal. In the Kremlin, we were allocated a suite of rooms that had belonged to a senior official. Leon Davidovich's study was panelled in polished Karelian birch with a golden sheen. He treated the statuettes of Cupid and Psyche as figures of fun; these symbols of bourgeois bliss seemed totally anachronistic in our present condition. When I arrived with the children, Leon Davidovich seemed much amused by our sudden domestic splendour. "A decent place, at last," he joked. For some time, Lenin was our neighbour. Then he moved to some small rooms in another building immediately beside the government offices. The two men had frequent and friendly contacts, though they never had time for lengthy conversations. The Commissars' dining room was next to our apartment and the Politbureau sometimes met there – just ten old comrades getting together without any formality or ceremony. One day the children were fighting in one of the rooms and crashed against a door which had not been properly shut, so that they rolled, quite out of breath, into a Politbureau meeting. The supreme authority of the Party received them with delight.

'A suite opposite ours was occupied by Stalin. Enukidze and Kalinin lived along the same corridor as well. Stalin, who was uncommunicative, often sullen and unconcerned with good manners, had little contact with Trotsky and when he did, it was strictly on business. As for me, he either greeted me perfunctorily or cut me dead. His young wife, Nadia Alliluyeva, the daughter of a revolutionary Caucasian railwayman, was, on the other hand, a charming creature, both intelligent and spontaneous, qualities that would later cause her unbearable suffering and lead her to suicide. Abelii Enukidze, Stalin's boyhood friend and fellow exile in Siberia, was a balanced and prepossessing man of great character; his features mirrored his agreeable personality ...

'Particularly at the beginning, the occupants of the Kremlin dined more than frugally. Leon Davidovich used to say, "We must live no better than we did in exile." I agreed with him, as I knew very well what privations the workers were suffering. In any case, I was too busy with my job to bother very much about food. The only people who still enjoyed a certain degree of prosperity were the few private businessmen and former property owners who lived off the black market. On one occasion, Trotsky sat down to a meal and noticed some butter. "Where did that come from?" he asked in astonishment. The secretary of the Central Committee, Leonid Serebriakov, who had been told about our diet by the doctor, had arranged this rare treat for us. It was not until many months later that the members of the government were able to live on an even half-way decent diet. Stocks of caviare, intended for export but not able to be sent anywhere, rendered sterling service ...

'At that time, quite a few government officials lived better than the revolutionary leaders because they knew how to "manage" and organized their lives accordingly. I learned by accident that there were special shops for different categories of "responsible militants". Innumerable abuses grew up in the distribution services and special privileges were established. The Politbureau talked of publishing guide-lines for the conduct of revolutionaries in authority ... But nothing was done – quite apart from the fact that it was difficult to draw up rules, it would have been impossible to impose them. Members of the government and other leaders were paid as much as the average qualified worker and, as far as possible, were issued with what other commodities they needed to do their job.

'Recreation and proper rest were unknown luxuries. Leon Davidovich would come home from the Commissariat for lunch at the Kremlin, and then stretch out on the sofa for three-quarters of an hour. His daughters, Nina and Zina, would sometimes come to see him during this break and be upset by his refusal to talk politics.

'Soon after we had moved into the Kremlin, Trotsky's father arrived in Moscow. The old man, who was seventy and had been ruined overnight by the Revolution, had left the village of Yanovka and covered the hundred and twenty miles of dangerous country from Kherson to Odessa on foot. On the road he had been stopped many times by various groups of partisans and had had to swallow their insults: to the Reds, to whom the name "Bronstein" meant nothing, the old man was a *kulak*, while the Whites recognized him as the father of that execrable Jew, Bronstein-Trotsky. Father and son greeted each other warmly. He told us that he had lost everything and had been happy to hand over all he had to the Revolution: land, buildings, horses and livestock. His sense of justice had made him support the cause of the people. Perhaps he was proud of the part his son was playing, but, if he was, he did not show it. With a little mischievous flash in his eyes, he said something like, "We fathers slave away all our lives to put something by for our old age, and then the sons come along and make a revolution." He was given a job in a state farm where he did well. He died in about 1922, in full harness at the age of nearly seventy-five ... He was large-boned, well-built, tall, with prominent features, a white beard and deep-set blue eyes. He was a man of great vitality and strength of character, and was singularly enterprising. I remember him as having one of those simple Russian faces painters so often give to mystics and village elders.'

VI. *Trotsky organizes the Red Army*

The stringent terms of Brest-Litovsk strengthened the general conviction that the Revolution was entering a bloody and pitiless phase. Civil war flared up in the Ukraine, on the Don, in the Urals, in Turkestan and Siberia. Trotsky devoted himself to creating the Red Army, which had to be built up from scratch, because all that was left of the Imperial Army was the hated memory of epaulettes, gold braid, negligence, brutality, defeat and reaction. The first new units were established to defend the Ukraine against its own pro-German nationalists and their foreign allies. Here, Antonov-Ovseenko and Muralov distinguished themselves both as organizers and also in the battlefield. Trotsky drew up vast new plans. The volunteer army would be replaced with young conscripts from all classes except the bourgeoisie; discipline would be cemented by firm conviction; the army would receive political education, and the command would maintain an egalitarian ethos and a sense of comradeship. There would be no ranks or titles and no privileged hierarchy. But first Trotsky, as chairman of the Revolutionary War Council and as Commissar of War and the Navy, had to recruit his own staff, and then set up regional War Councils. As he said in *My Life*, the task required 'great creative imagination'. A twenty-six-year-old army doctor, Sklyansky, an unassuming young man, 'conspicuous for his business-like methods, his industry and his talent for appraising people and circumstances', was appointed Trotsky's deputy and became one of the true organizers of the Red Army, 'the Lazare Carnot' of the Russian Revolution. He managed the Council's day-to-day work, while Trotsky toured the front lines, and kept in direct touch with Lenin, Chairman of the Workers' and Peasants' Council of Defence.

(Sklyansky died young, in a boating accident, while visiting the United States in 1925.) The most capable military leaders to emerge at this early stage were Antonov-Ovseenko, Muralov, Ivan Smirnov, Sergey Mrachkovsky, Markin, Raskolnikov, Blücher, Rosengoltz and Evgenia Bosch – together with Stalin and Voroshilov who had military ideas of their own.

Trotsky did all he could to rally career officers to the cause of the Revolution, since the art of the soldier cannot be improvised and senior officers are trained specialists. Unfortunately, Colonel Muraviev, the commander of a small army in the East, rebelled in July 1918, during the troubles in Moscow; he was shot at a session of the Simbirsk Soviet. Another staff officer, Vatzetis, turned out to be incompetent in the field but was given a job lecturing in a military academy. A third, Sergey Kamenev, became a valued colleague of Trotsky's and was appointed Commander-in-Chief in 1919. In May 1918, Trotsky ordered the arrest of Admiral Shchastny, the Commander of the Baltic fleet, and charged him with sabotage. Shchastny had been ordered to scuttle the fleet and to blow up the Ino fortress if there were the slightest danger of their falling into enemy hands, an order he attempted, at the behest of the Germans, to execute although there was no such danger. Testifying before the Revolutionary Tribunal, Trotsky said, 'When admirals or generals start to play their own political game at a time of revolution, they must be prepared, in case of failure, to take full responsibility for their actions.' Shchastny was sentenced to be shot by firing squad.

A twenty-six-year-old officer called Tukhachevsky, who had escaped from a German prisoner-of-war camp, was given command of the First and Second Volga Armies. In the autumn of 1918, a dozen Red Armies were holding a vast mobile front stretching from the White Sea to the Urals, the Volga and the Caucasus, and from the Baltic to the Don. Kalinin said in a private conversation, 'Leon Davidovich is pulling the cart of civil war all by himself.'

In May 1918, the Red Army could muster three hundred thousand men. By the end of 1920, its effective strength exceeded five million.

VII. *Internal dangers. Rising by the left-wing Social Revolutionaries. The Bolsheviks in full control*

The summer of 1918 ushered in a period of mortal peril and internecine struggle, both caused by the Treaty of Brest-Litovsk. The Social

Revolutionaries assembled their forces in the East, made common cause with the rebellious generals and the Czechoslovak Legion and set up a 'Democratic *Directoire*' which quickly made way for monarchist reaction and brutality. Various armed leagues conspired with the French military mission. They seized Yaroslavl, north of Moscow, massacred the Communists, and held it for a week, during which they provoked other killings, and then left the town in ruins.

During the war, Czechoslovak soldiers in the Austro-Hungarian Army had surrendered en masse and had formed themselves into an independent legion. Under the Treaty of Brest-Litovsk, the Soviet government was obliged to evacuate them from Vladivostok but, afraid of the presence of foreign troops along the Trans-Siberian railway line, the Council of People's Commissars ordered them to be disarmed. The legion decided to resist and, together with the Japanese, the Czechs and the White Guards, seized a large area, including Vladivostok. They also rose up on the Volga, in the Urals and in Siberia. At the same time, the right-wing Social Revolutionaries stirred up the peasants in Tambov. In the Ukraine, the Germans were rapidly losing control and the situation there grew chaotic, as anarchist guerillas rose up against them behind the lines and Ukrainian Nationalists engaged the Soviet forces. In the region of the Don and the northern Caucasus, the Cossack counter-revolution proved victorious, and a 'Volunteer Corps' was quickly raised under the command of Tsarist generals. British and French expeditionary forces landed at Murmansk. In the Bolshevik Party, a well-organized left-wing faction contemplated a split. It had its own newspapers and was supported by a good half of the party leadership, including Bukharin, Pyatakov, Bubnov, Preobrazhensky, Lomov, Sapronov, Uritsky, Unschlicht, Béla Kun and even Lenin's best friend, Ines Armand. They called for a revolutionary war against the German Empire and the immediate socialization of large-scale industry. They looked upon Lenin's 'opportunism' as treason against socialism. The left-wing Social Revolutionaries, led by Maria Spiridonova, though part of the government, also demanded an end to the 'shameful peace'. Soviet democracy was in danger of collapse.

At the Fifth Congress of Soviets on July 4th, Trotsky faced the storm. The Congress was attended by 733 Bolsheviks, 353 left-wing Social Revolutionaries, 17 Maximalists, 10 non-party delegates, 4 Anarchists, 4 Internationalist Mensheviks and 3 delegates representing the national minorities. Trotsky reported on the situation along the Ukrainian frontier, the threats against his friend Rakovsky, president of the Ukrainian peace delegation, and talked of assassination. 'All agents of foreign imperialism who call for offensive action and offer armed resistance to the Soviet authorities will be shot, and I ask the Congress to approve this order.' The left rose tumultuously with shouts of 'Kerensky! Executioner!' and the left-wing Social Revolutionary Kamov praised 'the large and healthy movement that is carrying Russian revolutionaries to the aid of their Ukrainian brothers'. Maria Spiridonova spoke of 'the martyrdom and betrayal of the Ukraine', and accused the Bolsheviks of working hand-in-glove with the Germans and of committing crimes against the peasantry. Lenin replied gravely, announcing new economic measures and maintaining that the cause of socialism must have priority over the sufferings of hungry individuals.

While these debates were still proceeding, two left-wing Social Revolutionaries, Yakov Blumkin and A. Andreev, visited Count Mirbach, the German Ambassador to Moscow, produced hand grenades and killed him. A special detachment of the Extraordinary Commission for Struggle against the Counter-Revolution – the *Cheka* – led by Social Revolutionaries, now staged an insurrection against the Soviet government. They occupied the Posts and Telegraphs and announced that the Left Social Revolutionary Party was henceforth the ruling party and that 'the people demand war against Germany'. The people of Moscow remained indifferent. The insurgents fired a couple of shots at the Kremlin but they were quickly overcome. Only one of their leaders was executed – Aleksandrovich, who, as Dzerzhinsky's deputy in the *Cheka*, had abused his office and organized the rising.

This act of political suicide on the part of the Social Revolutionary Party left the Bolsheviks in sole control. When Germany demanded that a security detachment be allowed into Russia to protect her Embassy, the Soviet government rejected the request categorically and Lenin made a speech in which he threatened total war. As a result, the Germans simply decided to move their Embassy to Pskov.

Czechoslovak intervention sealed the fate of the Imperial Family, who were then interned in Ekaterinburg (now Sverdlovsk). The Bolsheviks had intended to have the Tsar tried by a revolutionary tribunal in the Urals at the end of July, with Trotsky acting as chief prosecutor. However, the local Soviet under Belorodov feared that the Tsar might now be rescued by his friends, and decided on its own initiative to have him and his family executed there and then. During the night of July 15th–16th, the Romanovs and their retainers, eleven persons in all, were shot on the ground floor of the house in which they had been confined. The news did not reach the government until three days later, during a debate on public health. The executive of the Soviet approved the action of the Urals revolutionaries and then returned to its agenda.

VIII. *The Civil War. Trotsky's first decisive victory at Svyazhk*

The situation on the Volga front had grown extremely grave. When the Czechs and the Whites crossed Russia's most important river in several places, Trotsky decided it was high time he left for Kazan, and immediately gave orders to fit out the special train of the Minister of Communications for front-line service. On approaching the Volga, Trotsky heard that Kazan had fallen to the Whites. The train stopped at Svyazhk, a small town on the Volga, where its rear was threatened by a strong enemy detachment, consisting almost exclusively of officers and led by the monarchist Kappel.

Trotsky found his own forces badly demoralized, without regular supplies or proper communications; the local peasants were convinced the Soviet regime had been defeated. He decided to stand firm and to counter-attack, lest Kazan open the enemy's way to Nizhny-Novgorod, and Nizhny the way to Moscow. His revolutionary optimism was based on an assessment of the social forces engaged in the struggle, and the events quickly proved him right. At the other end of the telephone, Sklyansky promised food, munitions and reinforcements. But Trotsky knew it would not be a quick victory. Soon after his arrival, he came under very accurate enemy fire while inspecting a battery in the field, and when he returned to his railway carriage he found it pinpointed by no less deadly aerial bombardment. The thought of treason did not occur to him until much later.

Trotsky's train remained at Svyazhk for twenty-five days, and when it was all over, the Republic had been saved. Rosengoltz, Ivan Smirnov and some forty young Communists who made up the staff succeeded in restoring discipline, in re-opening the lines of communication and in raising morale. When the Fourth Latvian Rifle Regiment refused to fight, Trotsky ordered its commander and commissar arrested, and had them disarmed in his makeshift office in the presence of the train commandant. These two leaders of what used to be a crack regiment were later sentenced to imprisonment by a revolutionary tribunal. Trotsky then addressed the Latvians in terms both severe and uplifting: the enemy was less than a mile from Kazan and Kazan held the key to Moscow! They promised to stand firm.

Another regiment deserted its position, seized a steamship and made ready to sail. Markin jumped on board and called on the deserters to surrender. They did so. The revolutionary tribunal sentenced the commander, the commissar and a number of men, some of them Communists, to be shot.

Trotsky's appeal proved irresistible, and so did the example he set. Boots, medical supplies and field glasses appeared in quick succession, and pamphlets printed on the train were distributed as fast as they appeared. An anarchist pilot organized an air squadron, which flew reconnaissance sorties and bombed Kazan. When Kappel's unit mounted a surprise attack on the train, Trotsky took personal charge of the defences. Cooks, clerks, wireless operators, medical orderlies, anyone who could hold a rifle, took cover along the railway cutting and then drove off the Whites, who had twice as many men. The fighting lasted eight hours, and to show the enemy that he meant to stand and fight to the end, Trotsky had the engine uncoupled from the train.

This exploit marked a turning point. A few gunboats had just arrived from Kronstadt by canal, and the morning after the battle Trotsky and Raskolnikov boarded one, sailed down the Volga and entered the port of Kazan under cover of darkness. They were met with desultory gunfire, managed to set the enemy fleet alight, and, almost by a miracle, succeeded in returning up river in spite of a damaged rudder, their way lit by sheets of burning petrol. The workers in the Kazan gunpowder factory rose up against the Whites and were massacred. But on September 10th, 1918, the Reds recaptured Kazan.

IX. *The terror. Polemics with Karl Kautsky*

On August 30th, 1918, the right-wing Social Revolutionary Dora Kaplan fired a gun at Lenin just as he was leaving a factory meeting. Trotsky was recalled to Moscow but stayed for only a few days. Lenin was opposed to shooting the terrorist; the public was told she had been executed, but there are good reasons for thinking that she was sent to Siberia and that she may have been alive as late as 1951. This attack was one of a whole series: the young Bolshevik speaker, Volodarsky, was assassinated by a member of the right-wing Social Revolutionary Party in Petrograd, where a counter-revolutionary student also killed Uritsky; Nakhimson was assassinated in Yaroslavl. At the same time, the Whites unleashed a campaign of terror. On November 25th a band of Cossacks slit the throats of the members of the Taganrog Soviet. We have already mentioned the brutal murder of workers in the Kremlin arsenal. In May, General Mannerheim and the victorious Germans in Finland presided over the massacre of more than ten thousand workers and by the end of July 50,800 were in gaol. Moslem counter-revolutionaries and their British allies shot 26 Bolshevik commissars on September 20th without trial. The Civil War proved to be more vicious still than the World War, but even while the Whites were running riot the *Cheka* continued to hold back.

It was not until Lenin had been wounded that the Revolution took counter-measures. On September 7th, the Petrograd *Cheka* announced that 512 counter-revolutionaries had been shot, and many local *Cheka*s followed suit. The Party did its best to moderate the local hotheads. But while the Extraordinary Commissions (the *Cheka*s) had shot only 22 people during the first six months of their existence, more than 6,000 executions took place in the last six months of 1918, according to the official statistics which probably understated the true position. However that may be, the Red terror was still mild compared with the White terror in Finland. In the South, too, the counter-revolution organized large-scale massacres of revolutionaries, treating every worker as a potential Bolshevik. The Reds replied by killing officers and middle-class notables. Dzerzhinsky, the president of the *Cheka*, did his best to discipline the local Commissions, many of which had been infiltrated by sadists and criminals. He frequently telephoned Trotsky to discuss the fate of suspect officers.

At the beginning of August, Trotsky had, unbeknown to himself, escaped an attempt on his life, carefully organized by Social Revolutionaries. His train was to be blown up on the Kazan line, but he had changed his plans and had travelled on the Nizhny–Novgorod line, instead. And so he could continue to inspire and exhort his men.

'I give warning,' he announced at Svyazhsk, 'that if any unit retreats without orders, the political commissar will be the first to be shot and the commander will be the next ... Cowards, profiteers and traitors will not escape the bullet. I will answer for it before the whole Red Army.' Trotsky did no more than apply the rules of war adopted by all armies. But he was trying to enlist ex-officers in the Red Army, and to that end he had to defend them against slanderers, demagogues and detractors of all kinds. Colonel Vatzetis, the Commander-in-Chief, who was suspected and even kept under arrest for some time, was subsequently given an important teaching post in the military academy. A Bolshevik officer by the name of Blagonravov, whom Trotsky caught agitating against him, was dismissed from the train, but later made an excellent career for himself in the G.P.U. However, class animosity had grown so acute that Trotsky was frequently forced to intervene and to prevent the murder of prisoners and the wounded. He never stopped offering clemency to enemy troops who laid down their arms. Occasionally, he addressed deserters, and one day he made a point of facing a crowd of demoralized soldiers in the Kharkov district, accompanied by a single armed guard. He was greeted with shouts of 'Death to Trotsky!' followed by a threatening silence, but, as he began to speak, standing on a table, the mood of this strange assembly changed. In the end he received not only an ovation but the passionate promise that the men would resume the fight.

As his train travelled to and from every front, Trotsky found time to dictate a polemical work against Karl Kautsky, the German Social Democratic leader. Kautsky had condemned the dictatorship of the proletariat and the Red terror in the name of Marxism. In his *Terrorism and Communism*, Trotsky recalled the history of the English and the French Revolutions, the American War of Independence and the Paris Commune. None of them had been able to avoid violence, dictatorship or terror, except for the Paris Commune, on which the French bourgeoisie took such bloody vengeance. 'In revolution, as in war, it is the enemy's will that must be broken.' 'The bitterness of the struggle depends on internal and international circumstances. The more obstinate and dangerous the resistance of the defeated class, the more will repression be transformed into systematic terror ...' 'During revolutions, the class driven from power ... will not be intimidated by threats of imprisonment uttered by a regime they feel sure is bound to totter soon. This decisive fact alone explains the frequency of death sentences at a time of civil war.' 'A victorious war generally destroys no more than an infinitesimal part of the defeated army but demoralizes the rest ... The revolution kills a few people but frightens thousands.' 'You cannot condemn government terror unless you also reject all forms of violence, war or insurrection in principle ... ' 'In a revolution, greater energy means greater humanity.' Perhaps one other point should be made: the Russian revolutionaries knew that if they were defeated, the White terror would sap the living strength of the working masses and inevitably usher in an era of the most barbarous reaction.

x. *Trotsky's train. The 'Military Opposition'. Conflicts with Stalin*

Trotsky was to live in his mobile headquarters for nearly two and a half years, until 1920, during which time he covered something like a hundred thousand miles. 'Trotsky's train' became a legend: its approach alone invariably raised the morale of the tired troops. The train carried motor cars, fieldguns, arms, ammunition, provisions, medical supplies and pamphlets. It had two engines, a printing press, a library, a telegraph and radio office, a telephone exchange, and bathrooms. Trotsky was accompanied by his general staff, a tribunal, and a crack fighting unit in black leather uniforms. It was a strict rule that no women were admitted. A Latvian called Peterson was in charge of security and defence, and two private secretaries, Glazman and Sermux, were on hand to assist Trotsky. The train would appear at the front at the most critical moments or just before major operations. It travelled through the Ukraine, the Volga region, the areas round Smolensk and the Dvina; it could be seen in Rostov-on-Don and Petrograd during the most troubled days.

Throughout these years, Trotsky saw little of his family and had no private life. His life-history had become inextricably bound up in the history of the Revolution. He ran many risks without taking time off to discover what they were. He himself tells us that one night he was woken with a start by what felt like an earthquake. The doors of the coach were jammed and, scarcely dressed, he leapt out of a window, revolver in hand. Someone groaned in the dark, and there was the sound of splintering wood and crushing metal. The train had been derailed and eight carriages destroyed. Fortunately, there were no fatal casualties. Was it an accident or sabotage?

It was from his train that Trotsky ran the Red Army. He did not regard himself as a military strategist, but listened to the experts and then gave the appropriate orders.

He considered the social and political aspects of the struggle of paramount importance, and his quick grasp of them gave him the edge over the professional soldiers and also over a number of Bolsheviks, who were more temperamental than competent. From the summer of 1918, opposition within the Red Army arose 'against Trotsky' in general and his recruiting policy in particular.

Trotsky insisted on using the services of military specialists, that is, of officers of the old regime, for whose expertise the improvisations of workers and revolutionary intellectuals was no substitute. Moreover he believed that a great many ex-officers would serve their country honestly and well. The Central Committee decided to appoint political commissars alongside these men with instructions to watch them and to uphold the new spirit of comradeship among the ranks.

The 'Military Opposition' refused to look upon the old officers as anything but traitors; and bitterly resented the fact that even partial command should be given to men of this type. They greatly preferred the alternative of partisan warfare. The Republic held an area with changing frontiers, and at times was no larger than the old Duchy of Muscovy. Trotsky saw considerable advantages in this situation: with centralized railway and road networks and short lines of communication, the Red Army could concentrate its forces to strike with great effect at the dispersed enemy force with its very long lines of communication. To do so, the Red Army needed a central command and central control of all its resources. The Military Opposition demanded local autonomy for every army, and especially for the one under its control. That army was then engaged in the defence of Tsaritsyn (later Stalingrad and Volgograd); its commander was Voroshilov, a former ironworker from Lugansk, with Joseph Stalin, a member of the Central Committee, by his side, participating in the intrigues of the Military Opposition.

Tsaritsyn was being threatened by the Cossack army of General Krasnov, who, as the reader will remember, had given his word never again to bear arms against the Revolution, and who was now in command of nearly one hundred thousand men.[1] Tsaritsyn was putting up a brave defence but was squandering its resources, and it failed

---

[1] General Krasnov fled abroad after the defeat of the counter-revolution. During World War II, he helped the Nazis to form Russian quisling units, and was hanged in the U.S.S.R. at the age of eighty-eight.

to co-ordinate its actions with those of the other armies or to obey the orders of the Revolutionary War Council. The conflict grew so acute that Trotsky had to drop everything and rush to Tsaritsyn, where he discovered an extremely dangerous situation and total confusion. Stalin was recalled and seemed duly contrite, protesting that he and his friends had had the best of intentions. When Trotsky threatened Voroshilov with immediate arrest, he, too, apologized but continued to act as if nothing had happened. Lenin had to intervene time and again, and when he did he showed an undeniable bias in Stalin's favour, perhaps because he appreciated his qualities as a hard, non-intellectual, 'practical' man. In any case, the Politbureau and the government, though re-affirming their confidence in Trotsky, took only the very mildest measures against Stalin. It has generally been forgotten that Tsaritsyn, which held the key to the Caucasus and Asia, was seized by the Whites at the end of June 1919, and held by them for several months.

Stalin exploited the reverses of the Red Army to propose the mass dismissal of career officers whom, pathologically suspicious as he was even then, he regarded as potential traitors. Lenin referred the matter to Trotsky. 'Childish nonsense,' he was told. 'Do you know how many officers we have in the army?' 'No.' 'Thirty thousand at the very least ... For every traitor, there are a hundred dependable men; for every deserter, there are two or three professionals who have given their lives. How would we replace them all?' Lenin quickly dropped the matter.

But then Voroshilov and his friends began to call for the formation of an independent army group in the South. When Stalin sent the Central Committee a memorandum criticizing the 'conduct of the war', Trotsky, provoked, offered his resignation. The Central Committee rejected it on July 5th, expressed its continued confidence in him and gave him even wider powers. The decision was signed by all those present, including Stalin.[2]

It was during these debates that Lenin gave Trotsky proof of his full confidence. The execution of the commander, the commissar and some of the men who had deserted during the battle of Svyazhsk continued to give rise to indignant comments about 'Trotsky's severity'. During a session of the Politbureau, Lenin handed Trotsky

---

[2] The list of signatories was: Lenin, Kamenev, Krestinsky, Serebriakov, Stalin and Stasova. Kamenev, Krestinsky and Serebriakov were shot in 1936–7, and it is not known what happened to Helen Stasova.

a sheet of paper and said to him, 'I'll give you as many of these as you want.' At the bottom of the blank sheet of paper headed 'Chairman of the Council of People's Commissars' Lenin had written: 'Knowing the stern character of Comrade Trotsky's orders, I am so convinced, so utterly convinced of the rightness, expediency and necessity for the success of the cause of Comrade Trotsky's order, that I endorse it without reservation. V. Ulyanov-Lenin.'

The Stalin-Voroshilov group reluctantly bowed to the Party decision but failed to disband. We shall see how disastrous a part they played in the Polish campaign in 1920. Not in his wildest dreams could Stalin have seen himself as a rival of Lenin, who was ten years his senior, the founder of the Party and – on the strength of his ability, his integrity, his past history and the affectionate devotion with which he was surrounded – its unchallenged leader. But Stalin felt affronted by the standing of Trotsky, exactly the same age as himself and a newcomer to the Bolshevik Party, but also an orator, champion of the people, writer, politician and war leader. Their personalities could not have been more opposed. The one was an intellectual giant, as much at home in the West as he was in Russia, a gifted speaker, writer and man of action. The other, almost unknown outside Party circles, was inarticulate, lacking in personal charm, had spent his life serving on committees, involved in obscure projects, and had played no prominent part in the 1905 and 1917 revolutions. No wonder that, from 1918 onwards, he was consumed by ambition, and became a bitter and envious man.

xi. *The Civil War. Trotsky organizes the defence of Petrograd (1919)*

The general staff would work out operational plans and submit them to the Revolutionary War Council for approval. But though the voice of the chairman carried considerable weight in these discussions, Trotsky never imposed his personal opinions. In matters of general strategy, the Central Committee of the Party was always consulted, and when differences arose over the conduct of the war, Trotsky quite often found himself in a minority. The results proved him right on some occasions and wrong on others, but it never occurred to anyone to congratulate or to blame him. It was all in a day's work.

Towards the summer of 1919, the situation grew critical, so much so that few foreign observers gave the Republic more than a few months of life. While the towns suffered the slow agony of famine, the countryside was in the grip of typhoid and typhus with occasional outbreaks of cholera. The Anglo-French blockade prevented all contacts with the outside world: not a letter, not a newspaper, not a single crate of medical supplies slipped through the net. The Japanese were harassing the Red Army in the Far East, the Czechoslovaks were spread out along the railway lines between the Urals and Vladivostok, the British had occupied Archangel, the Finns had invaded Karelia, a German Corps was operating in the Baltic, and the Rumanians and French first captured and then abandoned Odessa. White counter-revolutionary armies, supported and equipped by the Great Powers, surrounded the revolutionary forces. In the north, supported by the British, was General Miller; from the Estonian frontier General Yudenich was attacking Petrograd; in the west were bands of White Guards and a hostile Poland; in the south Denikin's large volunteer army lay in wait; the Cossacks were on the Don, and in the east Admiral Kolchak, 'the Supreme Governor' of Russia, had occupied Siberia and the Urals.

Kolchak and Denikin commanded very large forces between them, and once the Social Revolutionaries had helped them into the saddle, they quickly put an end to any vestige of democracy in the territories under their control. During the previous September the Constituent Assembly at Ufa, with a liberal majority, had elected a Directorate which included the Social Revolutionary leaders Avkenstsiev, Argunov and Zenzinov (the last two as deputy members). They had entrusted command of the army to Admiral Kolchak, who swore the necessary oaths of loyalty, then organized a *putsch* and unleashed a cruel reign of terror on the population. The experiment in liberal democracy now over, he threatened Moscow.

When the Red Army had defeated him several times, the question arose whether he should be pursued beyond the Urals and finished off in Siberia, or whether it was better to strike elsewhere and run the risk of his licking his wounds and then joining forces with Denikin in the South. Trotsky was in favour of the second alternative but he was outvoted in the Central Committee. There were also disagreements about the correct strategy on the southern front and here, too, Trotsky found himself in a minority, at least for a time. As a result, the Red Army launched an attack on Cossack territory, which yielded no positive results but enabled Denikin to drive towards Kursk, Orel and Tula. It was only in the face of this disaster that Trotsky's original plans were adopted.

But before Kolchak's defeat, the exhausted and starving Seventh Red Army had been forced to yield to General Yudenich, who advanced upon the very gates of Petrograd in October 1919. Zinoviev, the president of the local Soviet, became panic-stricken and advocated the evacuation of the city. Lenin agreed. Why waste troops on an engagement doomed to failure from the start? A Finnish offensive against Petrograd from the North seemed imminent and a British naval squadron was sailing up the Gulf of Finland. But the evacuation of the city would have meant abandoning its population to the White terror. Trotsky maintained that victory was possible and spread optimism wherever he went. He travelled to Petrograd in his train, and within a few days fostered the will to resist – if need be, to the bitter end. Barricades and field guns burgeoned forth all over the city while crack regiments were called back from the Polish front. In the colonnaded halls of the Tauride Palace, which had witnessed the momentous events of 1917, Trotsky addressed the assembled workers, the Soviet and the garrison in rousing cadences. He told the Finns that the road from Petrograd to Helsingfors was no longer than the road back, and, amid loud applause, announced the arrival of the Bashkir cavalry. He argued that if the Whites should succeed in breaking into the city – intersected as it was by canals, fortified at each crossroad, and provided with trenches and artillery – Petrograd would become their graveyard. His very presence fired the people with enthusiasm. He rode into the line of fire, escorted by only one cavalryman, and calmed and rallied the panic-stricken infantry, who, taken completely aback, cheered him loudly.

On October 23rd and 24th, 1919, less than thirty miles from Petrograd, the White Guard offensive turned into a rout. At almost the same time, Denikin was defeated before Tula and Kolchak was broken in the East. A most desperate threat had been averted. Everywhere the Red Army, supported by peasants in revolt against the Whites, was in pursuit of the enemy. They advanced to the Estonian frontier and the Black Sea; Kolchak, tracked down by Siberian guerillas and deserted by his Allied advisers at the last moment, was captured and shot in Irkutsk in 1920.

XII. *Polish aggression in 1920. Trotsky disagrees with Lenin about the attack on Warsaw. Stalin's role*

Shortly before these decisive and unforeseen events, the Soviet government had been more than willing to consider peace terms that would have been far from advantageous to itself. On January 23rd, 1919, the Paris Peace Conference, at the suggestion of President Wilson, had invited all groups exercising or attempting to exercise power in any part of former Russian territory to attend a conference at Prinkipo, an island in the Sea of Marmara, and to sign a peace that could only have resulted in the dismemberment of Russia. The Soviet government accepted the invitation. In his reply Chicherin stated that the Soviet government 'does not refuse to recognize its financial obligations to creditors who are nationals of the Allied Powers', that it was 'willing to grant to nationals of the Allied Powers mining, timber and other concessions', provided only that such concessions did not prejudice the economic and social order of Soviet Russia. The Soviet government was also prepared to make territorial concessions. Trotsky was chosen to head the Soviet delegation to Prinkipo, but the leaders of the counter-revolution still felt so strong and confident of the support of the Great Powers, as well as of the opposition by Poincaré and Clemenceau to President Wilson's initiative, that they refused to take part in the negotiations.

By 1920 the Civil War seemed to be drawing to an end. The British had evacuated Archangel and the French had pulled out of Odessa. In Siberia, the last White bands were being tracked down. Only a small counter-revolutionary army under Baron Wrangel was left in the Crimea. There were great hopes. The Council of People's Commissars announced the abolition of the death penalty, which had been retained as an exceptional measure in the war zones, and the Party was considering abolishing all other emergency measures. Soviet democracy was about to be born when Marshal Pilsudski made a determined bid to ensure its miscarriage. He felt the young Polish state was strong enough to annex the Ukraine and possibly even to topple the Soviet regime. Meanwhile, London and Paris were lavish in their support of Baron Wrangel.

The Soviet Republic had recognized the independence of Estonia and Latvia; peace treaties had been signed. Negotiations with Lithuania were in progress. But Pilsudski's Poland rejected all Moscow's peace overtures. On April 7th, 1920, the Marshal informed the Ukrainians that Poland was about to 'liberate' them, and, at first, he seemed as good as his word. Moghilev, Vinnitsa, Podolsk and Zhitomir fell in quick succession, and on May 6th, Polish forces captured Kiev. Trotsky was preparing a counter-offensive and a number of Tsarist generals, including Brusilov and Polivanov,

offered him their services. Pilsudski's first reverses came at the end
of May – Baron Wrangel's offensive in the southern Ukraine may
have slowed down the advancing Red Army, but failed to check it.
In June and July the Poles abandoned town after town until their
own frontiers stood wide open. Lloyd George told the Russians that
if they attacked Warsaw, he would order in the Royal Navy. At that
moment, the Second Congress of the Third International was meeting in Moscow and Trotsky found himself in opposition to Lenin.
Tukhachevsky, accompanied by Smilga, a member of the Central
Committee, was marching on Warsaw, and Trotsky advocated signing a favourable peace before the momentum of the counter-offensive
had spent itself. Lenin, on the other hand, believed that the capture
of Warsaw would lead to a proletarian uprising in Poland, carrying
the Revolution to the borders of Germany and frustrating the Treaty
of Versailles, which he regarded as a disaster for Europe. Lenin had
his way and the capture of Warsaw was ordered. But no revolutionary movement appeared in Poland – patriotism won the day instead. Moreover, during the critical days, when Tukhachevsky was
approaching the gates of Warsaw, the First Cavalry, commanded
by Budenny, and the Fourteenth Red Army, commanded by Voroshilov and Stalin, marched on Lvov instead of coming to Tukhachevsky's aid. As a result, Weygand and Pilsudski were able to launch
a counter-attack, which – much to their surprise – turned out to be
successful. It seems that Budenny, Voroshilov and Stalin, convinced
that the capture of Warsaw was a foregone conclusion, had wanted
to earn their own laurels at Lvov. The result was disastrous.

Trotsky returned from the Southern Ukraine, where he had organized the great offensive against Wrangel, which had ended with the
terrible battle of Perekop and the eventual destruction of the White
Army. His train made a detour to the Polish front. In the Central
Committee there were fresh differences of opinion. Several members,
including Rykov, favoured a regrouping of forces and a renewed
campaign against Poland. Trotsky and Lenin, the latter admitting
his previous error, favoured immediate negotiations, and won the
day. In October, Joffe, Kirov, Manuilsky and Obolensky signed the
Treaty of Riga, which gave Poland more favourable borders than
the Allied Powers had recommended.

The character of Trotsky, organizer and head of the Red Army,
was highlighted by these events perhaps better than by any others.
He never despaired during even the most desperate situations; his

decisions were tough but always based on appeals to the masses and on revolutionary confidence. The success of a particularly brilliant campaign never turned his head. Trotsky the politician always predominated over Trotsky the soldier, and the former had not the slightest inclination to indulge in adventures, to take unnecessary risks. As an internationalist he recognized the importance of military force, but his internationalism was never carried on the point of a bayonet.

XIII. *The German revolution. Trotsky's work in the Third International*

Neither the example of the Russian Revolution nor the Russians' appeals to the workers abroad had fallen on deaf ears. Precisely one year and two days after the Soviet seizure of power, the sailors of Kiel refused to continue the war, Hindenburg's soldiers formed revolutionary councils, and red flags appeared throughout Germany. However, it quickly became clear that the German revolution was based on a model quite unlike the Bolshevik. The influential, reformist German Social Democratic Party, which had supported the Kaiser, held on to its majority among the German working class and displayed what might be called its 'powerful impotence'. It feared nothing so much as the implementation of its own programme, which favoured a measure of workers' control; so at first it was careful not to resist the current demand for workers' councils, which merely wasted their efforts in a political vacuum. At the same time, the Social Democrats adopted a policy of appeasing and collaborating with the upper-middle class, the reactionary judiciary and the military caste, with which they at once made common cause against the revolutionary minority of the German people, led by Rosa Luxemburg, Karl Liebknecht, Karl Radek and Georg Ledebour. It later transpired that Fritz Ebert, 'Regent of the Reich', was negotiating with the German High Command at the very moment that the Kaiser was fleeing to Holland and Karl Liebknecht was proclaiming the republic from the balcony of the Imperial Palace. The aim of these negotiations was to form an anti-Bolshevik alliance 'supported by the army and the Reichstag'. This, Ebert felt, was the more essential, as the German Right was in disarray.[3]

[3] See Franz Neumann: *Behemoth: The Structure and Practice of National-Socialism*, New York, 1942.

German Social Democracy had thus taken the same path that finally led Kerensky to the Kornilov plot and drove the Russian Social Revolutionaries into the arms of the diehard monarchist, Admiral Kolchak. In January 1919, when the Spartacists rose up in Berlin, the Social Democrat Noske appealed for help to the patriotic *Freikorps*. The insurrection was crushed; Karl Liebknecht and Rosa Luxemburg were arrested and murdered in cold blood by a group of officers. In short, Weimar democracy was nothing but a sham – it appeased the working class by deception while giving the reactionaries a chance to regroup their forces. Political assassination was the order of the day: the extreme right-wing struck systematically at German freedom and massacred militant revolutionaries wherever the opportunity presented itself. It was a long and tragic affair, too often forgotten today. Noske was Hitler's forerunner; without the one, the other would not have arisen. These facts must be borne in mind by anyone trying to grasp the attitude of the Russian Revolution and the Communist International.

On October 3rd, 1918, Lenin, anticipating the collapse of the German Empire, wrote to the Soviet Executive Committee that 'the Russian proletariat must throw all its energies behind the struggle of the German workers ... Grain reserves must be built up for the German revolution, and the creation of a powerful Red Army speeded up ... ' Trotsky, for his part, said that 'history is being fulfilled, like it or not ... With her 420-mm guns Germany imposed her will on the world ... And now history, having first raised German imperialism to great heights and having hypnotised the masses, has plunged it precipitously into an abyss of impotence and humiliation, as if to say, "Look, it has been shattered; all that remains is to sweep its debris from Europe and the world" ... ' He showed that the salvation of Germany – and of Europe – lay in the seizure of power by the socialist proletariat.

> If the German proletariat goes over to the attack, it will be the bounden duty of Soviet Russia to ignore national frontiers in the revolutionary struggle. Soviet Russia is merely the vanguard of the German and European revolutions ... The German proletariat and its technology, on the one hand, and Russia, disorganized but so full of natural riches and so populous, on the other, will constitute an invincible rock against which the waves of imperialism will be smashed.

One year earlier, the Russian Social Democratic Workers' Party (the Bolsheviks) had renounced the discredited title 'Social Democratic', and, returning to the tradition of Marx's and Engels's *Communist Manifesto*, had decided to change its name to the 'Communist Party'. The Second International had disintegrated on August 2nd, 1914, when its member-parties, instead of making common cause against the war, had endorsed their respective governments' war policies. The Russian Revolution, by contrast, proudly proclaimed its internationalism by its slogan, 'Workers of the world, unite!' On March 2nd–6th, 1919, immediately after the Spartacists' defeat in Germany, after Noske's victory and the murder of Karl Liebknecht and Rosa Luxemburg, the First World Congress of the Third International met in Moscow. Trotsky left the front to attend it and to represent the Russian Communist Party at the side of Lenin, Zinoviev, Bukharin and Chicherin.

The rift between revolutionary and reformist Marxists had meanwhile become a gulf – the blood spilt by the Social Democrats and their allies, the monarchist *Freikorps*, in the streets of Berlin had seen to that.

Lenin proposed Zinoviev as president of the Executive Committee of the Third International. He was a first-class propagandist and popularizer, and had been one of Lenin's close collaborators for many years. From 1919–23, Trotsky devoted a great deal of his time and energy to the Third International. He drafted the manifestoes of the first four congresses, took part in drafting its rules, and worked in its commissions. From 1920 onwards the new International won a number of adherents throughout the world: the French and Italian Socialist Parties supported it in principle, and the U.S. trade unions, the Spanish National Confederation of Labour, the Norwegian Workers' Party and many others appointed delegates to it. In Germany, the old Sparticist nucleus developed into the German Communist Party and attracted a great many independent Social Democrats. Trotsky advocated uncompromising ideological consistency and a clean break with reformism, that is, bourgeois socialism. His main aim was to form a Marxist proletarian party, disciplined in action and dedicated to the struggle for socialism and active international solidarity. 'The war,' he said in 1924, 'did not bring about the victory of the proletariat in Western Europe. We can see only too clearly that what was needed for victory in 1919 and 1920 was a revolutionary party.' He looked upon such a party as the conscious instrument of history and midwife of events. It should be made up of courageous and determined men, inspired with a collective spirit, and totally opposed to fatalism, inertia, the line of least resistance, and personal ambition, but devoted to the higher, that is, the international, interests of the working class. The idea that the Communist parties might one day turn into bureaucratic organizations, propped up by secret services, incapable of critical thought but ready to support criminal acts and corrupt men with blind fanaticism, did not, in those halcyon days, occur to Trotsky or anyone else.

Trotsky was particularly interested in the problems of French and German socialism. He kept up a lively correspondence with his old friends, the French trade unionist Pierre Monatte, and the teacher Fernand Loriot; he broke with Jean Longuet, whom he attacked in a vigorous polemic, and he had Ernest Lafont expelled from Moscow for consorting with pro-Pilsudski socialists during his trip. He attacked Marcel Cachin and L. O. Frossard for their parliamentarian attitudes. In 1921, at the Third Congress of the Communist International, he endorsed Lenin's censure of German revolutionary tactics: minority action must inevitably lead to defeat; the masses had first to be won over by propaganda, persuasion, and a vigorous fight for their basic demands.

XIV. *'War communism'. The Revolutionary Army of Labour. The trade union question. Invasion of Georgia. The Kronstadt rising. New Economic Policy*

It was not the immediate intention of the leaders of the Revolution to proceed to the complete nationalization of production – on seizing power they had confined themselves to establishing workers' control, and not workers' ownership, of production and the banks. It was only the left-wing Communists who had called for total socialization and it was the Civil War that had come to their aid. The owners abandoned their factories or shut them down and workers' committees stepped in to take them over. On May 1st, 1918, six months after the October rising, legacies were abolished by decree. Two months later, on June 30th, another decree nationalized all major industries. On August 24th, private ownership of real estate was abolished in the towns. By then it had become clear that it was only by dispossessing the propertied classes that their defeat could be brought about. The left-wing Communists declared themselves satisfied at last and rallied to Lenin.

There was no question of touching peasant property, though a substantial minority of the peasantry, well-to-do and generally reactionary, constituted a middle class far more energetic, more numerous and more formidable than the urban. The chaos into which the Civil War had plunged industry and transport and the inflation which had begun under the previous regime had made the towns dependent on the rural black market. As a result the peasants had begun to milk the townsfolk of their possessions – furniture, clothing, utensils and even works of art – in return for a handful of flour and potatoes. The rations of the army, the navy, the workers and the government had to be procured by requisitions, and rationing was extremely severe. Where the peasants had to choose between the Whites and the Reds, they generally – after costly hesitations and local skirmishes – chose the Reds; it was this fact that ensured the Revolution's ultimate victory over the counter-revolution. The question was whether – once this victory had been won – 'war communism', based on requisitions and hasty nationalization, could survive. The total industrial production of the country in 1920 was down by at least a quarter compared with 1913; in the iron and coal mining industries it was lower still. By the end of 1919, sixty per cent of the country's railway engines were in need of repair.

At that time, Trotsky was in charge of economic reorganization in the Urals. A telegram from Lenin asked him to take charge of the transport system, which he managed to improve considerably, though the experts had maintained that this was impossible. His work with the Red Army and his military train had brought him into direct touch with the peasantry, and he could see danger signals. In February 1920, a year before Lenin became converted to the idea in the face of imminent disaster, Trotsky proposed the adoption of the 'New Economic Policy'. He asked the Central Committee to replace the requisition of agricultural produce with a tax in kind which would leave the peasants a margin of profit large enough to encourage more intensive cultivation, and to supply them with industrial goods equal in value to the amount of grain they handed over to the state. In retrospect, it looks very much as if the adoption of these measures would have spared Russia the painful 1921 crisis and the Kronstadt revolt. As it was, the Central Committee rejected Trotsky's proposals by eleven votes to four.

For a whole year, Trotsky combined the posts of Chairman of the Revolutionary War Council, People's Commissar of War and the

Navy, with that of virtual dictator of transport. In *My Life*, Trotsky tells us that, having drawn a graph of the year 1920, the engineer Lomonosov indicated a point on it, and said to Lenin, 'Here comes death'. 'What is to be done then?' asked Lenin, to which Lomonosov replied, 'Even the Bolsheviks cannot perform miracles'. 'Still, we'll try to perform the miracle,' Lenin muttered drily. And it was in 1920, during the Polish campaign, that the transport system was in fact saved from paralysis. Trotsky had roused the transport workers to tremendous, often heroic efforts not only by repeated appeals to their conscience and by strict discipline, but also by improving supplies and co-ordinating all the services.

Victory posed the problem of demobilization. Could the soldier-ploughmen be sent back to their homes without a guarantee of enough food or a chance to work? Trotsky came up with a temporary solution: he proposed turning the Third Army in the Urals, which had just beaten Admiral Kolchak, into the First Revolutionary Army of Labour. A decree was issued and a general staff consisting of representatives of the Commissariats of Production, Agriculture and Supply, presided over by Trotsky, set the troops to work in the forests, the mines, the fields, the railways and the roads. Other armies followed and were not disbanded until 1921.

1920 was also a year of heated discussions concerning the role of Soviet trade unionism. Trotsky maintained that the unions should be integrated into the state and that they should play an active part in the administration of production and transport. Lenin and Zinoviev advocated a measure of autonomy for the unions; they preferred to see them as 'schools of communism' and as champions of the workers' more immediate interests. Trotsky countered that their argument was tantamount to admitting that the state and Party were inadequate teachers or guardians of the workers' rights. 'We do not have a workers' state but a workers' and peasants' state marred by bureaucratic distortions,' Lenin retorted.

The Workers' Opposition, led by Shlyapnikov, Medvedev and Alexandra Kollontai, also denounced the 'bureaucratic distortions' and emphasized the sufferings of the proletariat: near-famine, epidemics, forced mobilization, industrial chaos and the many cases of incompetence on the part of the middle and junior functionaries of the new state.

The first few months of 1921 were marked by a number of events that, in their several ways, indicated that the great revolutionary tide had begun to ebb. They were: first, the 'sovietization' of Georgia, second, the Kronstadt revolt and, third, the failure of the Communist rising in Berlin and the consequent change of tactics by the Third International.

Before the establishment of Soviet rule, the Georgian Social Democrats, who had played a most important part in the Russian working-class movement and whose leaders, Chkheidze and Tseretelli, had been among the leaders of the Russian democratic movement in 1917, had declared themselves in favour of the indivisibility of Russia, that is, of close federal links between their country and the great Russian Republic. However, immediately after the advent of Bolshevism, they had proclaimed their country's independence, subsequently confirmed by a peace treaty with the Russian Socialist Federal Republic. The Georgian Mensheviks enjoyed genuine popularity at home and did their best to rule democratically, but they repressed pro-Bolshevik agitation, occasionally with considerable severity. They were looking to the Western Powers for support, and Turkey had officially backed their independence.

Kirov was appointed Soviet Ambassador to Georgia and took up his post in Tiflis (Tbilisi). On February 17th, 1921, the Moscow government was faced with a *fait accompli*: the Second Red Army had invaded Georgia and had met with almost no resistance. Neither Lenin nor Trotsky, neither General Sergey Kamenev nor the Central Committee, had ordered the invasion; their only involvement was to acknowledge the deed when it was done. Trotsky did not consider that an independent Georgia was a source of danger. Like Lenin, he believed that the country would not break away from Russia without coming into the sphere of influence, or under the domination, of another power and that 'sovietization' was bound to come sooner or later; but he expected it to come from the efforts of the Georgian masses and not as a result of military conquest. Ordjonikidze and Stalin, two Georgians, decided otherwise. Their easy victory was to wreck the Revolution's policy towards the national minorities in the long run; meanwhile, it ushered in a period of bloody internecine struggle in Georgia. It was on the Georgian question that Lenin later broke with Stalin.

On March 1st, 1921, the sailors and workers of Kronstadt, after a clumsy harangue by Kamenev, rose in revolt, demanding the re-election of the Soviets, the legalization of all Soviet parties, the end of rationing, freedom for small traders and the release of political prisoners. The movement was inspired by anarchists and left-wing Social Revolutionaries. Former officers volunteered their services, and right-wing Social Revolutionaries were assembling in Estonia and Finland. The foreign press foretold troubled times for Russia. Kronstadt had considerable vantage points – the fortress, the arsenal and the Baltic fleet – and the uprising posed a direct threat to Petrograd, where famine had already led to a number of strikes.

The Central Committee charged Trotsky with quelling the rebellion, and he immediately left for Petrograd to study the situation for a few days. When his appeal to the insurgents went unheeded, he ordered Tukhachevsky to proceed against them without further ado. A first assault over the frozen Gulf of Finland was repelled with heavy losses. On March 18th, Kronstadt went down fighting, and many of its defenders fled to Finland.

Because this dramatic interlude has been a subject of sharp controversy, Trotsky had many occasions to discuss its underlying causes: the revolutionary masses had suffered dangerous exhaustion; Kronstadt was no longer the hotbed of passions and ideas it had once been; its citizens had been scattered all over the country – beyond the Caspian Sea, in Vladivostok and on all the fronts; with few exceptions, the old leaders were not among those who had remained behind. Elsewhere, too, resistance to the regime, reflecting the discontent and the weariness of the masses, particularly of the peasants, was growing apace; there were troubles on the Volga, and Makhno's anarchist bands roamed the Ukraine. South of Moscow, a peasant army led by the Social Revolutionary Antonov succeeded in massing nearly fifty thousand men in the region round Tambov, and was shooting Communists in the name of the Constituent Assembly. The original Kronstadt slogan of 'Free elections to the Soviets', had suddenly given way to another: 'Soviets without Bolsheviks'. Had Kronstadt not been recaptured before the thaw, nothing could have prevented the rebel fleet from sailing into Petrograd. The Revolution was being threatened by a handful of anarchists, a few left-wing Social Revolutionaries with anarchist tendencies, and behind them the old Parties, the émigrés and the old generals. Had they succeeded in overthrowing the dictatorship of the proletariat, the Kronstadt and peasant rebels would clearly have opened the door to reaction and the White terror. And what would the upshot have been? The lessons of the past few years were still fresh and painful in the Bolsheviks' memory. Wherever the Revolution had been worsted, in Finland, Bavaria, Hungary and, as now, in the Ukraine, on the Volga, on the Don, in Baku and in Siberia, all democratic elements had been suppressed and the most cruel reaction had visited bloody vengeance and terror on the poor, as witness the behaviour of Mannerheim in Finland, of General Hoffmann in Munich, Admiral Horthy in Hungary, Admiral Kolchak in Siberia and Baron Wrangel in the Crimea. To weaken was to perish.

While gunfire was still thundering across the Gulf of Finland, the Tenth Congress of the Bolshevik Party met in session. It censured the Workers' Opposition for its 'anarcho-syndicalist tendencies' and threatened it with expulsion from the Party. But there were no arrests; at that time, the very idea of arresting Party militants for their political opinions would have seemed monstrous. Lenin succeeded in having the New Economic Policy, intended to appease the countryside, adopted. It involved taxes in kind, concessions to foreign capitalists on strictly defined conditions and freedom for small-scale private enterprise. Trotsky fully supported these reforms which he himself had recommended a year earlier. The countryside was quickly pacified, even though large forces had to be mobilized to destroy Antonov's bands in the black lands around Tambov, and though fighting between the Red Army and the small 'army of insurgent peasants' led by Makhno continued in the Ukraine until the autumn. Makhno had fought alongside the Red Army to defeat Denikin and Wrangel. Trotsky had approved the pact between the Southern Army and Makhno 'on condition that it was loyally observed', and he had even discussed with Lenin the possibility of offering the Ukrainian nationalists some sort of territorial autonomy. But the pact was not loyally observed, for the two sides detested each other. Frunze, Gusov and Béla Kun were in command of this zone of operations.

At the end of 1921, another calamity shook the country – the great drought which caused the dreadful famine in the fertile Volga basin. But by the beginning of 1922, the New Economic Policy had begun to bear fruit. All fighting had stopped except in the Far East and in some remote corners of Central Asia. Nothing remained of the *ancien régime*. The imperial autocracy, the old caste system, the nobility, the Tsarist administration and civil service had all vanished without a trace, and so had feudal rule of the land, and with it the yoke of Russian and foreign capitalism. The latter had previously been so firmly entrenched that Russia might truly have been called a semi-colonial country. The first signs of agricultural recovery appeared in those regions which had been spared by the drought. Slowly but surely the paralysis of industry and transport yielded to renewed activity.

Peace treaties were signed with the Baltic states and Poland, and several countries recognized the Russian Socialist Federal Republic. Great Britain, without officially recognizing it, nevertheless received its diplomats. Among workers and socialists, a desire for reconciliation became apparent even among those who had been most hostile to Bolshevism. Talks between the Socialist Workers' International, founded by various left-wing groupings, and the Communist Third International were initiated. The International Trade Union Federation in Amsterdam appealed to all workers to lend their support to Russia because 'the defeat of the Soviet government would be the signal for a determined offensive by the counter-revolution ... The forces of reaction which, in Germany and especially in Bavaria, are behaving so arrogantly and which, in Spain, Rumania, Hungary and Yugoslavia, are imposing a rule of bloody violence on the working class, would triumph if the open and secret enemies of the Russian revolution were to succeed in replacing Soviet rule with a counter-revolutionary government under the patronage of West European capitalism ... ' Such was the language of even moderate trade unionists at that time.

The Bolshevik Party itself was in ferment. The Workers' Opposition, the Democratic Centralists ('Decemists') and the group round the *Workers' Truth* were all perturbed by the swelling bureaucratic tide, by the continuing state of siege and the strict discipline that was being imposed, and the leaders of the Central Committee had much the same preoccupations. The ranks of a successful revolutionary party are quickly swollen by the influx of adventurers, of men with an eye to the main chance and of reckless and unstable elements. The abuses, the excesses, even the crimes committed at the time, were due much more to them than to the militants, and it was against them that the first great party purge was directed. Out of 658,839 members, 159,355 were expelled. Others, who were discontented, left of their own accord. Expulsion amounted to censure, and resulted in the loss of so-called 'responsible' status. It had no other untoward consequences, provided no indictable crimes had been committed. Those expelled from the Party were able to continue in their jobs and were not molested in any way. In a number of cases, qualified workers and intellectuals earned more than they had done before because they were no longer limited to the maximum salary rates fixed for Party members – a very modest 185 to 225 roubles a month.

Disciplinary measures against Party members who criticized the Central Committee in public were limited to expelling the malcontents from Moscow, in some cases to remote areas where they were given responsible posts.

At the time, Lenin was the acknowledged head of the Party and government; Trotsky was in charge of the army, the navy, transport, economic affairs and of anti-religious propaganda; Zinoviev was president of the Leningrad Soviet, and Kalinin of the Moscow Soviet. Rykov headed the Supreme Economic Council, Bukharin was in charge of the press, and Chicherin of foreign affairs; Rakovsky was the equivalent of Prime Minister of the Ukraine, while Ivan Smirnov was in charge of Siberian affairs. Stalin combined two posts – the Workers' and Peasants' Inspectorate and the Commissariat of Nationalities. (It was in these departments that the most important conflicts were to arise.) Krasin was in charge of foreign trade and Lunacharsky of education. Serebriakov, Krestinsky, Preobrazhensky, Sokolnikov, Smilga, Pyatakov and Joffe made up the rest of the leading figures in the Soviet government. Zinoviev, Karl Radek and Bukharin held important posts in the Communist International.

Four · Opposition

1. *Lenin against the bureaucratic regime. Conflicts with Stalin. Last phase of Trotsky's collaboration with Lenin*

Lenin's speeches and writings in 1921–2, while still self-assured and authoritative, did not conceal his uneasiness and occasional bitterness. Reminiscences by his contemporaries show that Vladimir Ilyich was, like so many of the people he attacked, highly critical of the conduct and outlook of those Party leaders who favoured a bureaucratic dictatorship. At times, Lenin was brutally frank in his defence of the people – a brutality that no doubt reflected his anguish. 'What mistakes we have made!' he said repeatedly. 'It would be criminal to deny that we have exceeded all bounds...' Or again: 'Our attempt to implement socialism here and now has failed ... The dictatorship of the proletariat shows that never before has the proletariat been in such a desperate situation...' We must 'abandon the construction of socialism and fall back on state capitalism in many economic spheres.' We are 'uncouth'; we live in 'administrative chaos', in 'waves of illegality'. He coined words like *Kom-chvantsvo* and *Kom-vranio* (com-conceit and com-deceit, where 'com' was an abbreviation for communist); he compared some Party leaders to those brutal satraps of the old regime who had been dubbed *derzhimordas*, after the repulsive bully in Gogol's satire.

After their disagreements over the trade union question, Lenin and Trotsky had quickly resumed their excellent relationship. Both felt they had avoided disaster at the beginning of 1921, while yet safeguarding the essential achievements of the Revolution. Both recognized the immense problems ahead of them; both agreed on what to do about the arrested Social Revolutionaries. That party had fought in the Civil War on the side of the Constituent Assembly and had been responsible for several political assassinations, notably that of

111

Volodarsky, and the nearly successful attempt on the life of Lenin. Ten members of their Central Committee, all old revolutionaries, were in prison awaiting trial, and deserters from their ranks had helped to build up an overwhelming case against them. Death sentences seemed inevitable. Would they have to be carried out? Though less dangerous opponents had perished during the Terror, Lenin and Trotsky decided on clemency: none of the accused could be executed unless their Party resumed terrorist activities.[1]

In the Central Committee, Lenin waged a tireless battle for the reform of the revolutionary regime, until his health broke down under the strain. He was only fifty-five when he had his first stroke. In May 1922, while Trotsky was confined to bed in the Kremlin (he had sprained his foot on a fishing trip) Bukharin came to see him. 'Not you ill, as well!' he exclaimed in horror, as he entered the room. He told Trotsky that Lenin had just had a stroke, that he was paralysed down one side and could neither walk nor speak. The bad news had been kept from Trotsky for a few days, 'so as not to worry you ...' Bukharin embraced Trotsky and said affectionately, 'Don't you get ill too, I implore you ... There are only two men's deaths I think of with panic, Lenin's and yours.' Trotsky recalled Lenin's words: 'The old will die and the young will capitulate ... How many of you know what Europe is like or the working-class movement?' Lenin's body and his will to live were to fight on for twenty months, and we only recall the history of this agonizing last struggle because it forms an integral part of Trotsky's own life.

In 1922, at the Eleventh Congress of the Bolshevik Party, Stalin had been appointed its General Secretary. Lenin was then still in perfect health and though he defended Stalin against his critics, he did not, according to Trotsky, favour his nomination. The new post gave its holder no more than administrative authority; it was a purely technical, executive post and as such controlled by the Central Committee and the Politbureau. Lenin was determined to see that it remained so, but shortly afterwards he was struck down by his illness. He was up and about at the end of July, regained his speech and

[1] The majority of the members of the S.R.P., subsequently released and kept under surveillance, were later given responsible government jobs as economists or engineers. The 'brains' of the Party, Abraham Goltz, did excellent work for many years for the State Bank in the Volga region. Stalin had him tortured and shot in 1937.

movement and resumed his official functions on October 2nd, 1922. In the meantime, the new General Secretary had travelled to Georgia, where he had used his own authority to impose changes on the government and the party leadership. Leading Georgian Bolsheviks, including Mdivani, Okudjava and Kavtaradze, expressed their indignation at Stalin's unwarranted and brutal interference in Georgian affairs, and called on Lenin to protect their autonomy. Lenin was furious with Stalin, and, fearing a relapse in his health, dictated a confidential document dated December 25th, 1922, to the Central Committee in which he judiciously raised the question of his succession. This document eventually became known as his 'Will', and set out his views of the leading team: Zinoviev and Kamenev had a tendency to vacillate at critical moments; Bukharin was much too doctrinaire and 'undialectical'; Pyatakov was a man of very great ability, but was too prone to resort to 'administrative methods'. Lenin acknowledged that Trotsky's was the strongest personality, but said that he, too, was attracted to administrative solutions. What he undoubtedly meant was that Trotsky tended to resolve problems by directions from above. Lenin was afraid that the conflict between Stalin and Trotsky might one day lead to a split in the Party, and to avoid this he asked that the Central Committee be 'democratized' by an increase from twenty-five members and nineteen candidate members to a team of fifty or even a hundred.

Here are some quotations from this document:

Having become General Secretary, Comrade Stalin has concentrated immeasurable power in his hands and I am not sure that he will always know how to use that power with sufficient caution ... On the other hand, Comrade Trotsky ... has distinguished himself not only by his outstanding abilities ... He is certainly the ablest man on the present Committee, but is possessed of excessive self-confidence and has a disposition to be too much attracted by the purely administrative aspect of affairs ... These characteristics of the two most eminent leaders of the present Central Committee may, unintentionally, lead to a split if the Party does not take measures to prevent it ...

The importance of the first quotation – that the General Secretary had concentrated immeasurable power in his hands – cannot be stressed enough. Explicitly, Lenin did no more than note this fact, but he implied that this immense power had not been conferred on Stalin by the Central Committee. At the time, Lenin was angry with Stalin about his approach to the Georgian problem. On January 4th, he added the following strongly-worded postscript: 'Stalin is too rude and this fault, while quite acceptable in dealings between Communist comrades, becomes intolerable in the office of the General Secretary ... I invite the comrades to consider ways of removing Stalin from this post and appointing somebody who is better in all respects than Stalin, namely one more tolerant, more loyal, more polite, more considerate towards his comrades, less capricious, etc.'

Stalin's abuses in Georgia had suddenly opened Lenin's eyes and brought him to the point of inviting rather than ordering the comrades – for he did not share Stalin's rudeness – to consider the dismissal of the General Secretary. Dzerzhinsky, the head of the *Cheka*, and Ordjonikidze, the local representative of the Central Committee, had also compromised themselves by using strong-arm methods in Tiflis. (Ordjonikidze, a hot-headed Georgian with a violent temper, had formerly been a convict in the Schlüsselburg penitentiary and an exile in Yakutsk.) 'What depths have we sunk to!' Lenin said in a secret letter to the Central Committee. He accused Dzerzhinsky and Ordjonikidze of being converts to Great Russian chauvinism, of having no understanding of the socialist approach to national problems and of 'offending against the interests of proletarian solidarity'. He proposed to make an example of Ordjonikidze by suspending him from Party membership for two years and called for the 'repeal of the enormous number of unjust decisions made by Dzerzhinsky'. 'Stalin and Dzerzhinsky [must be made] to bear the political blame for this Great Russian nationalist campaign.' During March 1923 Lenin wrote to Trotsky on this subject several times and asked him to raise the national question at the Twelfth Congress. He also sent a note to the Georgian Bolsheviks, Budu Mdivani, Makharadze 'and others', saying, 'I follow your affairs with passionate interest. Am revolted by Ordjonikidze's brutality and Stalin's provocations. I am making notes for a speech ... ' The 'Old Man's' last energies were devoted to the struggle for the rights of the non-Russian nationalities. On December 12th, he had had a relapse: his right hand was paralysed and he had great difficulties in speaking. On December 23rd, he had begun to feel better and a few days later he had written his secret message to the Central Committee.

Some time before Lenin's relapse Trotsky had an important interview with him. 'Our bureaucracy is a monstrous thing,' Lenin said. 'I was shocked by it when I returned to work.' The conversation turned to the urgent 'shake-up' of the bureaucratic machine. Trotsky thought it was not only the bureaucratization of the State but also of the Party that had to be fought and that a start must be made with the organizational branch of the Central Committee. 'I promise to make common cause with you against bureaucracy in general and the organizational branch in particular,' Lenin told him. The organizational branch, too, was in Stalin's hands.

The new institutions were working badly; all of them lacked experience and lent themselves to abuses. A Workers' and Peasants' Inspectorate (*Rabkrin*) was set over them but achieved very little. At the end of January 1923, Lenin subjected it to severe, though polite, criticism. He called for its complete reform but added that 'the People's Commissar can – indeed, must – remain in his post'. Lenin had great faith in the Central Control Commission, a body parallel with, but independent of, the Central Committee, as a guardian of Party democracy. Lenin's critique was discussed in the Politbureau, where a majority argued, against Trotsky's opposition, that it ought not to be published. But then there were second thoughts about censoring Lenin. Kuibyshev suggested that the critique be printed in a single copy of *Pravda* which was to be sent to Lenin on his sick-bed. Kamenev supported Trotsky and, in the end, the article was published – the Politbureau recognized that it could not be concealed from the rest of the Party. A few weeks later, Lenin resumed the attack with his last article, 'Better Fewer, but Better'. In it he said, 'Things are so sad, not to say disgusting, in our state apparatus ... The *Rabkrin* has no shadow of authority. Everybody knows that there is no worse institution and that under present conditions nothing can be expected of it.' This was written on March 2nd. Lenin then said to Trotsky that he had prepared a 'bombshell' against Stalin, by which he meant a fierce attack on his Georgian activities, but that Kamenev should not be told, because Kamenev would tell Stalin, who would 'make a rotten compromise and then go back on it'. Lenin sent all his papers on the Georgian problem to Trotsky and also wrote a letter, breaking with Stalin. On March 9th, he had a third stroke, and this time he was no longer able to speak or to read. He was taken to Gorky.

'Leon Davidovich did not visit Vladimir Ilyich in his country retreat very often. But on one occasion he came back from Gorky angry and embarrassed. On leaving the house, he had found that the officials had filled his car with flowers, and he considered their action of stripping the hot-house more servile than kind. Moscow was suffering great hardship, and going hungry; Lenin was painfully trying to rally what little strength he had left ... The gift of flowers, which he could not refuse, greatly upset Leon Davidovich.'

This is perhaps the place to mention a special facet of Lenin's character. It was he who had decided to exile the Menshevik leaders, including Martov and Abramovich, to Western Europe. He still spoke of the right-wing socialists with implacable hostility and was not prepared to make any concessions to them, but when he heard that Martov, now in poor health, was living in very straitened circumstances in Berlin, he asked during a talk at which Trotsky and Stalin were present, whether it might not be possible to help Martov indirectly. 'Who cares,' Stalin said out of earshot of Lenin, 'let him croak.'

The man who said this about a defeated socialist, one of the acknowledged founders of the Russian workers' movement and one whose brilliant mind and inflexible integrity had become legend, was determined that he, for one, should be remembered. In 1922, his friends changed the name of Tsaritsyn – the Tsar's city – to Stalingrad. Other leading Bolsheviks expressed their astonishment, but did not bother to oppose this piece of self-aggrandisement which, after all, was a matter of very minor importance.

II. *Lenin's successors. Trotsky advocates the democratization of Party life*

Vladimir Ilyich's illness raised the question of his successor. Discreetly, Zinoviev, Kamenev and Stalin joined forces and formed the notorious 'Triumvirate', whose only bond was their common desire to oust Trotsky, the most popular Party member, and jointly to assume the 'heavy burden' of the succession. Kamenev, who had left for Tiflis with Lenin's instructions, heard on the way that the 'Old Man' had suffered a third stroke, and took good care to ignore his orders. At the Twelfth Party Congress, held in April 1923, the Georgian question was debated and a sham solution arrived at. Stalin repudiated his actions, but nothing changed. (The bloody Georgian uprising in the autumn of 1924 was the result, and Georgia was never, in fact, completely subjected.) Trotsky, submitting his report on industrial production, highlighted the complex economic and political problems facing the country. Industry was so crippled that the peasants had to pay nearly three times as much for manufactured goods as in 1913. (The exact figure was 2.75 times.) The terms of exchange were so disadvantageous to the peasantry that a major conflict threatened, which would result in agricultural stagnation. What was to be done? Agriculture must be put back on its feet by allowing the peasants a greater share of their produce, taxes must be lowered and simplified, and industrial production increased by putting an end to the prevailing chaos and the arbitrary methods of accounting – in short, by introducing overall planning. Piecemeal plans had been drafted before, but the idea of a long-term overall plan was entirely new, and fell on deaf and hostile ears. At the Congress, Trotsky was acclaimed with the usual ovations – there was nothing to show that the plotters were busily undermining his position, exaggerating his real and imagined faults, reminding people that he was not a true old Bolshevik, and privately accusing him of harbouring ambitions to become the country's economic dictator.

In fact, the Zinoviev–Kamenev–Stalin triumvirate had already begun to isolate Trotsky by various unexceptionable pretexts. His friends and old comrades had been sent to responsible posts abroad. Rakovsky, Chairman of the Ukrainian Council of People's Commissars since 1919, was appointed Ambassador in London, Krestinsky was posted to Berlin, Joffe successively to China, Japan and Austria, and Yureniev to Italy. Less well-known militants were removed with slighter honours by appeals to their devotion and Party discipline – the General Secretary's office knew all about shuffling personnel round.

The country was restless and the Party rank-and-file had begun to denounce the arbitrary whims of the various committees and bureaux, the stifling of opinion and the miserable condition of the workers. There were many strikes, and such protest movements as the Workers' Opposition of Shlyapnikov, Medvedev and Alexandra Kollontai, and the 'Decemist' group of Sapronov and Vladimir Smirnov. One of the more brilliant but less highly regarded critics was Preobrazhensky, the co-author with Bukharin of the *ABC of Communism* which had been translated into several languages. Forty-five of the most prominent Bolsheviks wrote a letter to the General Committee to protest at the gravity of the economic situation and the bureaucratic paralysis of the country. They all hoped for greater internal democracy. Instead of secretaries appointing assistant secretaries, and so on down through the ruling hierarchy, the general wish was expressed for a return to a system of elective office, of free criticism and of open discussion.

On October 8th, 1923, Trotsky wrote to the Central Committee and raised a number of disturbing points. He said that most of the delegates to the Twelfth Congress had been chosen by the central apparatus; that uneasiness in the Party and among the peasants was growing; that the Politbureau paid scant attention to economic problems; that the General Secretary's office was appointing men to leading industrial positions not on merit but for reasons of its own; that the Politbureau was considering reintroducing the vodka monopoly to raise revenue; and that the composition of the Revolutionary War Council was being altered so as to introduce people hostile to Trotsky. He demanded a return to Party democracy.

This letter was, of course, kept secret, as was the Politbureau's reply, which took the form of a diatribe against Trotsky. Events in Germany acerbated the differences. The German government, in an effort to frustrate the Treaty of Versailles and particularly the reparation clauses, had unleashed inflation on a fantastic scale. A postage stamp now cost thousands of millions of marks; inflation was ruining the middle classes and bringing hunger to the wage earners. Land and industrial plant, of course, lost none of their value; only the weaker firms went to the wall while the strong and the speculators benefited. The economic crisis called for a vigorous reply from the proletariat, and the executive of the Communist International, meeting without Lenin, considered the seizure of power by the German Communist Party and even fixed a date for it – November 7th, 1923. German and Russian Communist circles spoke of sending Trotsky to Germany to lead the insurrection, a task Zinoviev, as President of the Third International, felt he himself should be given. The bureaucratization of the International, no less than the low intelligence and incompetence of some of its officials, played an important part in thwarting the mobilization of the revolutionary forces. In Munich, a tiny party of anti-Marxist and anti-Semitic demagogues emerged briefly and farcically from the twilight to mount a *putsch*. It was led by old General von Ludendorff, and the agitator Adolf Hitler, at that time unknown. Soviet Russia had clearly missed her chance in Europe, and all the efforts of the International had culminated in a crushing defeat.

Trotsky wrote a series of articles in *Pravda* calling for a 'new course'.

A Politbureau decision adopted on December 5th, 1923, fully endorsed his demand for an overall plan and the democratization of the Party. For a moment, the Politbureau even toyed with the idea of implementing these decisions, but the Zinoviev–Kamenev–Stalin triumvirate was determined to have them quashed: the triumvirate knew full well that free speech and free elections would sweep them from power. A period of seething excitement began in the Party, especially in Moscow; it seemed as if real freedom was in the air.

III. *Life in the Kremlin. Trotsky's friends. Health problems. Travels in the Caucasus. An accident at Kislovodsk in 1924. Trotsky writes* Literature and Revolution

'Life had become more ordered in the flat we occupied in the Kremlin cavalry quarters – the same four rooms in which we had lived since our arrival but now adapted to our special needs. As always, Leon Davidovich was extremely methodical; he tried to combine maximum effort in his work with the least possible degree of exhaustion. He was, as he had been since youth, punctual and meticulous, and once he had drawn up a timetable, he would adhere to it rigidly and expect those round him to do likewise. Meetings and appointments had to begin on the dot. He had a horror of idle chatter and of careless or slovenly work, and surrounded himself with reliable men, so that at a time of the greatest disorder, the Commissariat of War, the Revolutionary War Council and the other offices of which he was in charge, as well as his personal secretariat, were models of efficiency, something that people in Moscow noted with approval or hostility, depending on who they were.

'He would get up at 7.30 and arrive at the Commissariat of War at nine o'clock sharp. He would often return to the Kremlin for lunch, at about 1.30, and sometimes take a rest in the early afternoon, laughing and joking with the family and relaxing from his current preoccupations. His late afternoons and evenings were often taken up with meetings and work in the Commissariat of War. When Lenin was in the chair, he would keep a watch in front of him to speed up discussions; the People's Commissars had two, three or, very rarely, four minutes to make their points, and even while they were speaking, further discussions were conducted on pencilled notes that were constantly passed round. When Leon Davidovich came home from the front lines or from committee meetings, he rarely had time to tell us all that had happened that day, but he would always make a point of praising those who had done a good day's work and even when circumstances forced him to make harsh judgments, he always did so objectively and impersonally. During the Civil War, he had met many remarkable though more or less unknown people, which had confirmed him in his confidence in the masses. One day Chapaev, the famous partisan from the Urals, had come to see Leon Davidovich in his train. The interview had begun with an argument and had ended in complete harmony. "I submit," the partisan had said and the two men had embraced. Later on, books and the cinema created a Chapaev whom Leon Davidovich did not recognize. The real Chapaev, he used to say, was infinitely more alive and a much nobler man than the legendary figure they had turned him into; he was a man who could face danger coolly and with instinctive good sense ... [Chapaev was killed on active service.]

'Leon Davidovich himself ran any number of risks without either seeking them out or avoiding them. A Latvian by the same of Peterson, who had been in charge of security on the military train, was now commander of the Kremlin guard, in which capacity he watched over Leon Davidovich's movements. The precautions and the itineraries he fixed sometimes irritated Leon Davidovich, who used to say, "I feel I am being turned into an object," but his sense of discipline made him comply. When we first came to live in the Kremlin, a sentry who did not know Lenin by sight refused to allow him into the cavalry building. Vladimir Ilyich tried in vain to persuade the sentry to let him through, and in the end he had to get a special pass from the guard at the gate. He was delighted by it all and was grinning all over his face when he presented himself in our flat.

'In those days, people used to say that Leon Davidovich was rather stand-offish. The fact was that he used the familiar form of address to hardly anyone, that we neither made nor received visits – in the first place we had no time – and that he went to the theatre only very occasionally. In short, our circle of personal friends was small and dedicated to work and the political struggle. But he established the warmest relationships in spite of that. Leon Davidovich's closest colleagues, who were younger than himself and whom he hardly ever saw except at work, were devoted to him and knew how attached he was to them. Sklyansky, Butov, Glazman, Sermuks, Poznansky and Victor Etsin remained steadfastly loyal to him and, after many years of nightmare existence, perished for their fidelity. Pyatakov advised Leon Davidovich to be "more sociable", lest he be thought haughty and arrogant. "You'll have to be more accommodating," Pyatakov insisted. But in 1926, when Leon Davidovich went to a New Year's Eve party at Kamenev's flat on the floor above ours, partly to find out about the mood of what was called the "Leningrad Opposition", he returned almost at once. "I can't stand it," he said. "Liqueurs, long dresses and gossip! It was like a salon." Nor did he care for the *double entendres*, touched with vulgarity, which were so freely bandied about. Radek, who used to make many of them up and tell them to great comic effect, would stop whenever he saw Leon Davidovich approach; although Trotsky, too, had a sense of humour, it was of a different kind.

'He did not smoke and drank only on special occasions. His day used to end between midnight and two in the morning. His only real distractions were hunting and fishing in the company of Preobrazhensky, Muralov and Pyatakov. Standing in the clear water among the reeds at dawn in the company of an old and experienced guide, who had learned what he knew from his father and grandfather; waiting for wild duck or spreading the nets; climbing the moraine-scattered slopes of some vast, icy forest after a brown bear – all this brought him peace of mind through close contact with the soil, the trees, the water, the snow and the wind. It was both a contest with nature and also a time for meditation.

'His circle of friends was small. It included, first and foremost, Christian Rakovsky, appointed Chairman of the Ukrainian Council of People's Commissars on Leon Davidovich's recommendation in 1919. They had known each other since 1913, when they met in Bucharest. Rakovsky was fifty (in 1923) and was a wonderful person, straightforward and charming. He had noble features, a quick tongue and a ready smile. He was Bulgarian by origin, French by education, Russian by culture and Rumanian by nationality. He spoke all the Balkan languages, had been a member of the Bulgarian, Russian, French and Rumanian socialist parties, and had made his first revolutionary speech in a church in Sofia at the age of sixteen. In Russia, he used to write under the pseudonym of C. Insarov. He was a born internationalist and had been freed by Russian revolutionary forces from Jassy prison in 1917. In the Ukraine, he became a soldier, a statesman, a radical sociologist and a good comrade – all in extremely precarious and dangerous circumstances. He was later to be an outstanding diplomat in London and Paris, but the rewards of office never turned his head.

'Nikolai Muralov (forty-six at the time) was a good-natured, mustachioed giant with rough peasant features. An old Bolshevik, known for his courage and good sense, he had fought in Moscow during the 1905 and 1917 risings, and eventually became military governor of the Moscow region. I can still hear Leon Davidovich tell Lenin over the telephone, "I need Muralov at the front. We must have someone strong and popular there. Nikolai Ivanovich can call people by their first names and swear at them like a trooper. He can handle them much better than I can."

'Ivan Nikitich Smirnov was forty, which made him two years younger than Leon Davidovich. He had been a Bolshevik since 1903, had taken part in the 1905 rising and could boast a long series of gaol sentences, deportations to Siberia and escapes. He had organized the Fifth Red Army in the Urals, and the victories over Kolchak, no less than the pacification of Siberia, were in large measure due to him. A former precision engineer, he was well-educated, thoughtful and a man of so much rectitude that people sometimes called him "the Party's conscience". He was tall and thin, with fine features and fair hair and wore glasses. He, too, was a good-natured man and very hard-working ...

'Yuri Pyatakov was only thirty-five but had become a militant at seventeen. He had distinguished himself on the Ukrainian and Polish fronts, and later during the early attempts to reorganize the economy. He had a lined, bony face and a shock of fair hair. He was an erudite Marxist, a born economist with a somewhat authoritarian and self-disciplined attitude. Leon Davidovich accused him of being superficial and of tending to gloss over the political and social aspects of problems with the help of rather far-fetched theoretical solutions. They had their differences and once even shouted at each other over the telephone, but Pyatakov called round to apologize handsomely and everything was forgotten. Leon Davidovich considered him "a fine brain".

'Adolf Joffe (aged forty in 1923), Leon Davidovich's friend from his Vienna days, who had crossed a battlefield near Petrograd under enemy fire with him in 1919, was usually abroad since he was a skilful negotiator – after concluding the various peace treaties, he travelled widely in the Far East. In 1923 he met Sun Yat-sen in Shanghai and won him over for the Russian Revolution ... Joffe, who was very ill, had imposing Assyrian features. He was completely incorruptible and had great independence of mind.

'Leon Davidovich also had cordial relations with Preobrazhensky, Tsviakov – whom he described as "a good brain and a fine judge of character" – Antonov-Ovseenko, and at times with Bukharin as well. He was good friends with Karl Radek, Kalinin, Alexei Rykov and Dzerzhinsky and had even closer ties with Krestinsky, Sosnovsky – a fearless character and a remarkable journalist – and Voronsky, a former prisoner and now editor of *Krasnaya Nov*, a literary journal that published the works of talented writers without any attempt to impose orthodoxy on them. Voronsky was fair-haired, rather short, gay, a lover of literature, and too intelligent for the days that lay ahead ... Leon Davidovich also valued Leonid Borisovich Krasin's qualities, but disapproved of his bourgeois way of life. For the same reason, he was rather cool with Sokolnikov, who had changed a great deal, now going to dances and generally amusing himself.

'During 1922–3, relations with Kamenev, who was probably still hesitant about siding openly against Leon Davidovich and who strongly criticized Stalin, were fairly good. Stalin had just ordered the arrest of Sultan Galiev, a Moslem Communist who had taken part in the semi-clandestine pan-Turkish movement. Kamenev at once telephoned Leon Davidovich. "We've allowed him [Stalin] to taste blood," he said. In those days, dissidents were not yet handed over to the firing squad, and the mere arrest of a Party member was against the unwritten code and created a sensation. (Galiev was no doubt shot in the end.) Stalin himself tried to make overtures to Leon Davidovich between his frenzied campaigns against "Trotskyism". But Trotsky detested Stalin's obsequiousness and preferred to keep aloof.

'During Lenin's illness, Leon Davidovich saw him only briefly – their meetings were most cordial and confidential – because the doctors insisted that Lenin must not be exposed to unnecessary strain. Lenin knew he could expect further strokes and that he did not have long to live. It was on the Georgian question that Lenin made his famous remark about Stalin in private: "This cook serves up nothing but peppery dishes."

'Leon Davidovich always had an inordinate capacity for work. He lived under great pressure, dealing with twenty different matters at once, reading documents, studying, and writing articles on literature, economics and domestic or foreign affairs. No wonder that his health began to suffer: he was laid low by debilitating fevers that frequently forced him to take to his bed or to retire to rest-homes in the Caucasus. The doctors, including our friend Dr Guetier, thought he had contracted some form of malaria, but were quite frank about their inability to make an accurate diagnosis. Apparently the constant conflict between Leon Davidovich's fine sensibility, nervous temperament and indomitable will brought on these attacks at moments of excessive mental strain. In the past, too, he would suffer from stomach upsets before addressing meetings and rallies. Now bouts of fever would assail him during his battles in the Politbureau, with the Party and, later, in exile. Even so, he would continue to work in bed, reading, making notes and dictating.

'When we stayed at Kislovodsk in 1923 and at Sukhumi in 1924, we quickly discovered that the atmosphere in the Caucasus was much more congenial than it had been in Moscow. The local authorities had not yet realized how precarious Trotsky's political position had become. His portrait still hung on the walls of clubs and offices beside Lenin's. Most Communists were delighted to meet him and invited him to deliver lectures. A small number, who knew the facts, were cool to the point of iciness ... We often asked ourselves, "Are we surrounded by smiling enemies or by good comrades?" At Sukhumi, on the Abkhaz coast, the Central Committee had provided us with a villa, and the head of the Abkhaz government, Nestor Lakoba, treated us with warmth and kindness. He was a cheerful, well-educated little man, who had proved himself in the Revolution but liked the good life. He was deaf in one ear and wore a hearing aid. He told us that in the thirteenth century his country had been ruled by a blind tsar; nowadays, it had a deaf commissar instead ... Later, when we had been isolated and were being treated as public enemies by most officials, Nestor Lakoba, on his visits to Moscow, still brought us big boxes of fruit ... He and his brother were shot in 1937.

'In 1924, we had an accident at Kislovodsk, which could have cost us our lives. In the event, we were lucky enough to escape with a few bruises. We had been on a shooting party in the mountains with Muralov and were coming down in a platform-car which suddenly jumped the rails as we were approaching the station and flung us all out into quite a deep ditch ... It might have been a genuine accident, or again it might not. Leon Davidovich's death would have greatly simplified matters for Stalin, although we didn't think of this until later.'

While convalescing and resting in the Caucasus in 1922, Leon Davidovich wrote *Literature and Revolution*, a book that aroused some controversy and had a considerable influence on the literary world in Russia and abroad. In it, he showed that it was impossible to produce great literature in a period of revolutionary dictatorship, and explicitly rejected the idea of 'proletarian culture', then in great vogue. 'There is no proletarian culture and there never will be ... the proletariat acquires power for the purpose of doing away for ever with class culture ... ' 'Revolutionary art which inevitably reflects all the contradictions of a revolutionary social system should not be confused with socialist art for which no basis has yet been laid.' 'The new artist will need the methods and processes evolved in the past, as well as a few supplementary ones, in order to grasp the new life ... ' 'The super-personal element is, above all, the social element. As long as man has not mastered his social organization, the latter will hang over him as his fate ... Babeuf's struggle for communism in a society which was not yet ready for it, was a struggle of a classic hero with his fate ... ' Leafing through the book today, the reader is brought face to face with another tragedy. A dozen modern Russian writers and poets are singled out for special discussion. Only three of them died natural deaths: Andrey Biely, Alexander Blok and Demyan Biedny. Two poets of the Revolution committed suicide: Yessenin and Mayakovsky. One poet, Kliuev, died on his release from prison. Voronsky was shot; several others vanished without a trace, Pilnyak amongst them.

IV. *Trotsky calls for the 'New Course'. The 1923 opposition is defeated by the Zinoviev–Kamenev–Stalin triumvirate. Lenin's death.*

Trotsky's *New Course* unleashed a storm of recriminations, attacks and polemics. For all that, it was a very simple pamphlet, and, apart from a few strongly worded pages, said very little that Central Committee speakers did not say themselves. It is true that there are always at least two ways of saying the same thing – with evident sincerity or with one's tongue in one's cheek. The anger of the Triumvirate and the uneasiness of the hierarchy showed how rotten the regime had become.

The *New Course* set out to do no more than justify a decision the Central Committee had taken in December 1923. Trotsky pointed out that, since the seizure of power, the Party had grown by leaps and bounds. For a time it had been necessary to maintain the dictatorship of the Bolshevik Old Guard, but now the new generation, which had grown up during the Civil War, ought to be given a greater say, and the power of committees and their secretaries diminished. The Party's bureaucratic machine, made up of thousands of officials, was tending to substitute itself for the Party as a whole, heralding 'the opportunist degeneration of the Old Guard, or of part of it at least'. This process may develop 'at a slow or even imperceptible pace, and then manifest itself quite suddenly'. The mere mention of this possibility was regarded by some as an 'outrage', and this fact itself was a sign of their 'bureaucratic arrogance'. 'The proletariat exercises its dictatorship through the Soviet state. The Communist Party is the leading party of the proletariat and hence of the state.' To avoid 'bureaucratic degeneration, a vigorous and active democracy [must be created] within the Party'. To prevent the emergence of organized factions, clandestine or otherwise, the Party must grant its members – now as always – freedom of criticism and opinion; otherwise the machine will pass into the hands of the most conservative elements, who will then impose a rule of silence. 'Bureaucracy is a social phenomenon, a technique for administering things and men' – men as things, it might be added. The evil was exacerbated by a general lack of culture.

Were Trotsky's theses tantamount to an attack on the principles of Bolshevism? We need only recall the history of the German Social Democratic movement, which, so great and brave in Bebel's time, had become ossified and corrupted by a conservative tradition determined to stifle its revolutionary will. Lenin's dynamic offered an infinitely more splendid alternative: the preservation of a tradition by constant renewal and enrichment.

Trotsky wrote in vain, for the organized clamour of the *apparatchiks* drowned his voice. Trotsky was insulting the Party, they screamed. He dared to besmirch the good name of the Old Bolsheviks and to compare them to the German Social Democrats, yet he himself had never been a member of the Bolshevik Old Guard and his 'past mistakes' had simply caught up with him. 'We are the true democrats, the incorruptible Old Guard, the true Party.' This theme recurred in innumerable speeches and reams of print.

In Moscow, however, the Party had responded so enthusiastically that the officials were terrified. Zinoviev later revealed that 'everybody lost their head' and that he was forced to form a (secret) committee of seven to weather the storm. Unfortunately, Trotsky was ill at the time and on his way to the Caucasus. The attacks on him grew so virulent that the Triumvirate, afraid of public confrontation, quickly denounced the rumour of Trotsky's imminent removal from office as 'malicious slander'. *Pravda* declared on December 18th, 1923, 'Nobody can conceive of the work of the Politbureau, the Central Committee or the State without the active participation of Comrade Trotsky.'

Before Trotsky boarded the train for the Caucasus, a number of Politbureau meetings were held in his flat. He tried to convince the others, speaking passionately to the set faces and closed minds. These meetings left him sweating and utterly exhausted.

'He said later that one of his conflicts with the Triumvirate arose as a result of his protests "against the systematic corruption of working-class leaders in Western Europe" initiated by Zinoviev, Kamenev and Stalin during Lenin's illness. Stalin and Zinoviev countered, "But the bourgeoisie is buying trade union leaders, parliamentarians and journalists. So why shouldn't we do the same?" Trotsky pointed out that corruption could only demoralize the working-class movement; it could never create revolutionaries. Lenin had warned against picking obedient dolts for the Communist International. Of what use were these all-purpose cynics, who would do whatever was asked of them until the very first moment of danger?'

The Triumvirate now published a list of Trotsky's errors: he was seeking to set the Party against its cadres and the young against the old; he was demanding freedom for factions within the Party and had accused Bolshevism of being in a state of degeneration. There were other charges as well. 'Trotskyism' was an unnatural creation, the very antithesis of infallible Leninist Bolshevism and as such riddled with pernicious errors. The newspapers were full of these accusations.

'At Tiflis station, Sermuks, a slender young man with reddish hair, and a trusted member of Leon Davidovich's staff, entered our carriage, looking ghastly and holding a telegram in his hand. Lenin had died on January 21st, 1924. Leon Davidovich's first thought was to go straight back to Moscow but a telegram from Stalin begged him not to: he would, in any case, arrive too late for the funeral, and the main thing was for him to get well. There was no point in endangering his health by returning. But Stalin was lying. Moscow was in the grip of a cold winter; Lenin was to be embalmed and the preparations for his funeral lasted a whole week. The Politbureau had decided on the embalming, on the glass coffin and on the mausoleum to be built in Red Square in front of the Kremlin wall.

'Mummy-worship became established ... When Leon Davidovich heard about it all, it was too late to raise any objections. "How Nadezhda Konstantinovna [Krupskaya] must be suffering," he said. "She knows better than anyone else what Lenin would have thought of such goings-on."

'In the event, Lenin's widow, overwrought and distressed, said nothing. She had just written Leon Davidovich a short letter. "I write to tell you that, a month before his death, Vladimir Ilyich was looking through your book ... and asked me to read him the passage about Marx and Lenin; he listened very attentively and then read it again himself. I also want to tell you that the way Vladimir Ilyich first felt about you when you came to us in London never changed right up to his death. I wish you health and strength and embrace you warmly." Though this last sign of Lenin's affection was a great comfort, Leon Davidovich's days in office were numbered. The Politbureau was reshuffling the War Council so as to isolate its President. Sklyansky, the Vice-President, was made head of the Moscow textile industry and was replaced by Voroshilov and Lazevich, of whom the former was close to Stalin and the latter to Zinoviev. Frunze, a first-rate soldier, and Unschlicht, transferred from the G.P.U., joined the Council as members.'

The animated intra-Party discussions died down while the whole country went into mourning for Lenin, and also because the Triumvirate had begun hypocritically to mete out a host of petty punishments to their opponents. Students were expelled from the Party and driven from the universities; workers were declared redundant and militants were posted to the North, Siberia and Central Asia. At the same time, the doors of the Party were thrown open to 240,000 workers who had not applied for membership until then – men who must have had reservations during the years when the Revolution was facing its greatest danger. Before the new recruiting drive, the Party had 350,000 members, of whom nearly 300,000 were officials (many of them ex-workers) and 50,000 continued with factory work. An influx of workers would have proved a boon had the regime been a vital force; but to a rigid and anxious bureaucracy, the new recruits were just so many servile tools.

When the Thirteenth Party Congress was eventually convened there were no grave disagreements. Leon Davidovich was greeted very warmly by an enthusiastic assembly. He insisted on the implementation of all the decisions concerning internal democracy, and stressed the paramount importance of the Party – which, despite its weaknesses, was the incarnation of all the hopes of the Revolution. 'No one wants to be right against the Party ... We can only be right with the Party, because history offers us no alternative. The English say, "My country, right or wrong" ... but we say, "My Party right or wrong" ... ' Despite all the symptoms of decay, the Party was not yet incurably ill: its prestige was still cemented by its victories, by the economic improvements – reflected in everyday life – it had wrought, by the peace it had achieved and even by the universal sorrow at Lenin's death. Party loyalty had always been the pillar of European socialism; it had knitted together the revolutionary parties in Russia; it was still a deeply ingrained sentiment and a great moral force.

In August and September the Georgian insurrection flared up and was ruthlessly repressed. Stalin who, together with Ordjonikidze, bore most of the blame, declared hypocritically: 'Either we allow the workers and peasants to criticize us or they will take their criticism into the streets ... either we renounce facile optimism and bureaucratic practices or ... ' etc. This was merely a paraphrase of what Marx had said about the blade of criticism and criticism by the blade, and, in any case, it was a piece of lying rhetoric.

v. *Trotsky's writings. The struggle in the Politbureau. Stalin's acquisition of power*

Trotsky looked forward to a period of intellectual renewal: educating the younger generation of the Party, talking to the country, not in polemical terms but by making history come to life. He published a sketch of Lenin and a little later, in October 1924, a sixty-page introduction to his *Collected Works*, in which he dealt at some length with the events of 1917. The title of this introduction was 'The Lessons of October'; it discussed the known facts and dealt with the part played by leading figures, and with their ability and relations with the working classes. It recalled that Zinoviev and Kamenev had been opposed to the seizure of power. Stalin was not mentioned, because it was impossible to establish exactly what he was doing during the crucial days. The Triumvirate, who had kept the Party congress in ignorance of the contents of Lenin's 'Will', considered themselves under attack – and so they were, but only in so far as any examination of the true facts could not fail to prove to their disadvantage.

Their violent reactions were predictable. Trotsky's book was called an attack on Party ideology, on Leninism (a recent invention), on unity and on Bolshevism. In other words, it was treasonable, though, as yet, nobody dared to describe it as such. Very soon copies of the book disappeared from public view; anyone found reading or discussing it was treated with suspicion. Newspapers, journals, conferences and meetings called by the most insignificant Party cells in the tiniest of villages – as well as in Paris, Prague, Berlin and other capitals – were devoted to one thing only: the condemnation of renascent 'Trotskyism'. Since this deliberately concocted 'ism' still lacked concrete doctrinal substance, letters were dragged out of the archives, even those written by the Tsarist police, together with anything else that recalled Trotsky's disagreements with Lenin in the years before the Revolution. In particular, the old émigré polemics were unearthed and a new legend was invented and spread: that Trotsky had 'underestimated the peasantry'. This was a good choice in a country where the peasants were far from satisfied. Lenin, tucked safely away in his mausoleum and venerated as a saint, had always sympathized with the peasants, but Trotsky had never understood them. Lest this simplification be thought a caricature of the real facts, it was shored up by innumerable incredibly dull and silly texts, all hastily embroidered on identical directives from the *Agitprop* section of the Central Committee. It has never been computed how many tens of thousands of tons of paper were wasted on this dismal war waged by a state machine against the brain and pen of one single man. Nobody, or hardly anybody, dared to point out that without sympathy for, and the support of, the peasantry, Trotsky could never have created the Red Army and led it to victory, or that Trotsky was the first to advocate the New Economic Policy in order to reconcile the peasants to the Revolution. But then, everyone could start on the ladder of a Party career by producing variations, however poor, on the official theme.

This period, too, saw the beginning of the end of the Third International, until then an association of revolutionary Marxist parties under the natural leadership of the Russians, but, within the past few months, perverted into a mere satrap to the ruling Politbureau coterie. Zinoviev, the chairman of the Executive Committee of the Comintern, sent anti-Trotskyist emissaries all over the world. They carried instructions and funds, they ordered expulsions, put 'reliable' men in charge of the newspapers, and selected party leaders, not on the basis of popularity or ability, but by the application of a single criterion: their hostility to Trotsky. The French, Belgian, German, Dutch, Luxemburg, Spanish, Italian, Czechoslovak and other parties were at first bewildered and did their utmost to restore harmony and unity, but their every resolution to that effect was treated as an act of defiance by the Executive Committee, who would immediately start campaigns to discredit the authors and institute sanctions against them. The editors of party papers were changed, and so was the Executive of the Third International which had come out against the new line and had given Trotsky a majority vote. The various national parties survived this crisis or, rather, they vegetated for years, more or less decapitated, disunited and debilitated but 'one hundred per cent bolshevized' as Zinoviev liked to put it. What this meant was that, thanks to their complete renunciation of the last vestige of autonomy and their continuous collaboration with secret agents, they had become the maids-of-all-work of a Comintern completely subservient to the Russian state machine.

On January 2nd, 1925, the Politbureau relieved Trotsky of his duties as Chairman of the War Council and as People's Commissar of War and the Navy, and appointed Frunze in his place. Trotsky was made Chairman of the Concessions Committee, of the Board of Electrotechnical Development and the Industrial-Technological Commission. He felt some satisfaction at losing responsibility for the army, for it put an end to the muttered accusations of 'Bonapartism'. He believed, and said so in private, that a socialist revolution must not rest on the army or police, but that it must constantly look to its inner resources, fortified by persuasion and by appeals to the masses.

In the Politbureau, he had become a lone voice. Zinoviev, Kamenev, Stalin and Bukharin (as well as their deputies Kalinin, Molotov and Dzerzhinsky) were publicly united against him, even though they had private differences on his account. Personal relations were polite enough, though extremely cool. One day, Bukharin said to him, 'It's because of you that there is no democracy in the Party,' thus indicating that he, for one, thought a breath of freedom would not come amiss. Trotsky and his popularity were so feared that Zinoviev and Kamenev recommended his expulsion from the Party and subsequent imprisonment. Because he felt less confident or possibly because he was already thinking of ousting his present allies, Stalin took a more cautious stand and opposed the recommendation – not, however, without first suggesting that, if the worst came to the worst, Trotsky could be got rid of by 'the Florentine method' – without any scandal and with a fine funeral thrown in. (Zinoviev and Kamenev later signed an affidavit to that effect.) Death now struck Trotsky's circle for the first time. One of his secretaries, Glazman, a loyal and devoted young man, who had been expelled from the Party on some pretext or other, killed himself in 1924. Glazman had often accompanied Trotsky to the front. In the Ukraine, not far from Kharkov, in 1918 or 1919, Trotsky's train had stopped in a derelict station full of deserters, the 'Greens', who were refusing to fight for either the Whites or the Reds and wore forest camouflage. The cry rang out, 'Death to Trotsky!' whereupon Leon Davidovich had climbed out, followed only by Glazman, who carried his rifle slung over his shoulder, notebook and pencil in hand and peered around amicably through his spectacles. The 'Greens' had begun to argue but had been won over in the end... And now *Pravda* was refusing to publish Trotsky's short tribute to his young comrade-in-arms. Nor was Glazman's the only suicide, for to young idealists expulsion from the Party could still be a deadly blow. Heartbroken revolutionaries who took their own lives also included Lutovinov and Evgenia Bosch.

The official reasons for the expulsions of the Trotskyists were never political. Instead, the control commissions, headed by Ordjonikidze, used such stereotyped phrases as 'demoralized petit-bourgeois element', 'corrupt person' or 'profiteer'. Sometimes a student was expelled on the mere grounds that he had procured a habitable room in Moscow or had new clothes, or had married 'the daughter of an ex-capitalist'. What was no crime in anyone else became one when it was committed by someone who dared to defend the *New Course* or to question the words of a Party official.

One author, who has studied these events in minute detail, has claimed that Trotsky completely misjudged Stalin. It is, of course, easy to be wise in retrospect, but, as Trotsky himself pointed out, the truth was rather that Stalin did not know himself, and must often have been surprised by his own power and success. His path was a series of curves and zig-zags. The Triumvirate had just one clear aim: to remove Trotsky from office, but there were reservations, and all three must often have wondered if their machinations would succeed. At times, they wished and hoped that Trotsky might agree to a compromise and join them in a subordinate position. Zinoviev and Kamenev discussed this possibility with a few reliable friends 'in a cave' during an excursion to Kislovodsk, in the Caucasus. As already suggested, Stalin, no doubt because he considered his co-triumvirs to be weak-willed, also sought a rapprochement with Trotsky. His overtures had been genuine, occasioned not so much by a love of intrigue as by the pressure of events. But then he found that he held such vast and unsuspected power that he had no need to share it with anybody. Stalin was, however, a pragmatist, one who changed his political outlook from day to day and from target to target, and he was still afraid to play the trump cards he held. When Sklyansky asked Trotsky, 'Who is Stalin?' Trotsky replied, 'The greatest mediocrity in our Party.' At the time, Zinoviev, one of the co-founders of the Bolshevik Party, a colleague of Lenin's since 1908 and now Chairman of the Communist International, regarded himself as the leading figure in the Triumvirate. Kamenev, who wrote so well, was an able parliamentary speaker, a skilful negotiator and a pleasant and even charming man, evidently came next. Stalin, relatively unknown in the country and even in the Party, a clumsy writer, a dull speaker with a pedantic style and a heavy Georgian accent, appeared to be more a man of action than of ideas, chosen by his two colleagues for his seeming mediocrity, his inflexibility and guile. This prevailing opinion of him certainly weighed on his mind and increased the force of his inferiority complex. For all that, his final victory should have taken no insider by surprise.

The country was tired. Three and a half years of war, twenty months of revolutionary fervour, more than three years of civil war, a major famine, continued privations, the extraordinary effort it took to re-build the economy – all these had exhausted the masses. The educated revolutionaries, particularly the Marxists, were in a minority, and most of them had been in the struggle for ten or twenty years before the Revolution. Many of the best of them had died in the Civil War, and most of the others, having been absorbed in the State and Party administrations, had lost touch with the masses. A reaction had set in – all that people wanted to do now was to rest, to relax and to live a quiet life. The defeat of the Communist International in Estonia, Bulgaria, Hungary and Germany appeared to justify a tacit rejection of international solidarity, an attitude of 'it's high time we looked after ourselves'. The ruling party now included profiteers, unashamed *arrivistes* and a good number of those conformists who climb to the top in any regime. It also comprised a large number of political illiterates, which made discussions of major issues difficult and at the same time favoured the rule of party officials. At the top, the

General Secretary appointed the regional secretaries: the mere fact that he was in charge of nominations enabled him to pack the committees with yes-men, many of whom were in his debt. These regional secretaries appointed others lower down the hierarchy, and so on, ad infinitum. The Party 'apparatus' was being 'Stalinized' long before the word had even been heard of. This was not so much a seizure of power as an invasion of every cell of the body politic, an insidious bureaucratic infection. The man responsible for it all had no clear plans for the future; he simply seized power because it was there for the taking with just a little cunning and a great deal of perfidy. By 1925, Bukharin had become Stalin's chief ideologist, and Zinoviev and Kamenev, out-manoeuvred and impotent, realized that their days were counted.

VI. *Stabilization of the bureaucratic regime. Zinoviev and Kamenev join Trotsky in Opposition*

When the Fourteenth Party Congress met in Moscow in December 1925, it was the most bureaucratically stage-managed of any so far, with all the delegations appointed by secretaries dependent on the General Secretary. The exception was the delegation from Leningrad, where Zinoviev was in charge of the regional committee, the Party, the Soviet, and of the Third International as well. An insidious farce had been played out at last: it had been rehearsed day by day for years, with signatures at the bottom of nomination forms in exchange for rewards ranging from petty privileges to prosperity in an impoverished country. The campaign against the Trotskyist phantom had helped to camouflage this swell of bureaucracy. As the bureaucrats continued to pay more attention to the packing of committees than to production, old Marxists could see the danger signals of which the general public was still unaware. The gap between the prices of manufactured goods and agricultural produce had not been closed, with the result that many peasants preferred to hoard their grain and to turn their backs on the State. The condition of the working class had improved slightly but not nearly enough – the level of consumption was only just back to what it had been before the Revolution, and not in all cases to that. Private trade proved to be more flexible and competent than the State sector. Ever since the 1922 financial reforms, which had established a stable currency, the *chervonets*, money had become a means of corruption – citizens gradually realized that the only way of getting anything done was to grease some official's palm. The N.E.P. (New Economic Policy) might have galvanized the country's economic forces, but these were now completely out of control.

At the Fourteenth Congress, long and confused theoretical debates were fought out before stolid delegations, all of whom had received firm instructions from officials schooled by the General Secretary. The fight against Trotskyism had undermined Party morale and helped to discredit the two most prominent leaders of the Polit-bureau, Zinoviev and Kamenev. Kamenev vainly denounced the revival of petty capitalism and called for a workers' share in the industrial profits. His words fell on deaf ears. True, much of industry was being run at a loss, but a new incentive for wage-earners might easily have wrought a radical change for the better. Stalin, for the first time, acted as spokesman of the Central Committee, thus stepping into Lenin's shoes, and when Zinoviev asked for the floor to speak on behalf of the Central Committee as well, his demand was construed as a crime against Party unity, and a clear sign of personal ambition. He was given a bitterly hostile reception, most of it engineered by the Party machine, which was by then highly experienced in such matters. Finally, when Kamenev roundly declared, 'We are against establishing a leadership principle ... We do not want the Secretariat ... to be above the Party ... We intend ... to subordinate the Secretariat to the Politbureau ... Comrade Stalin does not constitute the general staff of Bolshevism all by himself ... ' there was uproar, and the Leningrad delegation found itself isolated. Its members' shouts of 'Long live the Central Committee,' were drowned by a roar of 'Stalin! Stalin!' On the platform, Trotsky kept silent, but Lenin's widow, Krupskaya, solemnly announced her solidarity with the minority.

In his carefully worded reply, full of hyperbole, Stalin presented himself as a peacemaker and accused Zinoviev and Kamenev, his recent co-triumvirs, of favouring a policy of 'amputations' and of 'blood-lettings'. First they had recommended Trotsky's expulsion, and now they were out for Bukharin's blood. At the time, nobody, not even Stalin, could have openly considered shedding the blood of dissident Bolsheviks. Such words as *amputation*, *blood-letting* and *blood* served as graphic descriptions of purely political sanctions – dismissal from the Central Committee or, at worst, expulsion from the Party, which was also described as 'political death'. This was the time when such more or less liberal émigrés as the writer Alexey Tolstoy, such counter-revolutionary officers as General Slaschev, and many bourgeois intellectuals had been allowed back to Russia and given jobs; and when Mensheviks served in the commanding heights of the economy. The psychological significance of Stalin's continuous use of bloodthirsty metaphor was not to become obvious for another dozen years; in 1925, his eventual method of settling accounts was still quite inconceivable.

The clashes within the Triumvirate and its revelation before the Congress went a long way towards restoring Trotsky's prestige, which, in any case, continued to stand high among the masses, so much so that in April 1926, Stalin made further overtures to him. After Trotsky's theses had been read out at a meeting of the Polit-bureau, Stalin – visibly impressed – exclaimed, 'These theses are ninety per cent correct.' It was rumoured that Trotsky would be placed in charge of economic development.

Kamenev, now relieved of his office of President of the Moscow Soviet, and Zinoviev, whose organization in Leningrad had been broken up in the name of the Central Committee, also made over-tures to their former adversary. They now granted that Trotsky had been right to attack the bureaucratization of the Party, the stifling of Party democracy, and to call for a 'New Course' as far back as 1923. The Leningrad Opposition proposed an alliance and even a merger with the 1923 ('New Course') Opposition, and when some of the latter met to discuss the matter, Mrachkovsky, a man born in prison and persecuted for years, who had fought bravely in the Urals, spoke out against any alliance whatsoever with Zinoviev or Stalin, because, as he said, 'Zinoviev will leave us in the lurch and Stalin is bound to betray us.'

Trotsky believed that the adoption of a correct general line more than compensated for the shortcomings of individuals; that an appeal to the masses would rally the waverers and that, in spite of their recent past, Zinoviev, Kamenev and the Leningrad Opposition were right on a number of major issues: economic policy, the concentra-tion of power in the hands of the General Secretary, international policy and Marxist ideology. The bureaucracy had already begun to mutter about a new thesis – the 'building of socialism in one country', that is, of a socialist autarchy, incompatible with the idea of inter-national solidarity and even more so with economic reality. The Joint

Opposition arose finally out of the alliance between the Leningrad Opposition and the 1923 ('New Course') Opposition.

Zinoviev had several thousand adherents in Leningrad, bound together by the ties of old comradeship and the strength of the local Party machine. He could also count on the support of influential foreign leaders of the International: Ruth Fischer and Arkady Maslov in Germany and Albert Treint in France. But the left wing of the movement, of which Trotsky was the most authoritative spokesman, lacked a proper organization of its own. In Moscow, it had some six hundred members, in Leningrad about fifty, and in Kharkov several hundred, and though it was supported by active groups abroad, it had no funds or publications of its own. Moreover, all its members were economically dependent on the Party, and as there was a good deal of unemployment, most of them were reluctant to speak out for fear of losing their jobs.

Zinoviev was promptly relieved of the chairmanship of the Communist International. No new chairman was elected; Bukharin simply took charge of the secretariat. Zinoviev was also ousted from the chair of the Leningrad Soviet and appointed a co-director of Tsentrosoyuz, the commercial section of the co-operatives in Moscow, where, it was hoped, he would find it difficult to keep in close touch with Leningrad. All leaders of the Opposition were placed under discreet – or sometimes open – police surveillance.

VII. *Personal relations between the former opponents. The Joint Opposition against the bureaucratic regime*

Once resumed, personal relations between Trotsky, Zinoviev, Kamenev and the Leningrad group quickly grew cordial and even affectionate. The Leningrad leaders included Ivan Bakaev, aged forty, who had organized the Kamyshin rising in 1906, had fought in the October Revolution, had become a military commander during the Civil War and later Chairman of the Leningrad *Cheka*; Grigory Evdokimov, forty-four, an ex-sailor with a long history of persecution by the Tsarist police for his Bolshevik activities, now a member of the Central Committee and extremely popular with the workers of Leningrad; and Mikhail Lashevich, another veteran Bolshevik, an N.C.O. who had become a Red Army commander, and was well-known for his fearlessness. Bakaev was very young in appearance with a ready smile and had the typical look of a Russian worker; Evdokimov was tall, grizzled, and as taciturn as an ageing peasant, and had one great fault – he drank; Lashevich was a good-natured, fat little fellow. These men and quite a few more made up the immediate circle round Grigory Zinoviev (his real name was Radomyslsky), then aged forty-three. He was superior to all of them in education, in his intimate knowledge of Western Europe, and in his talents as a theoretician and popularizer. In addition he was a fluent speaker and writer in several languages and an acknowledged leader. Zinoviev was thick-set, with a rather pale complexion, Roman features, a huge, untidy head of hair and greyish-blue eyes. He had proved his physical courage on many occasions, but was known to crack up under prolonged strain and to need the support of someone less volatile than himself. He had links of close friendship with Kamenev (formerly Rosenfeld) who, at forty-three, had a thick, but already greying, beard. Before the Revolution, Kamenev had been in charge of the clandestine Bolshevik organization and had also spent a long time living abroad. He, too, spoke several languages and was a scholar. He had been leader of the Party faction in the Imperial Duma in which capacity he had opposed the war and had been exiled to Siberia. His nature was conciliatory, his manners pleasant and his attitude thoughtful and liberal. He was now Director of the Lenin Institute and was working on a biography of Chernyshevsky.

It quickly appeared that the campaign against Trotskyism, which had proved so great a shock to the Party and the International, also weighed heavily on the conscience of these men who had, in fact, begun it. Their break with Stalin filled them with tremendous relief and they showered Trotsky with attentions and warmth. All traces of the painful past were wiped out. There were still arguments, of course: revolutionaries cannot do without them. Good-humouredly, Trotsky's new allies revealed how they had invented the spectre of 'Trotskyism'. 'If you had not written *The Lessons of October*, we should have found some other pretext,' Zinoviev said. 'We had to tie in the old disagreements with current ones.' Lashevich waxed indignant about the mistakes he and those closest to him had made. 'After all,' he exclaimed, turning to his oldest friends, 'it was we who created Trotskyism.' And now the invention was threatening to backfire: since the workers of Leningrad had been inculcated with it, it might prove difficult to tell them that Trotsky had been right about the bureaucratization of the regime and the Party all along. However, the masses felt as relieved as their leaders: the end of an unpopular legend was welcomed as the healing of a wound.

'Endless conferences were held in the Kremlin, sometimes at our own place and sometimes in Kamenev's, Zinoviev's or Karl Radek's flat. Kamenev and Zinoviev were quite obviously sincere both in their new role and in their joy at being able to speak out freely once again, to be done with circumlocution ... Working with Stalin, with whom they had had to watch their every word and step, had been a great strain, the more so as the difference in their intellectual background, and his general lack of culture forced them to avoid theoretical discussions. Kamenev now took his revenge on Stalin in a host of little ways – by mimicking his clumsiness, his accent and his uneducated speech. Leon Davidovich did his best to turn the conversation away from personalities into more edifying channels. "Anyway," he said later, "the man is disagreeable enough to meet in person. Imitating him when he isn't there is really too much."'

Trotsky brought with him into the Joint Opposition, Pyatakov, Preobrazhensky, Muralov, old Boris Eltsin, who had been reared on Hegel and was one of the founders of the Bolshevik Party; Karl Radek, a man of tremendous nervous energy, well informed about world affairs in general and Central Europe in particular; Adolf Joffe, back from diplomatic duty abroad and now ill; and Rakovsky, Krestinsky and Antonov-Ovseenko, all three of whom still held diplomatic posts – in Paris, Berlin and Warsaw respectively. Sokolnikov and Smilga also rallied to the Joint Opposition, and so, with the exception of Bukharin and Tomsky, leader of the Soviet trade unions, did all those in the Party with any degree of talent. Nadezhda Krupskaya, Lenin's widow, was in deep sympathy with its aims.

Zinoviev and Kamenev had great hopes. They believed that Trotsky's popularity was so deeply established and so real that it would be easy to stir the Party out of its torpor, help to kindle a popular revival and set off a great new burst of enthusiasm. 'You have only to appear at meetings!' they told him. But Trotsky thought otherwise. 'The spirit of the times has changed,' he retorted. 'The masses are no longer the same as in 1917. They are tired ... The working class is confused and afraid of changes that might make things even worse than they are ... ' He foresaw a long political struggle followed by radical changes in the economic programme and in the country's foreign policy. He thought it possible that the Party and the Revolution might still be saved, but he did not underrate the dangers. 'Our

task is to explore every avenue of reform. We may end up like
Lenin or like Liebknecht, and we must be equal to either possibility ... '

Fear is the mainspring of legends and delusions. The Politbureau
feared a military coup since Trotsky's reputation in the army remained
high, and alluded constantly to the possibility. However, if the
Opposition ever considered resorting to arms, conspiracy or insurrection, it did so only to reject such ideas out of hand. It worked
completely in the open, except for some obvious precautions against
secret police infiltration. It opened a head office in Moscow and subsidiary offices in all the larger cities, much as the left-wing Opposition had done in 1918 and the Bolshevik faction of the Social Democratic Party in the days before the Revolution. It was proposing to
wage a battle of ideas, not arms, within the Party and hoped to create
a sizeable minority, capable of forcing through new legislation and
running its own press, until such time as it would be converted peacefully into a majority. It refused to appeal to workers and intellectuals
who were not affiliated to the Party, because it believed that counter-
revolutionary attitudes, whether conscious or not, were still rife
amongst them.

In July 1926, Dzerzhinsky delivered a passionate attack on the
Opposition at a meeting of the Central Committee. He was taken ill
as he finished speaking, lay down on a divan in the ante-chamber, and
died soon after of a heart attack.

VIII. *Economic problems*

This account would not be intelligible if we did not stop here to consider the problem posed by the 'dictatorship of the proletariat' in
1926–7. The fundamental question was: did that dictatorship still
exist? The Decemists (Democratic Centralists) under Sapronov and
Vladimir Smirnov were claiming that it did not; they pointed to the
privileged position of the bureaucrats and technocrats, the growing
influence of the secret police, the silence imposed on the workers and
their miserable wages. This was not the democratic dictatorship of
the proletariat but the bureaucratic dictatorship of the Secretariat.
Trotsky's answer was that the country's poverty was an inheritance
from the old regime and the war, and that by maintaining the
socialized ownership of the means of production and the power of
the Socialist Workers' Party, the bureaucracy was playing a positive

role in an unstable world, a world in which the U.S.S.R. was isolated and surrounded by enemies. Bureaucracy grew out of poverty and backwardness, and the Revolution would cure these ills by increased production and the revival of democracy within the Party. Moreover, the socialist revolution could never feel safe until it had spread to other industrial countries. What was needed was major internal reform. The alternative was Thermidor. Just as, during the French Revolution, the upstarts and the corrupt, supported by the exhausted masses, had decapitated the Jacobin party and stabilized the bourgeois regime at the very moment when Robespierre and Saint-Just were preparing to ameliorate the lot of the poor, so the Russian bureaucracy was preparing to steer hard to the right, possibly opening the way to a restoration of capitalism. The word 'Thermidorian' suddenly became part of the everyday vocabulary, to the utter exasperation of the Politbureau. Despite this, by 1926 Trotsky had published a booklet entitled *Towards Capitalism or Socialism*, in which he showed that the Soviet economy had solved its original problems and was now moving towards socialism.

Ever since 1921 and the peace, the country had been bursting with creative energy. Thanks to the determined efforts of the peasantry, agriculture was relatively prosperous and back to the 1913 level of production. A class of well-to-do farmers had arisen, and stock-breeders had acquired considerable fortunes.

The livestock population had been greatly increased and with it the general standard of prosperity in the countryside. In 1916, there were 35·8 million horses and 60·6 million head of cattle. By 1922, war and famine had reduced their number disastrously to 24·1 million and 45·8 million respectively, but by 1928, the figures were up again to 33·5 million horses and 70·5 million head of cattle.

The Party and the working class had succeeded in setting nationalized industry on its feet. Proudhon had been proved right: the workers were perfectly capable of running industry, transport and, to a lesser extent, the distributive branch of the economy.

To a Western visitor, Russia's poverty was striking enough but she was no longer destitute; in general hers was a tolerable level of poverty, with confidence that things were getting better. And, in fact, they had been improving ever since 1921. The monthly wage of a worker, in gold roubles (two gold roubles equalled just over one gold dollar), had risen from 24·3 in 1913 to 54·0 in 1925–6, and to 60·4 in 1926–7. True, the price of food and manufactured goods had gone up as well, but not in the same proportion – in terms of real wages the Russian worker's income was considerably greater in 1926–8 than it had been under the Tsar. In other words, the Revolution had, at long last, brought the worker some material comfort, and this despite the vast cost of the Civil War. The housing problem, however, was still very acute and there was unemployment. The unemployed received a benefit, which was adequate in most cases.

The Marxists in the Joint Opposition took stock of all of these economic developments. They realized that the period of reconstruction was coming to an end, and that the next stage had to be mapped out. Industry was still too weak to supply all the needs of the countryside, and large stocks of surplus grain and of other primary products were accumulating in the hands of the *kulaks*. The Politbureau decreed that wage rises should no longer be geared to general rises in production but to the output of the individual worker (who was already working to the limit of his capacity, with obsolete equipment). The price reductions gazetted by the government turned out, as one might have expected, to be fictitious, and what economies were imposed on government offices and the nationalized industry yielded little; private traders, more ingenious and flexible and also less scrupulous than the public sector, speculated in the products of socialized industry and resold them at extortionate profits; middlemen grew rich and the new capitalists were able to invest their surpluses in small businesses or to deposit them in the State Bank at a reasonably attractive rate of interest. These 'NEP-men', profiteers created by the New Economic Policy, were a parasitic and demoralizing social phenomenon. Unless firm and prudent counter-measures were taken, the Opposition foresaw a multitude of evils: a conflict with the *kulaks*; industrial stagnation; food shortages in the cities and in the army; the growth of a counter-revolutionary bourgeoisie made up of *kulaks* and 'NEP-men'; further bureaucratic encroachments on Party and State; and the final surrender of all the Revolution had stood for.

The Opposition proposed the following remedies: tax exemptions for all poorer peasants (fifty per cent of the total); heavier taxes for all well-to-do peasants, who would also be forced to make loans to the State on clearly stated and advantageous terms, thus facilitating the transfer to the towns of accumulated surpluses; a review of the industrial wage policy, a return to trade union democracy and the restoration of the worker's formal rights; consumer protection through measures against speculation and excessive profits by private enterprise; and the promulgation and implementation of successive five-year plans with a view to rapid industrialization. (All the Planning Commission had been able to do until then was to publish annual forecasts in the form of 'control figures'.) Industrialization was to be paid for partly out of the agricultural surpluses, partly out of the rationalization of the economy with attendant savings, and partly out of exports. Before the Party and the State could tackle these new tasks, however, it was essential that Party members, high and low, should recover their right to voice criticisms and to advance new ideas; only thus could popular enthusiasm be restored and the mental degeneration and ossification of the Party apparatus be overcome. Such, in brief, was the programme of the Joint Opposition, set forth in a large number of documents, notably the declaration of the eighty-three Old Bolsheviks, subsequently signed by three thousand Party members, and the 1927 *Platform*, which carried about ten thousand signatures.

Stalin had no economic programme. Trotsky has described his policy as one that 'progresses by stumbling against the wall under the whiplash of circumstance. If the whip cracks on the right, he turns left; if it cracks on the left, he turns right ... ' In particular, the General Secretary had condemned further industrialization. A remark of his about the vast hydro-electric power station planned on the Dnieper, the Dnieprostroy, was going the rounds: 'Russia needs it like a peasant needs a gramophone.' His tendency to do as little as possible was based on sound reasoning: the promise of a period of tranquillity made it easier for him to get his own way. He claimed the full support of Bukharin, Rykov, Tomsky, Kalinin, Voroshilov and Yagoda against the Opposition; the first three, who were sober political theorists, demanded a speedy development of agriculture and a slow rate of industrialization, at least while the international situation remained unstable. They enjoyed the confidence of the great majority of Party officials, who wanted nothing better than a quiet life and a smooth daily round. The Politbureau kept issuing a stream of pamphlets, full of doctored figures, denouncing the 'Trotskyist super-industrializers' as 'plunderers of the peasants', 'men of little faith', and 'petit-bourgeois intellectuals panic-stricken in the face of economic problems'. And who but a fool would heed them when all was for the best in the best of socialist republics? Workers' democracy was flourishing as was proved by the millions of affirmations at Party meetings. Torrents of official paper flooded the country, while the Opposition had to content itself with duplicating its appeals and circulating them among small groups of supporters.

IX. *The political struggle in the working-class districts. Differences over the Chinese Revolution (1926–7)*

During the summer of 1926, the Opposition decided to call a large number of private meetings, confined to Party members, and held mainly in the working-class districts. The idea was that Party members would be entitled to come together over tea in their homes for friendly discussions. Zinoviev, Kamenev, Trotsky, Preobrazhensky, Smilga and many others used to visit factory workers in their tiny rooms, where up to fifty of them would cram together after work. A long time before, Party leaders had given up all direct contact with the masses, who knew them only from their portraits but now received them with the utmost warmth. The most difficult problems were frankly discussed in a friendly atmosphere while students kept watch outside. Similar meetings were held in garages, woods and even in cemeteries, and it seemed as if the Party was beginning to come out of a long winter's sleep. The Politbureau was afraid to send in the G.P.U.; instead, it instructed local committees to set up activist brigades with orders to break up these private meetings, if need be by strong-arm methods. Lorries would bring in the groups of fanatics equipped with whistles and clubs. In order to avoid scuffles between comrades, and possibly more serious incidents, the Opposition decided on a compromise: on October 19th, 1926 it undertook to confine its speaking activities to Party platforms and to observe Party discipline. In return, it was promised a free and democratic discussion of its programme during the preparations for the next Congress. In all civilized countries and in every workers' party, the cut and thrust of debate was, of course, taken for granted; only reactionary governments curtailed the right to free assembly. However, as the Politbureau under Stalin, Bukharin and Rykov, could neither accept free discussion, which would inevitably turn to its disadvantage, nor invent legal sanctions at short notice, it resorted to methods reminiscent of the Italian blackshirts.

'Meanwhile, Trotsky, still suffering from his mysterious fever, had gone to Germany in the spring of 1926.

'Dr Krause, who had come to Moscow to treat various members

of the government, had suggested that Trotsky should enter his clinic for observation. We went to Berlin using the name Kuzmyenko, and only the German government was told of our real identity. Leon Davidovich had a tonsillectomy without an anaesthetic – and without the slightest effect on his health, either. We roamed about the streets of Berlin and were present at a workers' demonstration on the Alexanderplatz ... The White émigrés and the local police suddenly heard about our presence, there was talk of an attempt on Trotsky's life and we had to take refuge with Krestinsky in the Embassy. Leon Davidovich wrote his *Where is Britain Going?* during his stay in the clinic, when Britain was in the grip of a general strike.'

In the spring of 1926, a major event in deepest Asia had begun to influence the course of the Russian Revolution; the Party would soon be as split on the issue of the Chinese Revolution as it had been on internal political and economic questions. From Turkestan to the Pacific, the Soviet Union shared an immense border with China, a country against which the Russian Empire had pursued a systematic policy of conquest. Immediately after they had seized power, the Bolsheviks had called for an end to colonialism and the emancipation of all colonial and semi-colonial peoples with the help of socialist countries. Here we shall not try to make a detailed analysis of the links between the Russian Revolution and the awakening of Asia; they were spontaneous, direct and inevitable. At the end of his life, Sun Yat-sen told Adolf Joffe in Shanghai that the Chinese Revolution would fail unless it enjoyed the full support of the Soviet Revolution. The Kuomintang was in control of the Canton region only, where, with the help of Chinese Communists supported in turn by Red Russia, it had created a small modern army. A young nationalist leader was particularly outstanding as an organizer. His name was Chiang Kai-shek, and though he had staged a coup against the Communists, he had eventually reached a compromise with them in May 1926. From that time on, the Chinese Communist Party was under the strict control of the Soviet Politbureau, that is, of the Stalin–Bukharin group, which generally failed to keep the Executive Committee of the Third International informed of its decisions. Under the terms of the compromise, the Chinese Communists became affiliated to the Kuomintang, now officially a 'sympathizer' of the Communist International. Trotsky protested in vain against this dangerous step, which served to subject the movement of the masses to the leadership of the nationalist bourgeoisie. Stalin did not conceal the fact that he was engaged in a battle of wits with Chiang Kai-shek, whose son was sent to study at the Military Academy in Moscow. Russian military and technical experts were helping to organize and train the Kuomintang army and participated in its military operations – Blücher, for instance, a leader of the Ural partisans, who fought in China under the name of Gallen, and Rasgon, an army leader from Turkestan, who fought under the name of Olgin. Political advisers, among them Borodin (alias Aleksandrov, who had previously worked in Latin America) exerted pressure on the Chinese government; others, such as Voytinsky and Bubnov, directed the Chinese Communist Party or ran the trade unions. The Dutch Marxist, Sneevliet, was sent on several missions to China; so was the French Communist, Jacques Doriot, and the widow of Sun Yat-sen expressed her support for the Moscow line.

The Bolsheviks were convinced that the Revolution would culminate in the birth of a new China, that stagnation and oppression would make way for a bright future; that China would prove to be their natural ally; that the Chinese Revolution would weaken the old imperialism and that they were bound by deep links of international solidarity to China and the whole of Asia. This last feeling ran extremely deep and inspired even the lowliest Party members. Russian workers, badly dressed and underfed, would leave their workshops and engage in passionate discussions of the Chan-Ha peasant movement, the Wu-Han ministry and the problems of Shanghai. In Moscow, Karl Radek headed the Sun Yat-sen University. As an abundance of secret, confidential and direct information flowed in from China, the left-wing Opposition grew in influence, not least because it had predicted the inevitable disaster and had condemned Stalin's policy.

Stalin apparently wanted to seize power inside the Kuomintang, which meant to a large extent the sacrifice of the mass movement but had the advantage of lulling the suspicions of the Great Powers. To this end, his tame 'theorists' had evolved the idea of a 'Four-Class Bloc', a kind of premature Popular Front, which the Politbureau hoped to manipulate at will. In it, Russian bureaucratic methods of government had replaced Marxism and the idea of international solidarity; the aim was no longer to help the Chinese Revolution or to establish a new social order but simply to take over the leadership.

Chiang Kai-shek's and Gallen's (or Blücher's) Northern Expedition, which began in July 1926 and was directed against those Chinese warlords who had established control over vast tracts of territory, was supported by the working classes with extraordinary enthusiasm and devotion, and, despite the gravest obstacles, scored one victory after another. The campaign culminated in the workers' rising in Shanghai, led by the trade unions and their Russian advisers. But once the forces of the Kuomintang had occupied all the large cities in the Yangtse valley and entered Shanghai, reactionary generals, responsible to a government that included Communist ministers, unleashed a campaign of murder against the workers and peasants who had taken part in the insurrection. The Chinese Communists bombarded Moscow with appeals for help; they believed that unless they were allowed to stand up against their so-called allies, they would all be slaughtered. The Joint Opposition sided with them unreservedly and called for the establishment of Chinese People's Soviets, aid to the peasant movement, and full independence for the Chinese Communist Party. The alternative was certain defeat for the masses and victory for the forces of reaction. As the debate grew increasingly heated, Stalin, deliberately ignoring the warnings of Zinoviev, Radek and Trotsky, ordered all Communists in Shanghai to surrender or bury their arms. They obeyed and tragedy was the result.

In March 1927, Stalin delivered an address to the Moscow 'militants', that is, the Party officials, in which he attacked the Opposition. Of Chiang Kai-shek, he exclaimed, 'We have him well in hand; we shall use him and then we shall discard him like a squeezed lemon ... ' Somewhat expurgated, this speech was sent to *Pravda*, just when the news arrived that Chiang Kai-shek was disarming the workers of Shanghai by force or, more accurately, butchering the Communists. Overtaken by events, Stalin quickly withdrew his text from *Pravda* and blankly refused to tell Opposition members in the Central Committee what it had contained.

The impact of this defeat was such that many leading Party members, infuriated, felt certain that Stalin would be swept from power by a wave of mass indignation. Trotsky did not share their view. He believed, and said, that major defeats merely serve to discourage the masses, reinforcing their tendency to inertia and encouraging reactionary attitudes.

x. *The repression starts. Trotsky's last appearance in the Central Committee. He is expelled from the Party. The demonstrations of November 7th, 1927. Joffe's suicide*

And Trotsky was proved right by the events. While the Politbureau, the Central Committee and the Executive of the Third International were still staggering under the Chinese blow, the Stalinist machine systematically stifled discussion in the various committees and Party cells, substituting threats and sanctions that generally served their purpose. Veiled terror began to stalk the Party ranks. If opponents were given the chance to speak, it was for a few guarded minutes only, during which 'activists' selected by the secretaries heckled incessantly. The Control Commissions started a wave of expulsions for 'indiscipline' and 'factional activities', with consequent loss of work permits sometimes followed by arrest. Other members of the Opposition were posted in their hundreds to the frozen wastes or the desert regions. In September 1927, the Communist press in Moscow, Paris, London, New York and the rest of the world, by then completely under the thumb of secret agents, published a sensational story: a plot by the Opposition acting hand-in-glove with counter-revolutionary elements had just been discovered in Moscow, and a secret printing press had been seized; a former officer in Baron Wrangel's Army was implicated. A circular addressed to Party organizations mentioned a 'military plot'. Zinoviev, Evdokimov, Smilga and Trotsky immediately called on the head of the G.P.U., Menzhinsky, a sick man who received them at his bedside. They asked to be shown the incriminating documents but were told that all the papers had been sent on to the Politbureau and, in any case, had contained little incriminating evidence. Everything in the official bulletin had been composed of blatant lies or gross distortions and exaggerations. There had been no secret printing press – merely three or four typewriters in a poor working-class lodging. Trotsky demanded, 'Where is the counter-revolution? Where is Wrangel's ex-officer? Produce him!' The deeply embarrassed Menzhinsky made excuses: he was not responsible for the published versions; he did not control the press. An ex-officer in the White Army had indeed been associated with the discovery of the typewriters, but only because he was a G.P.U. informer and an experienced *agent provocateur*. The damp squib spluttered out miserably but neither the Central Committee nor the press published a retraction. A number of

Communists, including Mrachkovsky, one of the most respected and courageous of all, were already in gaol.

'Muralov, Ivan Smirnov and the others came to our flat in the Kremlin one afternoon, waiting for Leon Davidovich to return from a Politbureau meeting. Pyatakov arrived first, very pale and visibly upset. He poured himself a glass of water, gulped it down and said, "I have been under fire, but this – this was worse than anything I've ever seen! Why, oh why, did Leon Davidovich say that? Stalin will never forgive him or his children for generations to come!" Pyatakov was so overwrought that he was unable to tell us clearly what had happened. When Leon Davidovich finally came into the dining-room, Pyatakov rushed up to him. "Why, *why* did you say that?" Leon Davidovich brushed the question aside; he was exhausted but calm. He had shouted at Stalin: "Grave-digger of the Revolution!" The General Secretary had jumped to his feet, controlling himself with difficulty, and had rushed out of the room, slamming the door behind him. We realized that the breach between them was beyond repair.

'Pyatakov was pessimistic. He believed that a long period of reaction had started in Russia and the rest of the world, that the working class had come to the end of its tether, that the Party had been throttled and that the Opposition had lost the battle. He only persevered from a sense of principle and for the sake of solidarity.

'Leon Davidovich, overworked and tense, continued to feel weak and feverish and to suffer from insomnia. "My head seems hollow," he sometimes said. Even sleeping pills did not always send him to sleep. My sons and I suffered insomnia with him. In the mornings, at breakfast, we would watch Leon Davidovich open the papers ... He would glance at them and then throw them all over the table with disgust. They contained nothing but stupid lies, distortions of even the plainest fact or speech, hateful threats, and telegrams from all over the world, vying with each other to repeat the same infamies with boundless servility. What had they done to the Revolution, the Party, Marxism and the International! It was impossible to remain silent.'

There were a few reassuring episodes as well. The Opposition, to their surprise, managed to get hold of a theatre, where Kamenev was able to deliver an impassioned and intelligent address to thousands of militants. When the authorities cut off the electricity, the meeting continued by candle-light. In Leningrad, a silent crowd stood in the rain to wave to the leaders of the hard-pressed

Opposition. Fishelev, an old socialist printer who had returned from America at the beginning of the Revolution, managed to run off several thousand copies of the Opposition *Platform*. He was at once expelled from the Party, placed under arrest, charged with malpractice, misappropriation of paper and illegal publication, and sentenced by the G.P.U. to internment on the Solovetsky Islands.

At the end of October 1927, Zinoviev and Trotsky addressed the Central Committee for the last time, and *Pravda*, contrary to custom, published a mutilated version of their arguments, which indicated that the Opposition had become fair game and was, in effect, outlawed. From the tribune, surrounded by the last handful of his friends, Trotsky spoke in a clear voice and in measured sentences so as not to say one word too many. 'Why and how has the Party been taken in by those who have accused us of counter-revolutionary activities? ... You have made cuts in the transcript of my short speech about the Wrangel officer ... The Stalin–Bukharin faction has thrown men like Nochaev, Shtykgold, Vasilev, Schmidt, Fishelev into gaol ... it is stifling Party thought not only in the U.S.S.R. but throughout the world ... "Remove Stalin", Lenin advised us on his deathbed ... The ruling faction is striking at its own Party with unemployment, with bludgeons and with gaol ... The worker is afraid to say what he thinks or to vote according to his conscience ... Your policy does nothing but zig-zag ... You will get nothing out of the *kulaks* ... Behind the bureaucrats we can see the renascent bourgeoisie ... '
This speech was delivered amid shouted interruptions, shaking fists, whistles and jeers. Trotsky spoke on, unperturbed, raising his voice above the uproar until, finally, the members of the Central Committee rose to their feet in disorder as if provoked to assault. On reading the official report, we gain the disconcerting impression of a struggle between 'dead men on furlough' and one who alone foresaw their future. Most of those who tried to shout Trotsky down were later murdered by Stalin; they were already troubled spectres, powerless to stem their disastrous fate. Skrypnik, who shouted more loudly than anyone else, blew out his brains in 1933 to put an end to his persecution. Unschlicht, Chubar, and Petrovsky, who clamoured so furiously, were to disappear ten years later, shot, or immured in 'isolators'. Voroshilov was one of the very few survivors.

At the same session, Zinoviev was subjected to similar harassment, though the voices against him were not raised quite so high because he was known to be the weaker man. *Pravda* reported that, before being 'booed' off the tribune, he said, 'You will either have to let us speak to the Party, or you will have to throw all of us into gaol.' The official report speaks of 'laughter' at this, and of cries of 'That's enough! Get out!' In the end, Trotsky and Zinoviev were expelled from the Central Committee and hence prevented from addressing the Fifteenth Congress in December. They had been most effectively gagged.

The tenth anniversary of the October Revolution was about to be celebrated amidst a veritable flood of sanctions, vicious recriminations, sensations and threats. The Opposition decided to take part in the Moscow and Leningrad marches with its own placards and streamers bearing such slogans as 'Against the *kulak*, the "NEP-man" and the bureaucrat!' 'Honour Lenin's thought!' and 'For genuine Party unity!' Zinoviev and Karl Radek were in Leningrad, where lengthy scuffles developed between the militia and Opposition supporters who had assembled near the Winter Palace. The militia moved only half-heartedly against the men who so recently had been their leaders. Zinoviev, Radek and their group were eventually cornered in a courtyard. In Moscow, special 'activists' distinguished themselves by starting a whole series of brawls. Smilga, a member of the Central Committee, had put up portraits of Lenin and Trotsky under a red streamer on the balcony of his flat. They were torn down and ripped into small pieces. A group of workers marching past in district formation tried to unfurl a banner in Red Square, but the activists were on the look-out, tore the banner from their hands and knocked the bearers half senseless. Trotsky's car was caught in a swirling crowd and had two bullets fired at it. None of these incidents was serious in itself, but the over-excited atmosphere was reminiscent of a pogrom. Workers, expelled from the Party in their hundreds, provided a bitter commentary on this strange celebration of the victory of the proletariat.

Abroad and even in Russia – for the press had shed all inhibitions -- there was much talk of an organized show of 'insurrectional strength' on the part of the Opposition.

'That same evening, November 7th, Leon Davidovich decided that we should leave the Kremlin at once rather than allow ourselves to be evicted. We were trapped: expulsion from the Party could be expected within a few days and prison was the obvious next step. We asked Beloborodov, who was living in a House of the Soviets near the Kremlin, to put us up. He gave us a little room overlooking the courtyard, and two weeks later we were allocated a small flat by the Soviet accommodation bureau. Zinoviev, Kamenev and Radek had meanwhile received notice to quit their Kremlin apartments.

'The expulsion of Trotsky and Zinoviev from the Party was announced on November 15th, 1927. The next day, our friend, Adolf Joffe, put a bullet through his head. He had been suffering from a blood disease and the Central Committee went to great lengths to persuade him that his condition did not allow him to play as active a part in the political struggle as he would have liked to do. Before he killed himself, he wrote a long letter to Leon Davidovich which included the following lines: "If I may compare great events with small, I would say that the immense historical importance of your expulsion and Zinoviev's ... and the fact that, after twenty-seven years of revolutionary work in responsible Party posts, I have been forced into a situation where I have no alternative but to blow my brains out – I would say that these two events are characteristic of Party rule. And perhaps these two events, one great and one small, may between them serve to jolt the Party and cause it to halt on the road to Thermidor." He asked Leon Davidovich to do what he could for his wife and son (then seven years old).

'Joffe's letter was seized by the G.P.U. on the grounds that anything written by a Party member belonged to the Party. Leon Davidovich finally managed to get hold of a copy that was probably incomplete. The newspapers remained silent on this desperate protest by one who had been the first socialist to represent the Soviet Republic in Germany, China, and Japan, and who had prepared the way for peace with Poland. Several Communists were arrested and deported for having read manuscript copies of Joffe's letter. His young widow spent the rest of her life in prison and exile, and the boy later died in Central Asia. Joffe's funeral turned into an impressive display of solidarity, the last spontaneous and sincere demonstration of the spirit of the Russian Revolution. Thousands of Opposition supporters and workers followed the procession, and sang as they passed through the streets of Moscow, white with snow. At the gates of the Novodevichy cemetery, the militia tried vainly to stop the crowd from entering. The coffin, carried shoulder high, began to sway above people's heads and blows were barely averted ... Rakovsky and Trotsky spoke at the open grave, vowing that they, too, faithful to their duty, would follow the road of revolution wherever it might lead them ... These were their last speeches as free men on Soviet territory.'

Five · Persecution

1. *The Fifteenth Party Congress. Beginnings of totalitarianism. Zinoviev and Kamenev surrender. Trotsky's intransigence*

On December 2nd, 1927, the Fifteenth Party Congress opened, more triumphantly than any of its predecessors, under the official auspices of perfect unity, iron discipline, staunch Leninism and the widest possible democracy – or so the Soviet press made it appear. There was, in fact, not a single member of the Opposition among the 1,669 delegates, all of whom were local officials and ostensibly represented some 1,210,000 Party members. Stalin spoke for nearly seven hours. Resolutions designed to solve all existing problems were readily adopted; one by Molotov provided for moderate collectivization of the land, while others called for an industrial five-year plan, equally moderate in its provisions. The Congress unanimously condemned Trotskyism, which, it claimed, was 'Menshevik in tendency, ready to capitulate to the bourgeoisie at home and abroad, and in practice, allied to the third force and hence against the dictatorship of the proletariat'. (The 'third force' was a synonym for the middle classes which were said to be incurably reactionary.) Rakovsky, relieved of his post as ambassador in Paris, and Kamenev were still members of the Central Committee and hence allowed to address the Congress. When they testified that the Leningrad Opposition was unswervingly loyal to the Party, its programme and its aims, they were ordered to recant in public. At that, Kamenev exclaimed, 'Do they really expect old revolutionaries to abjure in the evening what they believed in the morning?' These fine sentiments notwithstanding, he, together with Zinoviev and the majority of their friends, quickly announced their total submission. By contrast, Rakovsky, Radek and Muralov, representing the Trotskyist wing of the Opposition, stood firm and declared that they would remain faithful to the Party

153

and fight for its reform from outside its ranks. Stalin had meanwhile planned a master-stroke by which he hoped to offset his defeat in Shanghai: the Communists were to seize power in Kwang-Tung, the historic cradle of the Kuomintang, at the very moment that the Fifteenth Congress was meeting in triumphant session. To that end, his emissaries, Heinz Neumann, a German, and Lominadze, a Georgian, had whipped up a proletarian insurrection in Canton, where coolies, workers and artisans rose at a signal on December 10th. A batch of decrees, written well in advance, was published the same day. The Fifteenth Congress barely had time, however, to salute 'the immortal commune of Canton' before it was drowned in the vainly shed blood of several thousands of workers.

The Joint Opposition was now as good as dead and hopelessly fragmented. A small group round Sapronov and Vladimir Smirnov believed that a police state was imminent, that clandestine action must be prepared against it and a new proletarian party formed. The Leningrad wing (the Zinoviev faction) saw no chance of political life outside the Party, whatever its leadership and whatever insult the 'capitulators', as they were henceforth called, had to suffer within it. They believed that a crisis was bound to arise at some point, and that it would then be essential to belong to the Party. Until that time they would have to swallow their pride and humble themselves daily in the certain knowledge that, when the crisis came, their reluctant recantations would count for little with the masses. Thus they reasoned in private. The others, those romantic Don Quixotes, could go to gaol and rot there.

By contrast, the more intransigent wing, which included Rakovsky, Muralov, Sosnovsky – one of the most brilliant journalists of the past years – and Trotsky, were prepared to suffer persecution for the sake of their Marxist ideals, the revolutionary tradition and eventual reform. Trotsky was convinced that the Stalin regime could not last for long. 'His fall will be sudden,' he said. Imprisonment would do more for the cause than abject moral surrender. Was Trotsky wrong? In the years to come, Stalin was more than once on the edge of the abyss and maintained his position only by his use of administrative and police powers. Ten years later, he would save his regime by ordering the greatest political massacre in history. Trotsky's notes show that, from 1923 on, he had few illusions about the strength of Stalin and his reactionary clique, that he clearly foresaw the elimination of all opponents of the regime 'in six or seven phases'.

Pyatakov and several others surrendered because they believed 'there was nothing else to do', that the present was too bleak and the future too inscrutable, that working for the industrialization of Russia was better than mouldering exile. Some, like Radek, clutched at the illusory hope that the Party might yet embrace more positive policies. Finally, there were those who preferred cowardly vacillations, self-interested recantations and privileges, to the bitter road to Siberia. In every case, however, emotional attachment to the Party of the Revolution was an important consideration.

'Before the final blow, Alexandra Kollontai used to visit us quite often. The 1920 Workers' Opposition, of which she had been one of the leaders, was allied to our movement. When she was appointed ambassador to Norway, she came to take her leave of us and offered to take out Opposition documents in her diplomatic bags to hand over to foreign groups. When I took them to her a few days later, I found her completely changed, confused and absolutely terrified. "Really, I can't take anything, I am sorry," she kept repeating ... Soon afterwards, she published a complete refutation of her past in *Pravda* – the price for keeping her job. Krestinsky, our ambassador in Berlin, capitulated straightaway. His wife visited us a few days later, just before we were deported. She was an old militant, educated, upright and sincere, who hated having to attend diplomatic receptions. She tried to justify her husband's behaviour and her own with obvious embarrassment. "What else could we have done? After all, one's got to live." We refrained from suggesting that one might live with a clearer conscience beyond the Arctic Circle.'

11. *Repression. Trotsky arrested, condemned without trial and deported to Alma-Ata*

'We were prepared for our deportation. As Stalin and Bukharin feared the impression that outright repressive measures might make abroad, particularly in those Communist Parties that had not yet been fully indoctrinated, the Central Committee invited the best-known members of the Opposition to accept posts in remote regions. It was suggested that Leon Davidovich should move to Astrakhan "voluntarily". He declined. The official Tass Agency indignantly denied all rumours about repression in the U.S.S.R. "The

Party is not resorting to punitive measures," the *International Press Correspondence* [Inprecor] declared in French, English and German at the very moment when the G.P.U. was busily hauling people out of bed, throwing expelled workers into filthy prisons and proceeding, with just a little more civility, to deport the best known pillars of the Revolution. Leon Davidovich's enforced departure for Alma-Ata was originally fixed for January 16th, 1928, but on that day thousands of citizens invaded the railway station and a large crowd of factory workers blocked the line, while other workers searched the entire train for Trotsky. The militia was afraid to intervene. A telephone call postponed our departure for two days.

'Early next morning, the G.P.U. turned up. Our departure had been brought forward by 24 hours and now there were no longer any pretences. The G.P.U. agents produced a warrant for Leon Davidovich's arrest, as well as a copy of the sentence pronounced on him in secret and in his absence by the Political Security Council. The agents seemed excited and confused. The Politbureau had charged Trotsky under Article 58 of the penal code, which applied to counter-revolutionary activities. We refused to leave. Trotsky had no intention of giving even the slightest impression that he was acquiescing or passively submitting to so odious and arbitrary a measure. Together with our son Lyova, Joffe's widow and the wife of Beloborodov (who had recently been ousted from his post of People's Commissar for the Interior and was also about to be deported), we locked ourselves in a room. One of the officers, a man called Kishkin who had more than once accompanied Leon Davidovich to the front, set about breaking down the door. At the same time, he shouted, "Shoot me, Comrade Trotsky!" He was ashamed of what he was doing but felt compelled to obey orders; a bullet would have put him out of his misery. His shouts later cost him his life: what better evidence could there have been of his subconscious Trotskyism! When the door was eventually forced, Trotsky refused to leave and soldiers had to carry him out. Sergey and Lyova called out the neighbours, all of them high-ranking officials. Frightened faces appeared at the doors ... The car did not take us to the central Kazan station but to the small, deserted one at Faustovo. The secret police had to drag Trotsky on to the train, where we found ourselves in a carriage full of special G.P.U. troops in uniform. A bleak snowscape spread out all around us; it was a freezing day. We had not had enough time to take a single book or even a towel. We were told that our luggage would follow on another train and that we would get it in twelve days' time at Frunze (Pishpek) in Kazakhstan on the Sinkiang frontier ... We said goodbye to Sergey: Lyova was coming with us, and not being a prisoner was free to stretch his legs on station platforms and make small purchases. At the door of our compartment, a silent sentry kept watch on behalf of the Politbureau. The Red Army men were friendly and would evidently have preferred some other task ... The convoy was under the command of a man called Barychkin, who in former times had sometimes gone shooting with Leon Davidovich. He was an obliging and resourceful officer but there was something about him we did not much care for. While Leon Davidovich was being arrested, he had been very reserved and correct and now he seemed to be ashamed and, as a result, extremely cool. Leon Davidovich, on the other hand, was good-humoured and at times even gay. He slept little ... While lying down on the seat of the compartment, he suddenly said to me, "I didn't want to die in a bed in the Kremlin ... " Neither of us knew exactly where we were going.

'From Frunze to Alma-Ata, we covered some hundred and fifty miles by bus through wastelands and snowstorms. Part of our luggage was lost – or stolen by the G.P.U. Alma-Ata was a large village without drains or lights, stricken with poverty, malaria and all the diseases of Central Asia. The G.P.U. put us up in the only hotel in the place, which was reserved for officials. Our room had no modern comforts but it was clean and overheated to such an extent that we had to leave the door to the corridor open. Three of Trotsky's secretaries had decided to join him in exile; in theory there was nothing to stop them settling in Alma-Ata and working for a deportee. One of them, Sermuks, had the audacity to demand a room in our hotel. I used to catch sight of his tall figure, his fine fair head and his friendly face in the corridor. We managed to speak to him only once ... He was arrested and spent the rest of his life in gaol or exile. Poznansky suffered the same fate. Georgy Butov, the third of Leon Davidovich's secretaries, fared even worse. This young engineer had been in charge of the secretariat of the War Council. Thin, smallish, pale and unhappy in his private life, he had proved to be a tireless organizer, although neither his origins nor his interests seemed to be such as to predispose him to revolutionary activity. Almost all War Council and High Command papers had passed through his hands. When the wave of persecution began, quietly at first, he knew that he would be one of its targets, for what better person was there to incriminate Trotsky? "I know I shall perish," he said. He had been arrested before our departure and presented with an indictment that he rejected in disgust. He proved to be a resolute fighter, and responded to continuous threats and psychological torture with a hunger strike that ended in his death in October 1928, after fifty days of desperate struggle. We did not hear about all this until much later ...

'News of the deportations quickly leaked out. The official Tass Agency published a denial which was repeated by the *International Press Correspondence*, the official organ of the Comintern, and by Bukharin who produced a special declaration ... Moscow-inspired newspapers, including *L'Humanité*, carried accounts of Trotsky's trip to Turkestan in a luxury train ... But a fortnight or so later, in the face of working-class revulsion and world press reports, Moscow admitted that some Party members had been deported or gaoled, though it naturally played down the numbers involved. Smilga and Serebriakov had been sent to Semipalatinsk in the Kazakhstan desert, Ivan Smirnov to Kizil-Orda, Sapronov to the Onega region, Rakovsky to Astrakhan and from there to Barnaul on the Obi in Central Siberia, and Preobrazhensky to the Urals. Lesser known members of the Opposition had been gaoled in their hundreds, often thrown into G.P.U. cellars in the company of criminals and, if they were women, of prostitutes ... The wave of arrests did not spare the sick, the pregnant, heroes of the Revolution, or the maimed. All were carried off in secret, and their names were rarely, if ever, published. In Moscow, the wife of a deportee was left behind with three young children and was quite unable to cope. When the G.P.U. was informed of her problems by telephone, they ordered: "Leave the children, take the mother ... " Nobody was tried, let alone defended – the G.P.U. reached all decisions by means of summary proceedings and its officers acted as inquisitors. At first, deportations to some township in Turkestan or an icy village in Siberia were the rule, but later the exiles were rounded up and thousands of supporters of the Opposition were thrown into special prisons called "isolators" and given three-year sentences that could be extended at the whim of the G.P.U., that is, of the Politbureau.

'From figures published by the Central Control Commission of the Party and from our own enquiries we were able to put the number of Opposition supporters arrested, deported or imprisoned in 1928 at a minimum of eight thousand. At that time, the victims were still allowed to read and to write. They accepted the privations, the cold, hunger and the break-up of their families, and at the same time tried to make the best of their lives. Animated ideological letters were passed between the various colonies peopled by deportees. The G.P.U. read, photographed and collected everything, and abstracted messages, as a result of which the Politbureau was kept informed of its opponents' views and could compile a list of its most unyielding adversaries ... In his *My Life*, Leon Davidovich noted that, from April to October 1928, "We sent out from Alma-Ata about 800 political letters, among them quite a few large works. The telegrams sent amounted to about 550. We received about 1,000 political letters and about 700 telegrams, in most cases from groups of people." In October, the correspondence suddenly stopped ... The Stalin–Bukharin clique was still terrified of its prisoners; repression was so unpopular that members of the Government continued to deny its existence against all the evidence, and the Central Committee made frequent overtures to those members of the Opposition who were most likely to capitulate – and not without success in a number of cases. On the other hand, economic problems were proving increasingly intractable, thus confirming the prophecies of those who had been expelled, and against whom a vast extermination campaign was even then being mounted in complete secrecy.

'We were living on what we had put by in Moscow against the day of our deportation. Our funds were sufficient for our needs but fast becoming depleted.

'Our life in Alma-Ata was fairly well organized. I wrote in my diary: "A town of earthquakes and floods at the foot of the Tyan-Shan range on the borders of China, two hundred and fifty kilometres from the railway and four thousand from Moscow; a year spent with letters, books and nature ... " It was also a year of secret and precious tokens of sympathy and devotion, a year of intellectual and moral communion with a revolutionary elite, men possessed of truly exceptional human qualities. We rented a small house close to the G.P.U. offices, almost in the centre of the town, that was being made ready as the seat of the Kazakhstan government. Leon Davidovich buried himself in a mass of newspapers and manuscripts that covered every table and spilled over on to the rest of what sketchy furniture we had. A typist took dictation from him every day, and all of us knew that this charming young woman had to make long reports about her work to the G.P.U. .... We went on a week's shooting trip into the snow-covered mountains. In the spring, Leon Davidovich occasionally went fishing, and in the summer we took a house in the country – as always not far from those of the G.P.U. officials – surrounded by an orchard in blossom. The blue mountain slopes could be seen behind the white and pink of the apple trees and the sky had the softest kind of light. Our host, a peasant, was naturally an informer, but our G.P.U. neighbour introduced himself as a sympathizer of the Opposition – true or false? – and overwhelmed us with attentions. Another official, D., established secret contacts with Leon Davidovich ... A comrade arrived from Moscow and set up as a carter in Alma-Ata, where he used to meet Leon Davidovich in the public baths. We worked out a system of signals by putting washing or flowers in our windows. One day the sign in their window looked most peculiar. I met D.'s wife in the native market and she passed me a note: her husband had just been arrested. Volynsky, one of the G.P.U. chiefs, had called for a list of Alma-Ata intellectuals and had picked out the name of our friend ... The carter also disappeared. We never heard from either of them again ...

'During the October celebrations that year, the G.P.U. men were plainly embarrassed. Leon Davidovich had been Lenin's close companion in the years of victory and was now a deportee. Should he be offered their compliments on this great occasion or should it pass in silence? This was a period of great sorrow for us. Nina, Leon Davidovich's younger daughter by his first wife, had died of tuberculosis in Moscow. She had written to us when her condition became critical, but the secret police had kept her letter back for seventy-five days to give the young woman, who was twenty-six, time to die before her father could apply for permission to see her for the last time ... Nina had been married to a young intellectual who had served in the Red Army, and left two children. Her husband, Man-Nevelson, was in exile or in gaol, where he evinced unflagging courage: his fearless *Open Letters to Stalin* were passed from hand to hand. Nothing more was ever heard of him.'

III. *Trotsky's banishment and deportation to Turkey (1929)*

'In the autumn of 1928, no further letters were delivered to us, and the snow of our isolation turned to ice. In December Volynsky, the G.P.U. representative, delivered an ultimatum to Leon Davidovich: unless he promised to discontinue his political activities, the Government would be obliged to make it impossible for him to engage in them ... "Political activities" obviously referred to Trotsky's correspondence with other deportees. We felt sure we would go to gaol. On December 16th, Leon Davidovich sent his reply in writing. He said that he absolutely refused to "renounce the struggle for the cause of the international proletariat which I have been waging continuously for thirty-two years, during the whole of my conscious life. The attempt to represent this activity as 'counter-revolutionary' comes from those whom I charge, before the international proletariat, with violating the fundamental principles of the teachings of Marx and Lenin, with infringing the historical interests of world revolution, with renouncing the traditions and precepts of October, and with unconsciously, but all the more menacingly, preparing the Thermidor." His indictment of the regime ended as follows: "You wish to continue with policies inspired by class forces hostile to the proletariat. We know our duty and we will do it to the end." We had no doubt that the majority of Opposition sympathizers were either already in gaol or about to be sent there.'

By 1929, no more than three well known members of the Opposition were at liberty – however precariously – in the entire U.S.S.R. Needless to say, all three were kept under strict surveillance. They were the Spaniard Andrés Nin, in Moscow, Alexandra Bronstein (Trotsky's first wife) and myself, [Victor Serge], in Leningrad. So thorough were the secret police and so complete the Party's files, that it is safe to assume the authorities knew the names and whereabouts of every Opposition sympathizer, including, of course, all those wives of deportees who had been allowed to stay on in the big cities.

'On January 20th, Volynsky called again, accompanied by G.P.U. agents who occupied our house, and watched our every move. Some of them were alarmed themselves. The following decision was communicated to us: "*Considered:* the case of Citizen Trotsky, Leon Davidovich, under article 58/10 of the Criminal Code, on a charge of counter-revolutionary activity expressing itself in the organization of an illegal anti-Soviet party, whose activity has lately been directed toward provoking anti-Soviet actions and preparing for an armed struggle against the Soviet power. *Resolved:* Citizen Trotsky, Leon Davidovich, to be deported from the territory of the U.S.S.R." When he was asked to sign a slip of paper acknowledging that he had been informed of this decision, Leon Davidovich wrote, "The decision of the G.P.U., criminal in substance and illegal in form, was communicated to me on January 20th, 1929."

'Where could we go? What country would admit us? What traps had been set for us? The G.P.U. messenger could tell us nothing since he knew nothing himself. The officer, who appeared sympathetic to us, was full of solicitude. "Where are they taking you?" he asked Lyova furtively. We had scarcely twenty-four hours to pack our papers, books and the few personal things we owned. Two days later we were driven across the snow-covered plains and through icy mountain passes. The powerful tractors meant to tow us across had to struggle hard through the frozen snow that blocked the Kurday Pass ... A train was waiting for us at Frunze and when we were on our way, Bulanov, the new G.P.U. representative, divulged our destination: Constantinople. We demanded to be allowed to take leave of our son Sergey and our daughter-in-law Anya, Lyova's wife, and they were brought from Moscow. Leon Davidovich refused to leave the U.S.S.R. voluntarily, which placed the Politbureau in somewhat of a quandary vis-à-vis the Turkish authorities. Meanwhile the engine dragged our carriage and our large escort of troops with difficulty over deserted railway tracks into the snow-covered forests of Kursk. Here we were completely cut off from the rest of the world, though at least we had our children with us. The papers reported the arrest of friends – it was now the turn of the Georgian Opposition (Mdivani, Kavtaradze and Okudjava) ... We passed the next twelve days quietly as if suspended in time. The German Republic, in 1929 the most democratic country in the world, where the strongest party was still the Social Democrats, had – apparently – refused us asylum, so that Turkey was where we would have to go whether we liked it or not. We saw nobody but the officials, constrained and formal in manner towards us, and we were not allowed to get off the train.

'Sergey and Anya decided to stay behind. They loved Russia and especially Moscow, and Sergey wanted to finish his engineering course. He promised to visit us later in Constantinople. Both realized full well that by staying in Russia they were risking their lives, but then nobody knew what the future held in store for us in our new exile and we could not insist they stay with us ...

'One night, at long last, we reached Odessa, where we boarded an empty cargo ship lying at a deserted wharf on the edge of the frozen sea. It was ironic that the ship was called the *Ilyich*, Lenin's patronymic ... Our new prison-ship, empty, freezing and funereal, weighed anchor at the dead of night and was towed out by an ice-breaker ... On February 12th, 1929, we arrived in Constantinople. Leon Davidovich handed a letter addressed to Mustafa Kemal Pasha (Kemal Ataturk), President of the Republic, to the first Turkish official who presented himself. The letter said, "I have arrived at the Turkish frontier against my will and I will cross this frontier only by submitting to force ... " But by that time everything had already been settled between the Kremlin and Ankara, and the Kremlin certainly did not play a pretty part in the arrangements. The letter was ignored ...

'At the end of our journey, the G.P.U. representatives, Bulanov and Volynsky, had begun to appear almost friendly. Bulanov, a thin, fair man, suggested I put on a shawl before stepping on to the bridge ... "I know that you have one, Natalia Ivanovna ... " It crossed my mind that a policeman had to notice everything, for professional reasons. He promised Leon Davidovich to obtain permission for our secretaries, Poznansky and Sermuks, to join us. "If they don't turn up, you can call me a blackguard," he said. Leon Davidovich replied, "How would that help me?" (Poznansky and Sermuks were never released, and died in prison.) Volynsky, who was civil and discreet enough, assured us that he was "our friend" before he shook hands with us for the last time. A senior G.P.U. officer by the name of Bulanov figured in the Moscow trials of 1937; he made a standardized confession and was shot. He was probably the Bulanov we had known. Had he too grown disillusioned, or was it simply that anyone present during our deportation had become an embarrassment?'

IV. *Life on Prinkipo. Work. Blumkin's execution*

'In Constantinople, we were put up in the Soviet Consulate. The Russian government had allowed us some fifteen hundred dollars. Although the Consular staff was respectful and almost friendly, we feared that the secret service might steal or confiscate the documents we had brought with us: our correspondence with Lenin, our collection of photographs, our correspondence with members of the Opposition and various souvenirs. We could not move to a hotel because the old Turkish capital had a large quota of White Russian émigrés. Minsky, who combined his function of Consul with that of G.P.U. official, hastened our departure from the Consulate after various incidents, including the arrest and brief detention of Lyova.

A Russian airman, to whom Leon Davidovich had shown kindness in the past (and who was now a G.P.U. informer) helped us to rent a small and rather dilapidated villa in the Prinkipo Islands, a summer resort for the rich. Here we were reasonably safe, all the more so because the place was almost uninhabited during a large part of the year. The waves of the Sea of Marmara lapped the shore a few steps from our new home. It was a beautiful place, spacious, peaceful, set in the blue sea and bathed in golden sunlight most of the time. We were to live there for several years in near-isolation, and had no contact with the Turkish authorities or the cosmopolitan society of Constantinople. Two policemen watched over us from a discreet distance. Leon Davidovich visited Constantinople only once, but our son Lyova, who ought now to be referred to by his full adult name, Leon Sedov (after all he was married, 23 years old, an experienced revolutionary, and a member of the Opposition – he had been the organizer of an underground youth movement in Moscow) was free to come and go as he pleased.

'We had vainly applied for political asylum in Britain and Germany, but since neither the Labour Party nor the German Social Democratic Party had been prepared to extend to us the blessings of modern democracy, it seemed futile to approach any other country. "The planet without a visa," Leon Davidovich used to say.

'Expressions of sympathy and requests for interviews, articles and books reached Leon Davidovich from all over the world. Friends came to see us, not a great many, to be sure, but in large enough numbers for us not to be lonely and to discover some loyal collaborators. Molinier and three French comrades went out of their way to make us comfortable on Prinkipo. Our old friends, Marguerite and Alfred Rosmer, lived with us for some time, and so did Pierre and Denise Naville and Pierre Frank, all members of the French Communist opposition, Rudolf Klement and Otto Schüssler, two young German militants, and Leon Davidovich's French translator, Maurice Hoertel, whose *nom de plume* was Parijanine. He was well read, in poor health, affectionate and yet bitter ... A Latvian by the name of Franck also spent five months on Prinkipo; we later learned that he was a G.P.U. informer, as was a certain Sobolevich or Sobolevicius, another Latvian, who paid us a much shorter visit. (Sobolevich's brother, Roman Well, was an *agent provocateur* among Opposition circles in Paris and in Central Europe, a fact that was not discovered until later.)

'Leon Davidovich wrote a series of articles for the American press on the political motives of his expulsion from Russia; he let it be known that he would hand over his fees to the Opposition press. Contracts with publishers in several countries helped us to make ends meet and we were even able, with the help of subscriptions, to publish a Russian periodical, the *Opposition Bulletin*. In 1929, Leon Davidovich wrote the three volumes of *My Life* (1879–1929), and during the next year the four long volumes of his *History of the Russian Revolution*. He also began a biography of Lenin but only completed Part I ... The books were published almost simultaneously in French, English, German and Russian as well as in several other languages. What with his daily correspondence, editing the *Bulletin*, and his theoretical and practical contributions to Soviet politics – the Opposition was fighting on – he had his hands full. Meticulous as he was, he would check every translation down to the last comma, surrounding himself with documents and reference books before writing a single page, verifying every date and searching for the right word. There was little time left for his friends. His chief relaxation was fishing in the Sea of Marmara. When the catch had been good, he would return in excellent spirits and sit down to dictate for hours on end. "It is as if the brain were working all by itself," he used to say afterwards. "The brain has its own momentum and all I have to do is to follow it ... "

'In Russia, they used to tell an anecdote about his fishing exploits. "Leon Davidovich went fishing at the entrance of the Bosphorus, when one of his friends suddenly saw his face cloud over. 'What's the matter, Leon Davidovich, what are you thinking about?' 'Alas, I am thinking of poor Lenin. If he were still alive, he'd be right here fishing alongside us.'" That sort of story could earn you three years' deportation or more.

'*My Life* was written in one draft, and finished in a few months. Until our arrival on Prinkipo, Leon Davidovich had rarely had a moment to himself. Now he had plenty of time at last to formulate more general ideas. He wrote about "the role of the creative imagination in the revolution". He put the best of himself into such lines as:

Marxism considers itself the conscious expression of the unconscious historical process. But the 'unconscious' process in the historical and philosophical sense of the term – not in the psychological – coincides with its conscious expression only at its highest point when the masses, by sheer elemental pressure, break through the social routine and give victorious expression to the deepest needs of historical development ... The creative union of the conscious with the unconscious is what one usually calls 'inspiration'. Revolution is the inspired frenzy of history.

Every real writer knows creative moments, when something stronger than himself is guiding his hand; every real orator experiences moments when something stronger than the self of his everyday existence speaks through him. This is 'inspiration'. It derives from the highest creative effort of all one's forces. The unconscious rises from its deep well and bends the conscious mind to its will, merging it with itself in some greater synthesis. (*My Life*, Chapter XXIX)

'At the beginning, we still kept up a minimum of contact with Russia. Postcards sometimes reached us, even from those who had been deported. Sympathizers in the Soviet missions to Paris and Berlin sent us messages and various texts. Our post from the Verkhne-Uralsk prison was particularly copious. It was written in almost microscopic script on pieces of paper the size of postage stamps ... But gradually these communications grew rarer. By 1931, they had almost completely stopped.

'It was by letter that we learnt about what had happened at the Politbureau meeting when Stalin proposed and forced through our deportation from the U.S.S.R. The General Secretary had justified Trotsky's banishment on the following grounds: "1. It is essential to disarm the Opposition. 2. Trotsky must later be discredited on the grounds that he has become a servant of the bourgeoisie. 3. The Social Democrats will make use of his writings and ... 4. We shall then be able to denounce his treason." Bukharin, Rykov and Tomsky voted against, the first protesting with tears in his eyes, but Stalin, Kalinin, Voroshilov, Rudzutak and Kaganovich had their way. Ivan Bakaev proposed that the Zinoviev group lodge a protest, but as Zinoviev himself pointed out sadly, there was no one left to protest to. He nevertheless consulted Nadezhda Krupskaya, who merely said, "No one will listen to us." Trotsky's banishment had clearly sealed the total collapse of morale inside the Bolshevik Party.

' ... Leon Sedov was walking in Constantinople one day, when somebody hooked a cane round his neck from behind, burst out laughing and hugged him. It was Yakov Blumkin, one of the Red Army's greatest soldiers and one of the most remarkable Soviet counter-espionage agents in the East. He had been a Social Revolutionary terrorist, had assassinated the German ambassador to Moscow, Count Mirbach, in 1918, and had later joined the Bolshevik Party. He was an adventurous and intelligent man, something of a poet, and had written several studies of the great French strategists. His work as a secret agent had prevented him from taking part in the political struggle in Russia, but he shared the views of the Opposition. He came to see us twice and told us that for security we would need some twenty reliable men on the island. He warned that attacks on us were being planned and offered to take letters to the few friends we still had in Moscow ... On his return to Russia he was betrayed by a woman, and condemned to death without a trial. He was granted a brief stay of execution to enable him to write his memoirs ... He died as bravely as he had lived.[1]'

v. *Trotsky advocates Soviet reform*

'The whole history of the political struggles in Russia, of the battle of ideas and of the increasingly bloody slide of the bureaucratic dictatorship towards totalitarianism is related in the eighty-seven editions of the *Opposition Bulletin*, published in 1929–40, first in Paris and then in New York, under the direction of Leon Davidovich and of Leon Sedov. We did not often succeed in smuggling copies into the U.S.S.R., but Soviet officials abroad read it and the Central Committee imported hundreds of copies in the first few years and then later dozens for its own use ... Through these channels, our ideas penetrated as far as the prisons.

'Official accusations to the contrary, the Opposition refused to form a second party to challenge the power of the bureaucrats; that sort of "second party" would have rallied all the malcontents and so have become an unconscious tool of reaction. As it was, reactionary pressure was constantly being exerted by the various Stalinist committees, but Leon Davidovich never lost hope of reforming the regime from within. "It is wrong to think that the Thermidor has come to stay in Russia," he wrote in 1928, "because the proletariat has not yet had its last say ... We must recapture the positions it

[1] On Blumkin, see Victor Serge, *Russia Twenty Years After*.

has lost ... A period of reaction may set in, not only after a bourgeois revolution, but also after a proletarian revolution ... " Rakovsky complained about the indifference of the masses, about the formation of a new privileged social class – the bureaucracy – and about their thirst for power, and went on to describe the present state, not as Lenin had done, as a "workers' state ... with bureaucratic distortions", but as a "bureaucratic state with working-class remains ... " The Opposition accordingly called for "Soviet reform" and a return to revolutionary methods. They believed that Soviet institutions could be gradually freed from the bureaucratic stranglehold by a return to the secret ballot, first of all within the Party, then in the trade unions and finally in the Soviets, thus ensuring that the leadership of all three was elected by a truly democratic poll.

'To achieve Soviet reform, the intransigent Marxists kept alive the traditions of Bolshevism and of Lenin, suffered persecution, set an example of steadfast and unflinching devotion and refused to make even the slightest concession of principle. The brutalities and crimes committed by the bureaucratic regime did not shake their loyalty to the Revolution or to its Party. The breach between them and such "capitulators" as Zinoviev, Kamenev and, later, Ivan Smirnov, Preobrazhensky, Radek and Smilga, was complete – all personal and political contacts were broken off. Leon Davidovich scoffed at Zinoviev's skin-deep leftism ("Each time a bit of muscle is needed, Zinoviev flinches"), and at the inveterate opportunism of Kamenev, the ideologist of conciliation. When people objected that he must surely have known what kind of people these former allies of his really were, he would answer, "We'd have made a pact with the devil himself to serve the proletariat."

'Even in prison Trotskyists and capitulators had no truck with one another, the former because of their contempt of the latter, and the latter for fear of compromising themselves by socializing with such stubborn enemies of the regime.'

Bitter controversy had begun to rage round the new thesis of 'building socialism in one country' which the Politbureau had elevated to the level of unassailable dogma. Professor Eugene Varga, a Hungarian and the Comintern's most servile economist, one day described it to Trotsky as 'a pious lie invented because the backward masses need it'. This pious lie, propagated with a false show of optimism, epitomized the bureaucrats' arrogant belief that they could attain peace and national self-sufficiency in a rapidly developing industrial world. Such self-sufficiency meant smothering the revolutionary spirit, was bound to lead to war, and was, in any case, an outright rejection of the great internationalist slogan, 'Workers of the world unite!' The underlying social philosophy was not only bureaucratic but infantile. The capitalist mode of production had firmly established itself throughout most of the world; it was based on a world market; how then could there be a new, socialist, mode of production that would be permanently confined within the frontiers of one country? And since the writings of Marx and Lenin, whom the bureaucrats liked to quote at such length, clearly refuted the whole idea, Marxist teaching had to be distorted and trivialized. Now that twenty years have passed, now that Stalin's dream of national self-sufficiency has vanished in the wake of a cruel war and now that the interdependence of industrial states is a fact no one can possibly deny, this particular issue has been settled once and for all. Today we know that no economic system, be it totalitarian or socialist, can exist in isolation, and that any claim to the contrary is a mere stratagem.

Needless to say, the theoretical controversy was, as always, bound up with immediate problems, the most pressing of which was whether or not the U.S.S.R. should work for the creation of socialist or semi-socialist governments in Central Europe, even if this involved considerable risks and sacrifices. The Opposition advocated militant internationalism; the official thesis opened the way to a policy of wait-and-see and to the dubious and disastrous compromises of which the Molotov–Ribbentrop pact of 1939 was merely the most glaring example.

The defeat of the Opposition was greeted with relief by the bourgeois world and by reformist socialists. Trotsky often quoted a remark by Sir Austen Chamberlain (reported in the New York *Nation*) to the effect that Britain and the Soviet Union could not establish regular relations until 'Trotsky has been put against the wall'. The Opposition was generally believed to consist of disruptive and hopelessly Utopian fanatics. Even socialists regarded Stalin as a more moderate and sensible political leader than Trotsky, and one less given to international adventures ... Bolshevism was running out of steam, and Germany was no longer in the grip of the 'Red Peril'. Nobody would see that the worst that could befall the world would be the consolidation of Stalin's despotic regime in Russia, and the defeat of socialism in Central Europe.

VI. *The mores of the Russian totalitarian regime. The Stalin School of Falsification. Thought control. Repression of Trotskyism*

There was an inexorable logic about the birth of Russian totalitarianism. The bureaucracy, over-privileged in the midst of general poverty, tolerated no criticism, and this precisely because socialism allows of no privileges. When denounced by the elite of the Old Party, the bureaucrats were unable to defend themselves except by imposing silence – they were too ignorant to do anything else. Demands for democracy had to be stifled at birth. The G.P.U. arrested no serving Party members, but the loss of the little red book, which amounted to expulsion from the Party, was similar to what in the Middle Ages was called 'handing heretics over to the secular arm'. An ex-Party member, picked up in the small hours, would spend some time in gaol – under passable conditions if he were influential enough and under unspeakable ones if he were a mere worker. A G.P.U. official would exhort him to recant, to submit to the Central Committee and then to denounce his more steadfast comrades. If he refused, he would be sent to Narym, Kansk, Ust-Syssolsk, Sol-Vychegodsk, to some settlement buried in the Arctic forests or the inhospitable desert sands. Soon afterwards they would come for his wife, lest she tell her workmates that her husband was being persecuted in secret for reading Lenin's Will.

The press was controlled more and more tightly to prevent any hint of this wave of secret persecutions. On rare occasions, when there was too much of a scandal or when the foreign press had already mentioned it, a *Pravda* editorial would welcome the arrest of a group of a hundred Trotskyists, and the readers would understand that these figures had to be doubled, tripled or even quintupled. The panic-stricken censors were terrified of missing some new heresy concealed under an umbrella of intellectual camouflage and redoubled their vigilance, so much so that they began to smell Trotskyist subversion in books on music, chess and dentistry. An article about the world economic crisis would set their heads spinning. Treasonable thoughts might sprout in every line but how could they be sure? Controlled as it was by Party secretaries, all thought became stultified, distorted, confused and constricted. The only certain way of remaining above suspicion was to regurgitate the official catch-phrases and to echo the insipid pronouncements of the Leader. Statistics were as threatening as hand grenades, and their votaries in no less a quandary than the economists.

Histories of the Revolution and Soviet novels are full of great figures who have since been declared outcasts – there was certainly no account of the Civil War that did not mention Trotsky by name. As a result, all historians bore the taint of heresy. Those studying the French Revolution, Robespierre, Thermidor, the English Revolution, Cromwell and the Levellers, or the tyrants of classical antiquity, were compromised from the outset and eventually in danger of their lives. Most of the young Communist historians had a tragic end; of the older ones, Evgeny Tarle was the only one to survive – thanks to an agile balancing act – but even he did not escape imprisonment in Leningrad, with the death sentence hanging over his head followed by a spell in Alma-Ata, all of which helped to convince him of the benefits of impeccable orthodoxy. By order of the Central Committee, the most colossal and barefaced campaign of 'correcting' history was begun. Memoirs were censored and expurgated; documents were concealed or destroyed, and encyclopedias re-written. Even the greatest living Russian writer, Maxim Gorky, was drawn into the campaign of falsification, and made to alter the page in his *Recollections of Lenin* that dealt with Trotsky: he cut out Lenin's praise of Trotsky and hinted instead that the older man had always distrusted the younger. This cavalier treatment of facts and documents, let alone of the readers and writers of this type of book, was repeated in countless millions of pages of print. People like Raskolnikov, Gusev and even Yaroslavsky – the official historian of Stalinism who, paradoxically enough, was later accused of 'unconscious Trotskyism' – as well as a host of others, wrote the exact opposite of everything they had written before. No history of the Revolution must breathe one good word about Trotsky, and the Bolshevik victory in the Civil War had to be attributed to Stalin, impeded by Trotsky's sabotage. Trotsky wrote a short, factual book on the subject. He called it *The Stalin School of Falsification*[2] which, needless to say, very few people in Russia had a chance to read. In it, he recalled that when he had warned Lenin to record certain decisions lest future historians misrepresent them, Lenin had replied, 'They'll never stop lying, whatever we do.'

The campaign to 'house-train' writers was pursued relentlessly. Voronsky, the Bolshevik critic and novelist, was flung into prison; Valerian Polonsky, the Bolshevik biographer of Bakunin, was being victimized but died of typhus before he could be arrested; the liberal

[2] Pioneer Publishers, New York, 1937.

novelist, Zamiatin, was persuaded to emigrate. The remarkable Soviet novelist, Boris Pilnyak, was repeatedly attacked by the press and subjected to dire threats, and though he drained the cup of humiliation and self-abasement time and again, he eventually 'disappeared', never to be heard of again – try as he would, he could not purge himself of the heinous crime of possessing too much talent. The poet Vladimir Pyast hanged himself in exile. This was merely the beginning of a long list of writers who figured in the vast book of martyrs. The young were dealt with even more harshly. A 'General Secretary of Proletarian Literature', Leopold Auerbach, who was related to Yagoda, the G.P.U. boss, ruled over the literary roost with considerable verbal flourish. (He was later shot at the same time as his powerful protector.) The writings of all those expelled from the Party were withdrawn from the libraries and frequently burnt. Stalin started his destruction of books long before the Nazis lit their bonfires, though he set about it much more discreetly.

A new and terrible psychological syndrome made its appearance in the Communist International both at home and abroad; it went by the name of *dvuruchnichestvo*, which may be roughly translated as 'double dealing'. The symptoms included having two faces, a private and a public one; two distinct sets of behaviour patterns, one to accord with one's unfortunate convictions and the other with the dictates from above. All those who were loath to be sent to the Arctic Circle, and to leave their families behind in wretched misery, spoke loudly in favour of the general line and passed votes of thanks to the Leader, couched in the most extravagant terms, regardless of what they were thinking and sometimes even murmuring in private. But it did them no good, for the authorities guessed what they were thinking and often heard what they were murmuring. Most of the old 'capitulators' remained under suspicion no matter how loudly they protested their new-found faith. To humiliate them even further, they were pressed to recant their errors in public, and to attack and betray their friends. They obliged, but since duplicity had become the general rule, the edge of their repeated recantations was blunted, especially as the recantations were sometimes rendered nugatory by the occasional cry of revolt. There was the case of an old revolutionary who had signed the Opposition *Platform*: he was hauled in front of the Control Commission in the middle of the night and recanted, but as soon as he returned home, he sent a moving message to his comrades begging them to forgive his cowardice and another to the Central Committee in which he once again declared his support of the subversive *Platform*. Later he retracted once again – and all this within the space of three days! It was common knowledge that at least four out of five Stalinists loathed Stalin personally, just as much as they hated and feared his policies; these men stood behind Bukharin, Rykov and Tomsky, the so-called 'right-wing deviationists'. Bukharin was still head of the Comintern and was still thought of as the theoretical master of Stalinism; Alexey Rykov was Lenin's successor as Chairman of the Council of People's Commissars, while Tomsky was the President of the Soviet Trade Union Congress. They were at the height of their powers and national popularity when, on the orders of the General Secretary, the press and the entire bureaucratic apparatus unleashed a campaign of vilification against them, muted at first but gradually becoming more violent.

VII. *Economic disaster in the U.S.S.R. The Right-wing Opposition (Bukharin, Rykov and Tomsky). Forced collectivization of agriculture, industrialization and terror*

The members of the Opposition had scarcely been expelled from the Party when their economic and political prophecies came true. In January 1928, *Pravda* published news of a grain crisis: there was trouble with the peasants who had been receiving worthless paper money in exchange for their produce. Supplies of food to the cities and the army were fast running out. It also became evident that the Trotskyists had been right to describe the proposed Five Year Plan as grossly inadequate, and that industrialization would have to be stepped up considerably. But these revelations only served to incense the Stalin–Bukharin Politbureau still further against their imprisoned opponents. The tiller was put hard over to the left and punitive measures against the grain-hoarding *kulaks* were promulgated – an obvious violation of the original Five Year Plan. When this happened, some five hundred members of the Opposition sent a conciliatory message to the Central Committee, signed among others by Rakovsky, Vladimir Kossior and Okuzhava. In August or September 1929, they expressed their support for the new line, adding a rider about the need for workers' democracy. Trotsky, too, expressed his approval, but complained that at the very time the Politbureau saw fit to adopt Opposition policies, repression was being continued. Stalin's response to these conciliatory moves was to execute Blumkin.

In its writings during 1926 and 1927 the Opposition had emphasized that the Politbureau included a strong right-wing faction that apparently turned a blind eye to the rise of a petit-bourgeoisie in the countryside and to the stagnation of socialized industry. This, they said, was tantamount to opening the way to capitalism, so much so that the right wing, led by Bukharin, Rykov and Tomsky, posed a greater threat to the future of the Revolution than the bureaucratic and opportunist centre led by Stalin. In this attack on the Right, the Opposition may well have gone too far, for, in retrospect, it is clear that the right-wing faction had preserved much more of the spirit of socialism than the Stalinist faction. Still, whenever Stalin, Rykov and Bukharin managed to shelve their disagreements to deal with some immediate danger, they would vie with one another to protest that 'the Central Committee had never been more united' or more 'monolithic'.

After July 1928, the dissensions within the Politbureau came into the open. The Right, which was more knowledgeable and, above all, more concerned with socialist problems than Stalin, argued correctly that the Soviet economy was approaching a very grave crisis and condemned the new measures against the peasantry.

Many suffered grave qualms of conscience, because by now all the promises and aims of the October Revolution had been betrayed. They called for a peaceful settlement in the rural areas, an end to 'accelerated' – that is, forced – industrialization, and a campaign to rescue the working class from the abject misery to which it had been reduced. In short, the Right, too, had at last begun to press for greater democracy. Unfortunately, although it seemed to have the masses behind it, it never dared to join openly in political battle with the Stalinists. Neither the persecution of its followers nor the humiliations that Stalin heaped upon it in the press and at Congresses stung it to action; the worm simply refused to turn. Perhaps it was too late in any case. The Bukharin faction had a majority in the Executive Committee of the Communist International, but when Palmiro Togliatti (Ercoli) of Italy betrayed them, they did nothing at all about it.

Perhaps it was its very feebleness that allowed the right-wing Opposition to survive for ten years, until the 1937 massacres. Perhaps, too, although it enjoyed the support of the mass of the people and even of a majority in the Party during 1932–4, it could not take up the fight without being crushed by the two forces which counted in the totalitarian state, the Party's administrative machine and the G.P.U.

Nikolai Bukharin, writer, economist, orator, 'Lenin's favourite', the darling of students and author of *The A.B.C. of Communism* and of the less well-known but perhaps more important *Precis of Dialectical Materialism*, was unquestionably the finest and most determined brain on the Right. Stalin, who relied on him, once said to him, 'You and I, we are like the Himalayas.' Bukharin was, however, very emotional, easily moved to laughter and tears, and what ambition he had was purely intellectual. As he weighed up the dangers to the country and the Revolution, and put together his intimate knowledge of the General Secretary and his sound assessments of the other Party leaders, he was terrified by what he saw. Before their arrest, the 'Moscow Opposition' had been able to get hold of transcripts of several conversations between Bukharin and Kamenev, which they published as a leaflet. In July 1928, the right wing of the Politbureau had apparently been anxious to enlist the support of the Zinoviev–Kamenev faction in an effort to topple Stalin. 'Yagoda is with us,' Bukharin had declared, 'and so are Kalinin and Voroshilov, though Stalin has some stranglehold over them ... If we make a public stand, he will accuse us of engineering a split and will finish us off; if we do not take a stand, he will scheme to finish us off anyway and blame us for the grain shortage as well ... If the country is destroyed, we shall go under with it, and if it escapes destruction, Stalin will play one of his tricks and we shall go under all the same. He is the new Ghengis Khan of the Central Committee ... The Party and the State have become as one, that's the real root of the trouble ... Stalin is interested in nothing but power ... He has only one method and that is vengeance ... the dagger in the back ... The Politbureau has become the scene of savage violence ... Stalin is leading the country to the abyss ... into civil war ... He will have to drown the [peasant] uprisings in blood ... That "swine Molotov", nicknamed "Stonebottom", supports him blindly.'

Kamenev remarked later that Bukharin, as he said all this, and more, had the desperate air of a man at bay. Bukharin confessed that he, the leader of the Right, had himself drafted the Central Committee resolution on the culpability of the Right. What was to be done? He prepared a draft for a new *Platform*, which he subsequently published.

At another secret meeting held late in 1928, Pyatakov, Zinoviev,

Sokolnikov and Lenin's widow expressed their distress at the latest turn of events. Ordjonikidze, the chairman of the Central Control Commission, later interrogated all of them in his official capacity, though in private he had given them to understand that he was sympathetic to their views and was himself undergoing a crisis of conscience. According to more recent reports, Ordjonikidze eventually broke with Stalin, and died in a clinic under close G.P.U. surveillance (February 1937).

It is extremely difficult to compress a very complex series of events into a few brief pages. At the end of 1928, the Government re-introduced bread rationing in the cities. In the country the policy of ruthless grain requisitioning had met with fierce, sometimes bloody, resistance. The Politbureau, which was divided within itself, could see no other solution to the peasants' policy of non-cooperation than the forced transfer of all agricultural land to agricultural co-operatives, or *kolkhozes*, under direct Party control. As a result the peasants were robbed not merely of the fruits of their labour but also of all their initiative. Agricultural co-operatives produce no benefits unless they are equipped with modern machinery and unless the peasants gain some tangible advantage. But there was no machinery for them to have, and the peasants put up an extremely fierce struggle: there were hundreds of local revolts, and full-scale uprisings occurred in Uzbekistan and the Caucasus, with hundreds of casualties. This was 'the peasants' enthusiastic reception of collectivization', extolled by *Pravda* and such fellow travellers as Henri Barbusse. Sooner than deliver their livestock up to the *kolkhozes*, the *muzhiks* chose mass-scale slaughter of their beasts, and kept this up over a period of several years. In 1928, the U.S.S.R. had a livestock population (according to official statistics) greater than it had been in 1913, and amounting to 35·5 million horses, 70·5 million head of cattle, 146·7 million sheep and goats, and 26 million pigs; by 1934, after five years of Stalinist collectivization, the figures were down to a disastrous 15·7 million horses, 42·4 million head of cattle, 51·9 million sheep and goats, and 20·4 million pigs. The Government announced that it would replace horses with tractors though the required factories had not yet been built. For the first time, the most remote agricultural hamlets as well as the cities were in the grip of famine – there was an acute shortage of grain, fats, meat, hides and skins, milk, sugar and flax. Stalin's answer was the 'annihilation of the *kulak* class' – any peasant who resisted or disobeyed his sagacious directives was immediately labelled a *kulak*, deprived of his modest possessions and deported with his family to the icy forests of the north. Never before had a civilized country expelled so many of its own citizens in so cruel a manner. By 1931, when the terror was still in full swing, foreign observers in Moscow estimated that four to five million peasants had been selected for the 'special colonization' of remote wastes. Figures throw a cold light on these atrocious events. In 1929, there were 25·8 million peasant families each with four or five members; by 1936, 20·6 million were left. In seven years, 5,200,000 families, or some 25 million people, had vanished. (These figures, too, are culled from the official statistics.) The overpopulated and strictly supervised cities could certainly not have absorbed more than a small proportion of the migrants. Things had come to such a pass that, on March 20th, 1930, Stalin was forced to sound the retreat. He did so in an article bearing the cynical title, 'On Dizziness from Success'. Collectivization was to be confined to sixty-eight per cent of all peasant holdings, and the anti-religious campaign was to be called off, since, as he declared with all the authority of the Kremlin, the destruction of churches was not a Marxist act.

The first Five-year Plan for industry, which was revised several times, demanded tremendous sacrifices during a period of famine, chaos and terror. In 1928, as we have said earlier, real wages, including social insurance benefits, were above the 1913 level and the ten-hour working day had been cut to eight. Real industrial wages had risen by 4·6 per cent from 1913 to 1928; by 1934 they had dropped 30 per cent below the 1913 level. In 1935, they began to rise slightly but remained 15 per cent below the 1913 and 20 per cent below the 1928 levels until World War II. Inducing people to work under such conditions was not easy. Terror became the only spur and the concentration camps filled and expanded to cover entire regions: the White Sea area, Karaganda and the northern Yenisey. From 1928 right up to 1939 the crescendo of terror never once abated. Together or in turn, Trotskyists, *kulaks*, the old bourgeoisie, believers, technicians, 'intractable and profiteering' workers, *shkurniki* (self-seekers), right-wing Communists and Party officials judged to be either too timid or too zealous, were hunted down en masse. As a result, the whole nation became brutalized.

In 1930, forty-eight specialists in the meat supply industry were shot, including Professor Karatygin. On August 7th, 1932, came a fresh decree to protect the 'sanctity of collective property': any peasant withholding grain from his *kolkhoz* would incur the death penalty. At the end of 1932, as starving workers were fleeing from the factories and as waves of migrants spread out all over the U.S.S.R., internal passports were introduced for the first time. From then on, the urban population was strictly controlled by the police and by the secretaries of housing committees. Draconian legislation bound each worker to his place of work and severe punishments began to be meted out for 'unjustified' absences and lateness. In March 1933, thirty-five Communist leaders and agricultural specialists were shot because the agricultural policy pursued in the Ukraine had turned out to be an unprecedented disaster. But as everyone knew, and as Opposition members in prisons throughout the country said openly, the real culprits were Stalin and his coterie. In order to clear his name, Stalin invented acts of sabotage, espionage and foreign intrigues; the G.P.U. found suitable victims among those farmers, technologists, administrators and Party leaders who had indulged in aggrieved outbursts, proved their guilt and then shot them without trial in the G.P.U. cellars.

The great public trials, which were mounted after careful preparation and rehearsal, served the same purpose and were intended for mass consumption at home and abroad. When production fell disastrously in the coal mines of the Donets basin, fifty engineers were arraigned in the so-called 'Shakhty trials' and made to confess acts of sabotage – five of them were executed. In July 1928, another batch, this time of only four people, was shot, but the terror had only just begun, and it was, of course, much more convenient to shoot people without trial. In 1930, the trial of engineers accused of being members of the 'Industrial Party' ended with seven death sentences, but nobody knows what happened to the two thousand 'associates and accomplices' mentioned in the official files. Engineer Ramzin and his co-defendants had pleaded guilty both to sabotage and to conspiring with Poincaré and Briand to plan a war against the U.S.S.R. Ramzin himself, who repented and appears to have been an over-zealous *agent provocateur*, was later rehabilitated and decorated for his contribution to the successful industrialization campaign. Let those who can, make sense of all this.

A trial of economists and Mensheviks followed in 1930. Those in the dock included the historian Nikolai Sukhanov, author of one of the most important works on the February Revolution, and the economists Gorman and Ginzburg, who were members of the Planning Commission. Their true crime was that they had sent the Politbureau repeated criticisms of its economic policy and warnings about the consequences. They were accused of conspiring with the Second International in an attempt to make war on the U.S.S.R. The Menshevik leader, R. Abramovich, was said to have visited Moscow in secret – at the very time that he was in Germany being photographed with a large number of other socialists from all over the world. The accused at this trial were not sentenced to death; they disappeared instead into the 'isolators' and were never seen again. In the Verkhne-Uralsk prison, Sukhanov told members of the Opposition about the bargain he had made with the G.P.U.; when they failed to keep their promise to release him, he went on a long hunger strike and was eventually taken to an unknown destination (1933–4). Ryazanov, the historian of Marxism and founder-director of the Marx–Engels Institute, and one of the oldest veterans of the Russian Socialist Movement, died in exile after having been deported for protesting to Stalin about this faked trial.

In 1932, the blackest year of the famine and the Stakhanovite treadmill, a host of tiny opposition groups sprang up within the now Stalinized party. Syrtsov, the Chairman of the Council of People's Commissars in the Russian Socialist Federal Soviet Republic (R.S.F.S.R.), disappeared under mysterious circumstances – it was rumoured that he had dared to criticize the forced collectivization of land. Two old Bolsheviks in senior posts, Vladimir Tolmachev and Nikolai Eysmont, members of the Regional Committee for the Northern Caucasus and Ministers in the R.S.F.S.R. Government, expressed their indignation about what was happening in Kuban; both disappeared and so did many of their associates. The former Secretary of the Moscow Committee, Ryutin, and some of his friends published a political manifesto denouncing tyranny, economic blunders and the incredibly wretched state of the workers. After expressing his astonishment that the General Secretary should have reduced the Revolution to its present parlous state by his inhumanity and incompetence, he went on to compare him to the *agent provocateur*, Azev, and concluded by paying homage to the resolution and foresight of Trotsky. The G.P.U. condemned Ryutin to death in secret but, for the time being at least, he was not executed.

All these dissenters had until recently toed the official line. In addition, there were 'the young Stalinists' (Lominadze and Jan Sten), whom Stalin had regarded as his special disciples before they finally turned against him. At the beginning of 1935, the Ukrainian Communists also came under attack. Skrypnik, who had distinguished himself by his bitter hostility to Trotsky, reacted by taking his life, while Shumsky and a number of others were sent to concentration camps.

Zinoviev and Kamenev were expelled from the Party once again and, at the end of 1932, deported for the crime of having knowledge of Ryutin's document without reporting him to the G.P.U. They abased themselves once more, offered humble apologies and applied for reinstatement.

All these developments are worth bearing in mind in detail, if only because they throw light on their sequels in the blood-stained future.

VIII. *Trotsky's writings and their influence. Trotsky opposes 'Stalinist industrialization'*

The political struggle continued. Trotsky's writings had a considerable influence, despite the fact that few of the imprisoned Oppositionists had the chance of seeing them in print. However, most senior officials and members of Soviet missions abroad made a point of reading the *Bulletin*, memorized its contents and some even carried its message back to Russia word for word. Since many were sent to prison for their trouble, the 'Trotskyist' cadres in the 'isolators' were able to discuss the points raised at some length and some of their deliberations were even carried back to Turkey. Senior officials, People's Commissars and members of the Central Committee read the *Bulletin* avidly, because savage reality was increasingly confirming the exile's most ominous prophecies. As a result, Trotsky was able to extend his influence even to the ruling circles of the U.S.S.R. During the first year of his exile, the official press continued to quote him from time to time if only to refute him, but as the ten lines from Trotsky, which were surrounded by three hundred lines of abusive commentary, were the only ones that mattered to a large number of readers, the newspapers were eventually instructed to cease quoting him altogether.

Outside Russia, Opposition groups on the fringes of the Communist Parties grew stronger and multiplied; their critiques, reports, prophecies and revelations proved a source of great anxiety to the orthodox. Trotskyist publications appeared in the United States, France, Germany, Austria, Argentina and China, and there were Trotskyist groups in almost every country. This growing international movement was persecuted by reactionary regimes as well as by the Stalinists (who beat a number of Trotskyists senseless in a prison in Bulgaria). The Opposition groups were often divided amongst themselves on ideological grounds, but intellectually and morally they stood head and shoulders above their Stalinist adversaries. And although he was always short of money, Trotsky helped the movement whenever and wherever he could.

In his many published works Trotsky dealt mainly with two parallel series of problems: the Soviet economy and Stalin's regime, and the international policies of the Russian Revolution and of the Comintern. Here we can do no more than adumbrate his ideas on these two subjects.

From about 1929 the bourgeois and socialist press in Europe and America had argued consistently that by collectivizing agriculture and forcing the pace of industrialization, Stalin was simply implementing Trotsky's ideas. This argument contained a grain of truth, but no more, for circumstances had indeed forced a reluctant Stalin to follow the path the Opposition had mapped out.

But when he eventually did so, he resorted to absurd, senseless, and criminally hasty methods. The best way of torpedoing an idea is to have it implemented by its enemies. The democratization of the Party and the trade unions, a basic demand of the Opposition, was totally incompatible with Stalin's rigidly totalitarian system of government. His own economic policy and the terrorization of the workers was so harsh and oppressive as to border on insanity. Its brutal excesses were perhaps its worst feature. Where the Opposition had merely called for such fiscal measures against the *kulaks* as would encourage the development of smallholdings and of agricultural cooperatives, Stalin preferred to dispossess and deport millions of peasant families; where the Opposition had called for a Five Year Plan as a rational means of improving the workers' lot by steady industrialization, Stalin preferred the confused, even chaotic programme of forced industrialization. This programme, based on the hasty and constantly revised plans of terrorized experts, led to a precipitous drop in real wages. In 1931–4 real wages were down to at least half the 1927 and 1913 levels, with consequent famine in the industrial regions. All this could have been avoided and was the direct consequence of the regime's mistakes, ill-conceived improvisations and crimes.

In March 1930, Trotsky declared that the Plan was not matched to the country's resources, that the natural interdependence of agriculture and industry was being ignored, and that it was madness to attempt the construction of a 'national socialist' society in so great a hurry. He called for an end to the senseless 'adventurism', an end to the dispossession and deportation of the *kulaks* and to 'galloping' industrialization; he insisted that the condition of the working classes must be radically improved, and that heed must be paid to the quality as well as the quantity of industrial products; that inflation must be checked, honest statistics reintroduced and closer collaboration with the world market restored (message to the Central Committee dated March 20th, 1930). Stalin, by choosing that very same day to order the immediate cessation of forced collectivization, seemed to be heeding his adversary's advice to the letter, so much so that ruling circles in Moscow began to ask themselves, only half in jest, when Trotsky would pass on his next directive. Even so there was a strict ban on any references to the raging inflation – admitting its existence was tantamount to saying that it was in the nature of things for money to lose its value in a socialist society.

Trotsky did not paint everything in sombre colours, black though the general picture was. He was careful not to point out to what great extent Stalin's gross economic and political errors had sapped the strength of the U.S.S.R., and even acknowledged that the industrialization campaign had, in part, been successful – though it had needed administrator-policemen to spur on an exhausted proletariat, new industries were, in fact, springing up. He remained convinced, however, that genuine socialist methods would enable the country to do much better, cut costs and help to turn the U.S.S.R. into a shining example of socialist achievement instead of, as it was now to anyone who knew the truth, a frightful object lesson in the dangers of socialism. No wonder that when Joaquin Maurin recommended the Soviet method of industrialization for Spain, but failed to mention its drawbacks, Trotsky reacted with indignation.

The international slump which had started with the Wall Street crash the year before, had meanwhile thrown millions out of work in the industrial West. Trotsky realized that unemployment would seriously weaken the working class, especially in Western Europe. The only remedy was a new plan made 'on genuine Marxist foundations and not on the specious theory of a single socialist state'. The U.S.S.R. could give a lead in reducing world unemployment, by importing machines and agricultural equipment on a massive scale, particularly from Germany and Great Britain with whom a barter arrangement could be arrived at. To that end, it was essential to draw up a plan that was intelligible and acceptable, even if only in part, to both the Russian workers and their comrades abroad. The reformist socialist governments under Ramsay Macdonald in Britain and under Hermann Müller in Germany were 'more likely to make common cause with the U.S.S.R. in a struggle against unemployment at home than against imperialism abroad'. In any case, the growing crisis would force them to do so. Unfortunately, Trotsky's appeal, made on March 14th, 1930, fell on deaf ears in Moscow.

IX. *The Nazis in power. Trotsky attacks the 'Stalinist Comintern'*

In 1929, having been duly briefed by Stalin and Molotov, the Communist International called for the 'radicalization' of the masses and a more determined revolutionary approach. In so doing, they hoped to silence left-wing critics of 'socialism in one country' but, in fact, grossly misjudged the political climate of the crisis-torn West. This was the so-called Third Period theory, which Trotsky called a 'third period of errors'. When Molotov told the Tenth Plenary Session of the Comintern Executive, 'We have stepped with both feet into a period of tremendous revolutionary events of international significance', Trotsky called it 'a flat-footed argument'. Again, when the official *Bolshevik* spoke of a 'tide of revolutionary fervour in Germany, France and Poland', when Molotov predicted that the Communist Party would seize power in France, when Jacques Doriot, a member of the French Politbureau, said that the French peasants – of all people – would soon take over the land 'at gun-point', Trotsky attacked their lamentable demagogy at length. Such fantasies were all the more dangerous because they were an excuse for Molotov to declare that all overtures to the reformist socialists were out of the question. Soon afterwards, the Stalinists began to refer to Social Democrats as 'social fascists' and to argue loudly that the only way of crushing Hitler was to destroy the moderate socialists first.

The German tragedy had begun. In the country with the strongest and best organized workers' movement, where socialism was most deeply rooted in the minds of millions, the Nazis had started their ugly march to power amidst the threatening collapse of capitalism, and with the blatant support of high finance and heavy industry. The fact that famine and terror seemed to have become a permanent feature of Russian life had caused the German petit-bourgeoisie and a large section of the working class to turn away from socialism. In this sense, Stalinism may be said to have given indirect encouragement to the rise of Hitler; worse still, the Comintern played the enemy's game more directly. It was on this point that Trotsky spoke out with unprecedented bitterness, the more so as the Soviet press refused adamantly to recognize the dangers and continued to publish news of encouraging 'victories' by the German Communist Party, and the Comintern Executive ordered Thaelmann to adopt a bizarre and suicidal strategy. Thaelmann had become leader of the German Communist Party for the simple reason that he was an obedient tool; himself under a cloud of scandal, he was just another example of the bureaucratic corruption of the 'apparatus'. In November 1930 Trotsky called upon the entire German working class – Communists, Social Democrats and trade unionists of all hues – to make common cause against Hitler. In September of that year, the Nazis had collected six million votes. During the summer, they had called for a referendum, by which they had hoped to overthrow the Social Democratic Government of Prussia under Otto Braun; on that occasion Thaelmann, duly instructed by Stalin, had ordered the Communists to vote with the Nazis! Trotsky pointed out that in its pamphlets the German Communist Party had tried to show that, taken all in all, there was no great difference between the Nazis and the 'social fascists', the Social Democrats. This was a flagrant aberration, an invitation to disaster. What the Party should do instead, Trotsky wrote, was to issue a clear warning: 'Communists fighting shoulder to shoulder with Social Democrats, Christian and unaffiliated workers will defend each and every worker's home from the Nazi menace.' (September 1931)

If that were done, Hitler could not hope to rise to power by democratic means, but would have to resort to force. It was against this eventuality that Social Democrats and Communists must combine forces; for the rest, the Communist Party must be careful to guard its political independence: 'No agreement except for the common fight.' (December 8th, 1931) 'The left-wing Opposition is ready to place itself completely at the disposal of the Communist International for the most humble, the most difficult and the most dangerous tasks ... provided only it is allowed to uphold its ideas ... ' (June 16th, 1932)

'The key to the international situation is found in Germany,' Trotsky wrote in December 1931. 'The climax is coming: the pre-revolutionary situation will turn into revolution or counter-revolution... The destiny of Europe and of the entire world, for many years to come, will hinge on its outcome ... The leadership of the German Communist Party is carrying the proletariat to disaster ... to capitulation before fascism ... The victory of German fascism will inevitably drag the U.S.S.R. into a war ... Hitler must be opposed without mercy by armed resistance ... The strength of Nazism lies in the division of the working class ... We must unite the working class.'

But when the Communists collaborated with the Nazis once again, this time in the so-called 'Red Referendum', Stalin justified their action when addressing a meeting of Party officials in Moscow. Moreover, the Stalin-Molotov Politbureau, deaf to exhortations and blind to the facts, proceeded to instruct German Communists to support the Berlin transport strike called by the Nazis in November 1932.

'Under the knout of the Stalinist clique,' Trotsky wrote, 'the terrorized and disorientated Central Committee of the German Communist Party ... is delivering the working class up to Hitler and crucifixion ... ' The entire Comintern press called Trotsky the 'henchman of the social fascists.'

Their vicious attacks on the 'social fascists', that is, the Social Democrats, who, they claimed, had to be crushed before the Nazis could be ousted, and their continued accommodations with Hitler whose gangs never ceased murdering Communist workers - all these insensate and criminal distortions of ideas and facts were the seeds of the harvest reaped during the last series of free elections held under the Weimar Republic, when millions of unemployed voted first for the Communist Party and then switched to Hitler. Those who try to dupe the starving and confused masses do so at their peril.

By the beginning of 1933, the die had been cast. Hitler had seized power, Thaelmann was in prison (never to emerge again), German Communists and militant workers were being tracked down. But so deluded were the Comintern that *Rundschau*, their official organ, saw fit to declare, in April 1933, that there was no cause for concern. 'The revolutionary tide will continue to rise ineluctably ... The Fascist dictatorship, in destroying all democratic illusions, is ridding the masses of noxious social democratic influences and hence accelerating Germany's march towards proletarian revolution ... Only fools will say that the German Communists have been defeated ... ' The Stalinist hack who penned these incredible sentiments on orders from above, one Heckert, was shot by Stalin several years later.

Trotsky summed up the situation. 'The most powerful working class in Europe, whose strength derives from its industrial output, its social importance and its organizations, has offered no resistance to Hitler's march to power ... This is a fact that must dominate all our future strategies.' But this very fact produced such panic in the Kremlin that the announcement of yet another about-turn – a Comintern call for a united front with the Social Democrats – came when it was far too late, and was first published in *L'Humanité* so that it could be date-lined Paris instead of Moscow. Trotsky took note of this piece of cowardice, but added the hope that the lesson would not be lost on Austria, which was now bearing the brunt of the fascist assault. He called for working-class unity in every country on Germany's borders, and repeated that the U.S.S.R. would inevitably be drawn into a war. *Pravda* called him a warmonger.

x. *Visit to Copenhagen. Suicide of Trotsky's elder daughter Zina*

It would be impossible to give here even an abridged account of Trotsky's international activities; all we can hope to do is to set out some of the most salient features. In 1929, Trotsky advised members of the Chinese Opposition who consulted him to support a democratic Constituent Assembly. When the Spanish monarchy collapsed in 1931, he advised the Politbureau (on April 24th) to recognize the weakness of the Communist Party in Spain and to make common cause with all revolutionary forces in that country. The alternative would be 'the inevitable defeat of the Spanish Revolution which would lead inexorably to the triumph of Mussolini-style fascism in that country. It is unnecessary to point to the possible consequences for Europe and the U.S.S.R. The growth of the Spanish Revolution, by contrast, at a time when the world (economic) crisis is far from over, would open up a vista of vast new opportunities.' The Politbureau did not bother to reply; all in all, it paid scant attention to what was happening in the Iberian Peninsula, and some of the pronouncements it did make on the subject were very strange.

On the other hand, Stalin was hypnotized by the danger in the

Far East, where he expected war from Japan. Here too, the disagreement between him and Trotsky was complete. Trotsky, who was often interviewed by the American press, said that the U.S.S.R. had little cause to be nervous on that score. Japan's aim was the colonization of China, he told journalists, and even that was more than she could accomplish at present. The key to the world situation was not in Mukden but in Berlin, and Trotsky had no doubt that Berlin was preparing a world-wide conflagration. On February 25th, 1932, he declared, in an interview with United Press, that the United States would be increasingly affected by the political and economic crises, wars and revolutions that were about to sweep the entire world; America would develop the most powerful military system imaginable on land, sea and in the air. The U.S.S.R. would adopt American technological methods, and Europe would turn Communist or collapse into barbarism. (United Press, February 25th, 1932.) The outcome of the next war would be decided by technical superiority, he added in an interview with the *Chicago Daily News* published on April 23rd, 1932.

On February 20th, 1932 the Politbureau announced that Trotsky and those members of his family who were abroad had been stripped of their Soviet citizenship. Trotsky replied from Turkey in an *Open Letter to the Central Committee*, the body officially responsible for this decision. A few lines from this letter deserve to be quoted here because they contain his own considered view of Stalin and a reminder of Lenin's: 'You know Stalin as well as I do ... His strength never lay in his own personality; it lay in the Party machine. Alternatively, it lay in him to the extent that he was the most perfect embodiment of bureaucratic automatism ... It is essential to trust the working class and to give the proletarian vanguard an opportunity of reforming, by open criticism, the entire Soviet system from top to bottom so as to cleanse it of all its accumulated filth. Finally, we must remember Lenin's last and insistent recommendation: Remove Stalin!' (March 1st, 1932.)

The *Open Letter* circulated among the Soviet leaders just as a Party crisis was coming to a head. The general situation was indescribable. The countryside was devastated; the cities were starving; industry was in a turmoil; the workers were exhausted and desperate; trouble was brewing in Central Asia and the Caucasus; trains were crowded with deportees; the cemeteries in the northern forests were crammed with little white crosses; hundreds of thousands of 'special colonists' and others condemned to forced labour by the G.P.U. were digging canals and building new factories. Increasingly, Party officials in Moscow and elsewhere were wondering, sometimes almost aloud, whether this monstrous betrayal of the Revolution could have happened by pure chance.

'On October 14th, 1932, we were at last able to leave Constantinople and pay a short visit to Copenhagen. Leon Davidovich had been asked to read a paper to a learned society there and we were quickly issued with visas. With us travelled our young comrades, Otto Schüssler (from Germany), J. Fraenckl (from Czechoslovakia) and Pierre Frank (from France). When the steamer docked at Athens, Leon Davidovich was cheered, greatly to our surprise. At Naples, we were allowed to disembark and to visit the ruins of Pompeii. At Marseilles, the police took quite extraordinary precautions. A motor launch came alongside and took us further down the coast. A plain-clothes detective travelled in our car, first as far as Lyons, and then on to Paris, and the press had no idea of where we were.

'After a day in Paris, we boarded a ship at Dunkirk, where we were so closely guarded that the police did not even allow the secretary of the stevedores' union to approach us. In Denmark small groups of Stalinists were waiting at all the stations on our route but they only managed a few shouts and cat-calls. Leon Davidovich addressed an audience of some 2,500 at the Copenhagen Stadium on the October Revolution. He spoke in German, and ended with a defence of socialism, "which represents a leap from the rule of necessity to the rule of freedom in the sense that it sets contemporary man, torn as he is by contradictions, on the road to a happier existence ... A man of genius, Sigmund Freud, has discovered the wells of what is poetically described as the human soul ... Our conscious thought is but a tiny fragment of the work of hidden psychic forces ... For the first time in history, man has begun to consider himself ... the product of semi-physical and semi-psychic processes ..." The Danish Government refused to have this lecture broadcast over the radio on the grounds that the King and Court objected.

'Our visa was for eight days only and we heard that the King was opposed to any extension. Some twenty political friends, all of them well known and holders of valid passports, had come to talk to Trotsky. This so-called clandestine conference, which was neither secret nor formal, aroused the anger of reactionaries and Stalinists alike. We were staying in a villa that belonged to a *danseuse* and was furnished in a most peculiar style. No one could enter or leave it without being observed ... Stauning's Social Democratic Government insisted on our leaving the country the very day our visa expired. As there was no boat, we had to pretend that we had left and spend the next 24 hours travelling about by car. Leon Davidovich had applied for a Swedish visa, and had heard from socialists in Stockholm that Sweden was perfectly willing to allow him to enter the country, but that the Soviet ambassador, Alexandra Kollontai, had raised insurmountable objections ... Our son, Leon Sedov, who was living in Berlin at the time, was refused permission to join us during our stay in Denmark, but we spoke to him on the telephone daily.

'We had expected to spend some time in France on our way back, but the French authorities demurred. We travelled through France by car accompanied by some friends. The Italian government allowed us to board a ship at Genoa, but when we got there Mussolini's police were in such a hurry to get rid of us that they tried to make us travel on a cargo boat. We refused. We had travelled about incognito, but all our comings and goings were nervously and fussily – although courteously – supervised by members of the various police forces. Leon Davidovich used my name and travelled as Mr Sedov. On the boat, as we passed through Greek waters, past Corinth, we suddenly saw a demonstration on the shore and heard cries of 'Long live Trotsky!' The passengers looked at each other in amazement; Mr Sedov's identity had been exposed, but we met with nothing but sympathy. All the same we kept mostly to our cabin ...

'We spent the last few months of 1932 in an uneasy atmosphere, within sight of the Bosphorus. An accidental fire had completely destroyed Leon Davidovich's library and the whole of our collection of photographs of the Revolution. Fortunately the archives were saved. The number of postcards from Russia dwindled rapidly, though we kept hearing, indirectly, of the grave internal crisis and the savagery of Stalin's reprisals against our friends and comrades. As soon as someone had served his term of imprisonment or banishment, the G.P.U. simply extended it, sometimes for another term of three or five years. In the "isolators", hunger strikes and violence continued all the time without the outside world hearing anything about it ...

'All in all, some seven thousand members of the left-wing Opposition had been imprisoned or deported and as the arrests of Trotskyists continued, the right-wing Opposition, too, began to join them on the roads to the Arctic, to Narym and to Kazakhstan ... It was enough for a working woman just to mention the ludicrous wages she was being paid for her to be dubbed a "Trotskyist" or "Rightist", to be flung into one of the unbelievably overcrowded prisons, to be starved, and finally to be sent to labour in the frozen Arctic forests. The last remnant of our friends in the left-wing Opposition (Bolshevik–Leninists) was ranged round Rakovsky, aged fifty-nine and now almost completely isolated; round Sosnovsky, treated more harshly than those under sentence of death in the Tomsk gaol in the days of the old regime; and round Muralov, who had been deported to the Tara region. Kamenev and Zinoviev, despite their countless recantations, had just been deported once again following the arrest of the Ryutin group [see p. 179]. Zinoviev was quoted as saying, "Our greatest error was to have abandoned the Opposition in 1927 ... " It was certainly rather late in the day to realize that. By the end of 1932, the process of exacting whole-hearted or half-hearted recantations had come to an end. Instead, the G.P.U. now made surprise nocturnal raids in the streets, on offices and on homes, and arrested all those old revolutionaries who had once belonged to the Opposition but had since humbled themselves before Stalin. We learned that this had happened to Smilga, Preobrazhensky, Mrachkovsky, Olga Ravich, Ter-Vaganian, the editor of *Under the Sign of Marxism*, and to Ivan Smirnov ... Repression had been intensified at the very moment that Hitler seized power in Germany.

'On January 5th, 1933, Leon Davidovich's elder daughter, Zina Volkova, who had just celebrated her thirtieth birthday, locked herself in her Berlin room and turned on the gas-taps ... She had had tuberculosis and had been given permission by the Soviet government to go to Germany for treatment.

'With a double pneumothorax and at times severely neurotic, Zina had watched the brownshirts taking over the streets; she had heard about the Moscow arrests, and had been left completely without news of her husband, Platon Volkov, a young working-class intellectual lingering in prison. She was incapable of adapting herself to life in the West, and the loss of her Soviet citizenship had proved the last straw ...

'Leon Sedov, who was also in Germany, was in danger of falling into Nazi hands. When he had been refused a Danish visa, I sent a successful appeal to M. Herriot asking for leave to see our son when we crossed France at the beginning of December 1932. We met him in Marseilles. This is perhaps the place to tell of his meetings with two old Bolsheviks in Berlin. In July 1931, while doing his shopping in the Kadewe department store on the Wittembergplatz, Leon Sedov suddenly found himself face to face with Ivan Nikitich Smirnov, of whom he had been very fond ever since childhood. Smirnov had made the obligatory obeisances to Stalin after being deported. He believed that political struggle against the Moscow regime had become impossible and that the only useful part old revolutionaries could now play was to help in the industrialization programme. The growth of production and consequent strengthening of the working class might perhaps save Russian socialism yet ... He had been put in charge of the new motor industry in Nizhny-Novgorod, and though Leon Davidovich severely condemned his abject surrender, Smirnov and Leon Sedov met once or twice more. Smirnov continued to defend his stand, but spoke freely about the parlous state of the U.S.S.R. He promised to supply Leon Sedov with statistics "so that the facts might be made clearer abroad". For over a year we had no further news of him. During the autumn of 1932, Golzman, another industrial leader, arrived in Berlin with a message from Smirnov for Leon Sedov. Golzman was sympathetic to the Opposition but took no active part in political life; he was an educated, honest, moderate and liberal Bolshevik. The economic data he brought along were published in No. 31 of the *Opposition Bulletin*; they contained no secrets of any kind. He himself read our publications very thoroughly because he wanted to communicate their gist to a few interested people in Moscow. But by then every known militant in Moscow was surrounded by spies, and the fleeting contacts between these two old Bolsheviks and ourselves became known to the G.P.U. It seems that Golzman was the first to be arrested, in great secrecy; Smirnov's arrest followed on January 1st, 1933, and he was sentenced to ten years' imprisonment without trial ... '

XI. *Anxious days in France. Trotsky expelled from France in 1934*

'In 1933, the Daladier Government granted us asylum in France. The first moves in that direction had been made by Leon Davidovich's translator, Maurice Hoertel (Parijanine). We arrived in Marseilles on July 24th, 1933, accompanied by our American friends, Sara Weber and Max Schachtman, as well as by two young secretaries, Jan van Heijenoort and Rudolf Klement.

'Both the reactionary press and *L'Humanité* protested furiously against Daladier's generous gesture. According to Jacques Doriot and other French Communist leaders, M. Daladier, a "radical fascist", wanted nothing so much as war against the Soviet Union, and his admission of Trotsky to France proved this better than anything else could have done. Because demonstrations in Marseilles were threatened, we left our ship at Cassis and were transferred to a launch, in which Leon Sedov, Raymond Molinier and a police commissar were waiting for us. From Cassis, we went by car, still accompanied by our three French friends and a police official, to Saint-Palais, near Royan.

'At Saint-Palais, the Moliniers had rented a villa for us. It was right by the sea, and its name, Les Embruns, [Sea Spray], suited it very well. On our very first day there, when we had only just arrived, it caught fire, entirely by accident. We had to take shelter in a car in the road while the fire was put out. We stayed, incognito, at Saint-Palais for about two months and our presence was only known to the Minister of the Interior, the Prefect of the Charente-Maritime Department and a fairly small number of friends. Leon Davidovich received some fifty guests, including André Malraux; the Dutch parliamentarian Sneevliet; Parijanine; one of the leaders of the British Independent Labour Party and several German refugees ... Then he fell ill and we moved to Bagnères-de-Bigorre in the Hautes-Pyrénées, where we lived in almost complete solitude for two weeks.

'The *Sûreté* had no objections to Trotsky's moving to Barbizon, which was near Paris, provided he remained strictly incognito. He shaved off his thick, grey goatee, so as to look like a middle-class French intellectual ... The local authorities were kept in complete ignorance of our identity. We spent more than three months in the calm of the Forest of Fontainebleau. Rudolf Klement used to bicycle to Paris to fetch our mail. One evening he was stopped on the road by a policeman because his lights were not working. Klement refused to give his address and was taken to the police-station ... Because we were constantly on the alert against attempts on the life of Leon Davidovich or any of our friends, we were extremely alarmed at Klement's disappearance. Next morning, another young comrade who had gone out to do the shopping failed to return. The police and the *gendarmerie* took up positions along the road and finally about a dozen of them called on us. The news of Trotsky's presence in Barbizon created a sensation and a crowd of curious onlookers collected in front of the villa. Inside the railings two guard dogs, made nervous by all the commotion, barked incessantly ... The newspapers announced the discovery of a hotbed of revolution in Barbizon; there was even talk of a secret printing press. Our peace had been shattered and, at the end of 1933, we went into hiding in Paris for a few days.

'Henri Molinier was tireless in the devotion he showed us. The French Government had no wish to molest us, but was afraid of our becoming embroiled in a scandal with the G.P.U., the Communist Party, counter-revolutionary émigrés, sensation-mongering journalists, the right-wing press, the indiscreet and the curious. To avert any possible trouble, Molinier then took us to a small hotel near the Swiss frontier, but we were recognized and had to make off once again, this time to a village near the Grande-Chartreuse mountains in the Isère. Spring had come and our little peasant cottage was surrounded by new foliage and flowers. We took long walks and made plans for the winter ... Suddenly, the newspapers revealed Trotsky's new place of refuge and we had to pack our bags once again ... For a few days a family *pension* sheltered us under the attentive eye of a *Sûreté* official. We pretended to be in mourning – I wore black – so as to get away from people and to account for our taking all our meals in our room ... Then, M. Beau, an elementary schoolteacher, kindly offered to put us up in his house, about twenty miles from Grenoble. We had two good rooms, enjoyed a friendly atmosphere and some contact with M. Beau's colleagues. When the United Federation of Teachers met in congress at Grenoble, Beau and his wife, Marguerite, organized a small meeting and asked Leon Davidovich to address it. We stayed with these excellent people for some ten months.

'Our residence permits were running out. M. Sarraut, the Minister of the Interior, who was being harried by reactionaries and Stalinists alike – this was soon after the rioting on the Place de la Concorde which was organized by the Right and supported by the Communist Party – issued an order for our expulsion. There was nowhere for us to go – the planet was still without a visa as far as we were concerned. The *Sûreté* informed us that we were being placed under special surveillance. Leon Davidovich later noted that "during the last year of my stay in France I was more isolated from the world than I had ever been on Prinkipo ..."

'A planet without a visa again! We left the Beaus to spend some time in the dilapidated little house Leon Sedov and his wife had rented near Paris. Almost daily, the police called to enquire about our plans ... A Labour government had come to power in Norway; friends in Oslo applied to it on our behalf and eventually succeeded in having us admitted.

'In May 1935 we learnt of the arrest in Moscow of our younger son, Sergey. He disappeared at the age of twenty-seven. His only crime had been that he was our son, believed in his father's integrity and refused to denounce him publicly, as he must no doubt have been asked to do. Sergey had never played an active part in politics – his only true interests were science and mathematics, and the only paper he had published – with two other young engineers – was one on lightweight gas generators ... I lodged a public protest which had no effect at all. A few weeks passed, and then an international money order which I had sent to Sergey's wife, Lola, came back to us marked with a sinister "no forwarding address". Lola had been arrested as well. She, too, was to perish because she knew that her husband was completely innocent and because she was familiar with the ideas and believed in the integrity of Leon Davidovich ... We never discovered what really happened to her.

'In June 1935, we embarked at Antwerp for Oslo. Vandervelde's Belgian Government refused to let us spend even a day looking at the city's museums.'

Six · Nightmare

1. Asylum in Norway. Vexhall, the Knudsens, isolation

'Quiet, rugged, handsome Norway! There, during the latter part of 1935 and the beginning of 1936, we enjoyed the illusion of genuine security while staying with honest people who became our close friends. Members of the Labour Government had advised us to accept the hospitality of the well-known socialist Riksdag member, Konrad Knudsen, who lived in the village of Vexhall near Honnefoss, some thirty miles from Oslo. The village was small and the house spacious with a huge courtyard in front. The main gate to the road was kept open day and night ... this could only happen in Norway! If we were watched or guarded in any way, we never noticed. The old leader of the Labour Party, Martin Tranmael, a trade unionist who had served on the Comintern for a brief space, paid us a courtesy call, as did the Minister of Justice, Mr Trygve Lie. These were our only contacts with the authorities.

'We had two comfortable rooms at the Knudsens', Leon Davidovich's study and our bedroom. We ate with the family. Leon Davidovich's secretary lived nearby. To begin with this job was held by Jan Van Heijenoort, later by a Czech intellectual, Erwin Wolf, who soon afterwards became engaged to our host's beautiful blonde daughter, Jordis Knudsen. She was a fine, decent, straightforward girl, and a picture of health. (She had no idea that she, too, would be exposed to intolerable moral pressures simply because she had known outcasts like us.) Her father, a moderate socialist, spoke a little English ... They were kindly people of inflexible probity.

'We had few visitors – several Norwegian socialists and some from abroad. The only way of reaching us was through the editorial offices of the Labour newspaper in Honnefoss, which was edited by Konrad

195

Knudsen. Our visitors had, by force of circumstance, to become the Knudsen family's visitors, as well.

'I used to do my shopping in Honnefoss. Sometimes we would accompany the Knudsens to the local cinema where we saw old films ... We began to feel so safe that Leon Davidovich would occasionally go for long, solitary walks through the woods ... He was extremely busy with his correspondence, analysing Russian and other publications, editing the *Bulletin* (published by Leon Sedov in Paris), and writing a book to which he attached the utmost importance: *The Revolution Betrayed* [1]. He had at last obtained direct news from Russia about the persecution of our comrades, political life in the gaols and the dramas of deportation ... Three supporters of the Opposition had, as if by miracle, managed to flee the Soviet Union during 1935 and the spring of 1936: Tarov, a worker dragged from gaol to gaol in Central Asia, with the screams of the tortured and the rifle-shots of the firing squads ringing in his ears, had escaped through Iran; Anton Ciliga, a former member of the Central Committee of the Yugoslav Communist Party who had spent several years confined in Verkhne-Uralsk, was expelled from the Soviet Union after a prolonged hunger strike; and Victor Serge, too, had been deported following protests by French trade unionists and intellectuals.

'The news from the U.S.S.R. was extremely confusing. On the one hand, the wave of persecution increased relentlessly; on the other, the revaluation of the rouble in 1935 – one rouble now bought one kilogramme of black bread – had served to alleviate hunger, the general economic situation showed signs of improvement and there was even talk about a democratic constitution and a general amnesty ... The U.S.S.R., as a member of the League of Nations, was pursuing a policy of peace, and foreign Communist parties were joining Popular Fronts. In comparison with the Third Reich, where Hitler had ordered the mass execution of a section of his own party on June 30th, 1934, the U.S.S.R. was still a "champion of European culture", a fact its apologists never tired of stressing.'

But Stalin was already staggering under the torrents of blood and the sinister contradictions of the Kirov affair. On December 1st, 1934, Sergey Kirov, who had taken over from Zinoviev in Leningrad and was a member of the Politbureau, was assassinated at the Smolny Institute by a young Communist called Nikolaev, who shot him with a revolver in the back of the neck. Stalin himself went to

[1] Doubleday, Doran & Co., Garden City, New York, 1937.

Leningrad to interrogate Nikolaev. None of the assassin's deposi-
tions was made public, and he was executed, together with all his
friends – fourteen young Communists – after a secret trial. During
the next ten days, one hundred and fourteen prisoners were killed
in various prisons. More than three thousand Communists, said to
be supporters of the Zinoviev group, were arrested, and the first of
a series of secret trials was staged. During it Zinoviev, Kamenev and
Evdokimov 'confessed' their moral responsibility for the crime: the
alarm and despondency they had spread might, they meekly agreed,
have helped to plant the idea of an assassination in the minds of
Kirov's murderers. They were given long prison sentences, and thousands of militants were sent to concentration camps. There was a
clumsy attempt to implicate Trotsky by claiming that he had sent
Nikolaev a letter through the Latvian consul, but as this accusation
was easily refuted, Stalin quickly dropped it. At the same time, the
G.P.U. passed comparatively mild sentences on the leading figures
of the Leningrad secret police, who had known all about the assassination plan and had done nothing to prevent it. This fact speaks
volumes about the real culprits. On Stalin's personal orders, the
G.P.U. next proceeded to a wholesale purge in Leningrad. It culminated in the deportation, during 1935, of hundreds of thousands of
ex-capitalists, officials, officers and intellectuals of the old regime,
members of Oppositionists' families, religious people and heretics
of all shades. The Politbureau had become obsessed with terror and
repression.

Up to that point, the Trotskyists had not been involved and for
good reason. They had for years been kept under constant surveillance by the G.P.U. both in gaol and in exile. Those who were released
after serving long prison sentences were immediately flung into 'isolators'. One of these, Rakovsky – now sixty-two years old and worn
out by seven years of privation, constant surveillance and isolation
at Barnaul in Siberia – made his peace with Stalin so as to play his
part in averting 'the threat of war and the Fascist peril'. He was kindly
received in Moscow, and the Politbureau entrusted him with a brief
mission to Japan.

11. *Trotsky writes* The Revolution Betrayed

'We spent the winter of 1935 at Vexhall, in perfect solitude. The Norwegian winter has a pure beauty, with its clear skies, glittering snow

and the dark snow-clad firs. At nightfall, flames of crimson spread over the white expanse and the sky blazes up for a few moments ... We sometimes went with the Knudsens to a mountain hut which could only be reached on skis. We would stay there spellbound by the austere magic of the winter cold.'

Trotsky's entire life was concentrated in his thought, which in turn was expressed in his writings with limpid clarity. His literary output during this period merits detailed attention, if only because the whole world was hovering on the brink of disaster, but we shall have to confine ourselves to adumbrating his main ideas. Towards the U.S.S.R., he adhered strictly to the views of the 1917 Revolution and of the 1923 Opposition. In March 1933, he was still calling for 'Soviet reform', 'an honest Party regime' and 'Soviet democracy'. (*Opposition Bulletin*, No. 33) Hitler's rise to power in Germany meant two things to him: it heralded a new war and reflected the bankruptcy of the Stalinist Comintern.

In October 1933 (*Bulletin* No. 37), Trotsky published an appeal signed by the German Socialist Workers' Party, the Dutch Independent Socialist Party and the Russian Bolshevik-Leninist Opposition. It called for the formation of a Fourth International which would uphold the revolutionary Marxist tradition now abandoned by the Comintern. 'There is no longer a Bolshevik Party,' the document said. 'Reform of the Russian Communist Party from within is no longer possible ... The Bolshevik Party will have to be built up anew ... The workers' state can only be saved by world revolution ... The Comintern has turned a deaf ear to the Revolution.' The implications of the new line were extremely wide and, it may be said without exaggeration, they caused an absolute panic in Moscow. If the Opposition really believed that a second party must be formed as the sole means of ousting the bureaucracy by revolutionary means, then the regime was exposed to a grave threat. For though the alternative party was still embryonic, especially in the U.S.S.R., it could count on the support of men of proven courage and known ability, while the official Party behind its façade of unanimity, was consumed with doubts, anxiety and secret rebellion.

In 1935, Stalin decided to call the Seventh Congress of the Third International. The last such Congress had been held seven years earlier – Stalin had not even bothered to keep up the constitutional appearances in a body that had long since ceased to have the least pretence to independence. 'The whole question is whether the bureaucracy still has need of the Comintern,' Trotsky wrote. Earlier, he had called the Stalinist machine, which corrupted, demoralized, confused and lulled the Communist masses, the 'syphilis of the workers' movement'; he now described it, in June 1935, as 'the greatest plague of the workers' movement'.

He developed the theory of 'Soviet Bonapartism', by which he explained the nature of the Stalinist regime with the help of Marx's analysis of the methods by which Napoleon and Louis-Napoleon had seized power in France. In *The Revolution Betrayed*, a book on which he worked daily at Vexhall, he put forward the most detailed and complete analysis of life under Stalin. He cited statistics to show that 'the national income per person in the Soviet Union is considerably less than in the West'. For this situation he blamed Russia's past. 'There was no other way out upon the road of progress except through the overthrow of capitalism.' He attributed the power of the bureaucracy to the low level of production, to rationing, poverty and backwardness and rejected the official thesis of the 'complete victory of socialism'. His economic arguments were based strictly on official statistics. He denounced the 'growth of inequality' and the tragic condition of the workers who often fought against Stakhanovism (that is, overwork) by sabotaging machinery, a fact acknowledged by *Trud*, the official organ of the Soviet trade unions. Stakhanovism, he pointed out, divided the working class into the privileged and the hungry: it was the policy of 'divide and rule'. He denounced the 'Thermidor in the home, and the family circle', the fact that women and young people were being reduced to their pre-revolutionary status, the imposition of thought control, and the abasement of culture and art. 'In reality, in spite of individual exceptions, the Thermidor will go into the history of artistic creation pre-eminently as an epoch of mediocrities, laureates and toadies'. In foreign policy, the U.S.S.R. had ceased to rely on the international proletariat, 'without whom the Soviets would not have lasted a year'. Trotsky denounced the 'wicked fiction' of Stalin's and Litvinov's disarmament proposals. Germany 'is rearming feverishly, mainly against the U.S.S.R.' 'The decree restoring the officers' corps in all its bourgeois magnificence' was 'a deadly blow to the principles of the October Revolution', because it had helped to destroy the socialist tradition of the Red Army. Trotsky took a soberly optimistic view of the coming war. Russia had many advantages, not least her vast territory and her reserves of manpower. 'The instability of the present Nazi structure in Germany is conditioned by the fact that its productive forces have long ago outgrown the framework of capitalist property. The instability of the Soviet regime, on the contrary, is due to the fact that its productive forces still fall short of the rules of socialist property.' 'Hitler has far less chance than had Wilhelm II of carrying a war to victory ... Only a timely revolution, by saving Germany from war, could save her from a new defeat.' Japan and Poland posed a far less serious threat to Russia, but 'the danger of war and a defeat of the Soviet is a reality ... If the revolution does not prevent war, then war will help the revolution ... Nobody demands of the Soviet Government international adventures, unreasonable acts, attempts to force by violence the course of world events. On the contrary, insofar as such attempts have been made by the bureaucracy in the past (Bulgaria, Estonia, Canton, etc.), they have only played into the hands of the reaction, and they have met a timely condemnation from the left-wing Opposition. It is a question of the general direction of the Soviet state. The contradiction between its foreign policy and the interests of the world proletariat and the colonial peoples, finds its most ruinous expression in the subjection of the Communist International to the conservative bureaucracy with its new religion of inaction.' 'The decline of Europe is caused by the fact that it is economically split up among about forty quasi-national states ... The task of the European proletariat is not the perpetuation of boundaries, but, on the contrary, their revolutionary abolition, not [the maintenance of] the status quo but a socialist United States of Europe!'

Trotsky went on to point out that 'the question of the character of the Soviet Union has not yet been decided by history.' It was neither capitalist nor socialist, but appeared as a 'contradictory society halfway between capitalism and socialism in which ... a further development of the accumulating contradictions can as well lead to socialism as back to capitalism ... ' The new Constitution was a false façade. 'In a country where the lava of revolution has not yet cooled, privileges burn those who possess them ...' 'Soviet Bonapartism' is 'a regime of crisis ...' 'A new revolution is inescapable ...' 'More than ever the fate of the October Revolution is bound up now with the fate of Europe and the whole world ... ' 'Bureaucratic autocracy must give place to Soviet democracy ... This assumes a revival of freedom of Soviet parties, beginning with the party of Bolsheviks, and a resurrection of the trade unions.' The book ends with a new refutation of the idea of 'socialism in one country' and a scathing attack on the 'official friends' of the Soviet Union, who have completely forgotten that 'the motor force of progress is truth and not lies'.

If we have summarized Trotsky's views at such length, it is because of the unprecedented and tragic campaign of slander and falsification that was about to be unleashed against him.

III. *The trial of Zinoviev, Kamenev and Smirnov. Thirteen executed. Trotsky accused. The judicial farce*

'Anxious days were upon us. Leon Davidovich had just finished *The Revolution Betrayed*; spring brought fresh new leaves, flowers, streams and clear, warm mountain air. We accompanied Konrad Knudsen and his wife on a fishing trip, and planned to spend a few days at a lakeside hut in a clearing in a wooded fjord. A car followed close behind ours; we were afraid of an accident or possibly even an attempt on our lives. Knudsen stopped and questioned the young people in the second car, who became confused and abandoned the chase ... Meanwhile young members of a Norwegian fascist organization had tried to break into our house and had been stopped by Jordis Knudsen. One courageous young girl had succeeded in driving off these boys who, though fascists or pro-fascists, felt incapable of resorting to violence. All the same, we realized that something unpleasant was brewing ...

'Several days passed quietly in our cold hut by the lake ... Then, during the night of August 14th or 15th, Knudsen, who was listening to the radio, heard a news bulletin from Moscow announcing the opening, in five days' time, of the trial of the "Trotskyist-Zinovievist Centre", accused of "terrorism" among other things. Now, by a decree passed one day after the Kirov affair, terrorism had been declared a capital offence; those found guilty of it had no right of appeal, nor even the time to plead for clemency, as they were to be executed one hour after the verdict. In the circumstances, the far-fetched charge of "terrorism" could mean one thing only: that Stalin was about to resort to judicial murder. The thirteen accused included Zinoviev, Kamenev, Ivan Nikitich Smirnov, Evdokimov, Bakaev, Mrachkovsky, who had been a military commander in the Urals, and Dreitser, who had been on Trotsky's train; the rest were less well-known ... "A trial!" Leon Davidovich exclaimed in astonishment. A public trial! They would have to find proof – and that was, of course, impossible. He knew the accused well enough to realize how monstrous the charge against them was. For the rest, as there had been a complete break between them for years, how could there possibly be a Trotskyist-Zinovievist Centre? Was it an invention of the Politbureau? But in that case the accused – old Bolsheviks that they were – would surely refuse to take part in a farce that might cost them their lives. Leon Davidovich had no doubt that Stalin was out for blood in order to finish off Lenin's old colleagues, and to achieve his ends ... The atmosphere had suddenly changed in our simple, gay little hut where we had felt so far away from any crime ... Even the lake had clouded over.

'We returned to Vexhall filled with forebodings. A batch of Soviet newspapers lay waiting for us. They mentioned the arrest of a large number of Party members and we knew that for every name published there were dozens of others. Our clear impression was of a police coup d'état against the entire body of Old Bolsheviks.

'The trial of the Thirteen opened in Moscow on August 19th, 1936. By the time we read the indictment in the Soviet press, it was all over. Leon Davidovich, implicated a thousand times over, had not the slightest chance to refute one single lie or to demand proof of one single allegation against him. He was like a man in a delirium during those days, as if plunged into an insane nightmare. He knew all about the corruption and ferocity of the regime and the twisted, but total, devotion of most of the victims to the Party, strangled though it had been by the General Secretary, but their headlong descent into the abyss completely bewildered him.

'Not so long before, it would all have been unthinkable. But now, the Soviet Press Agency and the official bulletins piled lie upon misconstruction, double meaning upon equivocation, falsehood upon falsehood, as anyone in the least familiar with the facts and the men involved realized full well. Yet how many people abroad knew the facts and the victims? And those who did in Russia were all doomed. Leon Davidovich could see, as could every other old revolutionary who had survived abroad, that the trial was directed against all Communists who had played an active part in 1917–23.'

The indictment mentioned some fifty accomplices. The reason a mere thirteen were brought to trial was that they were the only ones who had agreed to confess whatever was demanded of them. The others were never heard of again. The prosecutor, Vyshinsky, announced that the files of about ten of them were being examined separately. That was all. They all died without trial.[2]

The accused confessed to the most far-fetched and impossible crimes, babbling deliriously along set lines. At times, some of them, including Ivan Smirnov and Golzman, seemed to have second thoughts and, with a few well-chosen words, they could easily have brought Vyshinsky's house of cards crashing down around his ears. But they thought better of it; presumably the prosecution had made a secret deal with them after playing on their sense of Party loyalty, their duty to their families and their certainty that they would be shot if they refused to co-operate. Various traps were set for the accused: all of them counted on the fact that no Old Bolshevik had ever been shot for opposing the regime; that, quite recently, the 'foreign traitors and saboteurs and their accomplices', that is, Ramsin and the technical experts tried with him, had been pardoned and rehabilitated for their meritorious service to industry; that finally, a new decree had just been promulgated allowing the Thirteen to petition for a free pardon. Hence they must have felt that if they lent themselves to this vast judicial slander of Trotsky, if they accompanied their false confessions with eulogies to Stalin and his 'brilliant' success in building socialism in one country, their lives would be spared and, after a spell of solitary confinement in some isolated cell, they would be allowed to live a normal life once again.

In substance, they confessed that they had set up a kind of central committee – a 'centre' – in accordance with instructions from Trotsky acting in collusion with the Gestapo, and that they had planned Nikolaev's assassination of Kirov in December 1934 – at a time when Ivan Smirnov had been lingering in gaol for more than two years, when Zinoviev had been exiled to Kurultay in Kazakhstan and Kamenev to Minusinsk, both under close and constant surveillance. Moreover, their confessions came after several secret trials followed by a hundred and thirty executions had ostensibly wound up the Kirov affair. They also confessed to planning the assassination of almost the entire Politbureau with the strange exception of Molotov. (Could Molotov have objected to this farcical trial?) Minor figures confessed to entering the U.S.S.R. for the express purpose of engaging in terrorist activities under Trotsky's orders. Leon

[2] The thirteen were: Zinoviev, Kamenev, Evdokimov, Ivan Bakaev, Ivan Smirnov, Ter-Vaganian, Golzman, Rheingold, Dreitser, Moyse Lurie, Fritz David, Berman-Yurin and Olberg.

Davidovich knew none of these except Olberg, who had offered him his services as a secretary, but, as the old German revolutionary writer Franz Pfemfert had given him a most unfavourable reference, Trotsky had refused to engage him. He found Pfemfert's letter again – but too-late to put it to any use. The 'terrorists', who had allegedly planned a dozen assassinations, had never carried out even one; all they confessed to was the intention to commit a series of crimes. The written declarations of Kirov's murderer, the only authentic and indisputable evidence about the only actual assassination, remained in the archives of the Politbureau and their contents were never divulged.

'Few foreign observers were taken in by such ideological and political forgeries, least of all by Vyshinsky's claim that Trotsky had been preaching defeatism in the coming war when he had said, "We might do what Clemenceau did in France." Vyshinsky was relying on the fact that few people in Russia knew that Clemenceau, while bitterly attacking his predecessors, had consistently defended the war until Germany's surrender. There was nothing Vyshinsky would not stoop to; he knew better than anyone that his own head would roll if he fell short of total cynicism, all the more as he had been a Menshevik until 1922 or 1923, and hence a "counter-revolutionary". He now turned Trotsky's widely published plea for the removal of Stalin into a "call for terror". As that plea was taken verbatim from Lenin's Will, Vyshinsky was, in fact, indicting Lenin, though such small scruples never deterred him. But then the stage-managers made a serious mistake. Golzman who, as we saw earlier, had had a brief meeting with Leon Sedov in Berlin, now claimed he had been received by Trotsky at the Bristol Hotel, in Copenhagen, and that Trotsky had given him verbal instructions concerning Kirov's assassination. Golzman also claimed he had met Leon Sedov on that occasion. Leon Davidovich made enquiries and it turned out that there was no Bristol Hotel in Copenhagen; we were also able to prove that Leon Sedov had never been to Copenhagen but not until the trial was over, and by then it was too late. We could, furthermore, have proved that Golzman did not meet Trotsky anywhere else in Copenhagen during the week Leon Davidovich spent there in the company of a handful of people and closely watched by the Danish police, but what good would it have done? It was all madness, but it poured out from the world press, and the Stalinist papers in particular, and was followed by a special "summary" – certainly not verbatim – of the trial in several languages ... During the next months we gathered a mounting body of evidence proving conclusively that the prosecution had fabricated its entire case, and in this we had the help of many of our friends. We learned about Olberg's doings from Prague; Paris sent us news about such subsidiary figures as Lurie and Fritz David, both of them good Stalinist officials. The "terrorist" Lurie had been director of an historical institute ... what strange fate had selected him for his new role?

'In their confessions, the principal accused had also implicated the right-wing Opposition, particularly its leaders, Aleksey Rykov, Bukharin and Tomsky. Tomsky, head of the Soviet trade unions, did not wait to be arrested and forced to confess to crimes he had never even heard of; he shot himself instead. At the end of the trial, the accused, who had demanded such exemplary punishment for themselves and spun such a hideous web of lies, had obviously come to the end of their tether. There was a note of pathos in their final declarations, especially in Kamenev's. They still accused Trotsky, as they had to, but they now realized that they had dug their own graves and that they had abased themselves in vain. Golzman, it is said, refused to sign what he knew was a useless appeal for clemency. Perhaps he had lied about the Bristol Hotel on purpose, in order to expose the shamefulness of the whole farce. Vyshinsky's final plea was something no civilized country had ever heard. "I demand, Comrade Judges, that these mad dogs be shot, every one of them!" His call was echoed by thousands of meetings and demonstrations and by the world Communist press ... During the night of August 25th, thirteen skulls were blown to shreds by the bullets of a specially selected G.P.U. squad. Leon Davidovich and our son, Leon Sedov, were condemned to death in absentia. Stalin was on holiday in the Caucasus; he took walks on the Riviera along avenues lined with fragrant lemon-trees. He is said to have read the accounts of the trial with anger; he felt Zinoviev and Kamenev must have been mocking him when they declared, under the shadow of the gallows, that they "had no political platform whatsoever" and that it was only their "thirst for power" that had driven them on. The stage management of the trial, he decided, had been very poor. They would have to do better. Other trials would follow.

'Now, one name had not been mentioned at the trial, that of Yagoda, People's Commissar for Internal Affairs and head of the political police. It was this man who had made all the secret preparations for the trial on direct instructions from the General Secretary. If anybody knew the truth about the seamy side of the whole affair, it was Yagoda and his principal underlings. Hence, they, too, had to disappear.'

IV. *Trotsky at Sundby in Norway. Theft of his archives in Paris*

'The nightmare descended on the quiet house in Vexhall, and the nauseating stench of the blood shed in Moscow began to envelop us even here. Our friends and hosts knew the truth about us because they lived alongside us, but the reactionary press let itself go ... Leon Davidovich, frowning and often feverish, was deeply immersed in research work. Armed with red, blue and black pencils, he annotated accounts of the trial and jotted down notes on bits of paper. His study filled up with galley-proofs and manuscripts, every one exposing a profusion of crimes. Then, when he was exhausted, he would go outside, straighten his shoulders, walk towards the fir-trees and contemplate the mountain scenery and the incredible peace. One day, well before all this bloodthirsty madness had started, he said to me as we stood in the winter snow, "I am tired of it all – all of it – do you understand?" This was no lapse or weakness, but revolutionaries, too, are only human.

'He received journalists and gave interviews. Generally, we met with intelligent sympathy. The Moscow confessions seemed outside the bounds of probability and the deaths of the accused – after their protestations of patriotism and loyalty to the Party – beyond the bounds of human cruelty. People simply could not understand, and it was exceedingly hard to explain things to them. Just as many fatal diseases eluded the physician until the microscope was able to probe the mysteries of the living cell and of organisms that could not be seen with the naked eye, so the nameless disease that was gnawing at "Soviet" society had causes that could not be seen from a distance, the less so as the public prosecutor went out of his way to obscure them. Innumerable facts, passports and dates had to be checked, as well as a vast amount of testimony, and the accused had been executed before Leon Davidovich had time to do any of these things. A certain Berman-Yurin testified that he had visited Trotsky in Copenhagen ... We had absolutely no idea who he was, but Leon Davidovich remembered that he had received only one Russian-speaking visitor in Copenhagen and he had been clearly identified;

several witnesses who had never left us for a moment were able to testify to that ... Dreitser (who was subsequently shot) had testified that Trotsky had sent him a letter written in invisible ink, which he had "developed" and then sent on to Mrachkovsky in Kazakhstan; Mrachkovsky for his part had testified that he had received the letter "undeveloped". Obviously, the lies had not been properly co-ordinated ... The letter was said to have run to about a dozen lines, but all the same it had apparently contained "full directions for sabotage and terrorism". Perhaps forged letters purporting to be from Trotsky had been deliberately circulated, some "developed" and others untreated ...

'Leon Davidovich made some calculations. Of the original Politbureau, which at the time of the Revolution had consisted of seven members, one had died – Lenin; five had been shot, or sentenced in absentia, and Stalin alone remained in power. Eighteen members of the Central Committee had been, or were about to be, executed. One hundred and thirty-nine "terrorists" had been mentioned during the trial of the Thirteen: what had happened to them? All of them had belonged to the elite of the Revolution. In retribution for one assassination, that of Kirov, which had all the hall-marks of an individual act of protest or, at most, of an action planned by desperate young men, one hundred and sixty-five people had been executed, and that according to the official figures ...

'Worst of all was the moral degradation. The socialist revolution had fought hard against its enemies, but, to survive, it had to overcome mortal dangers and it had drawn its sword against other swords. It had pursued great, just and concrete aims; it spoke straight from the shoulder, in a language that many may have detested but whose sincerity and honesty few could have doubted. Now its surviving spokesmen were lying, covering themselves with obloquy and being massacred by their former comrades.

'Part of the mystery had been explained in the *Opposition Bulletin* (No. 51), which was dated July/August 1936 and appeared a few days before the trial of the Thirteen was announced. In the Verkhne-Uralsk prison, the Menshevik historian, Sukhanov, wrote down and circulated among the inmates an account of his meetings with Stalin's inquisitors. "You have asked me for the greatest possible sacrifice by incriminating myself," he had told the G.P.U., " ... and I felt I ought to comply in the greater interests of the U.S.S.R. Under the instruction of the officials we, the accused, learned our parts and rehearsed the comedy we were intended to play at a forthcoming trial. You promised us – and we naturally expected – a conditional or purely formal sentence ... But after having persuaded us to incriminate ourselves, you continue to keep us in gaol ... " (*Letter from a Comrade*, signed V.S.)

'A few days passed ... The Soviet Union handed Norway an ominous Note in which it contended that Trotsky's continued presence there was likely to impair friendly relations between the two countries. Puntervold, Leon Davidovich's Norwegian lawyer, told us that Yakubovich, Stalin's ambassador in Oslo, was threatening Norway with economic reprisals. (This same Yakubovich was soon to disappear in Moscow.) Mr Trygve Lie, the Minister of Justice in the Norwegian Labour government, demanded a written declaration from Leon Davidovich to the effect that henceforth he would refrain from writing about current political affairs and that he agreed to have his incoming and outgoing mail inspected ... Leon Davidovich flatly refused: he would not keep silent in the face of Stalin's crimes. "If it is your intention to arrest me why do you require my authorization to do so?" The Minister replied, "But arrest and complete freedom are not the only alternatives." "Whether this is a quibble or a trap, I should prefer arrest," was Leon Davidovich's conclusion. He later wrote, "The Minister obliged at once and issued the necessary orders for my arrest." Leon Davidovich's secretary, Erwin Wolf, was expelled from Norway without any explanation. He left and threw himself passionately into the fight against Franco in Spain. Another friend, Walter Held, a German refugee and now a naturalized Norwegian, was prevented from seeing us, too ... The reader should bear these two names in mind; we shall refer to their terrible fate in due course.

'At the beginning of September 1936, we were taken under escort to Sundby near Storsand and interned in a large house on the edge of a fjord. We were given the first floor and some fifteen policemen were installed on the ground floor; we were not allowed to leave the grounds. All our correspondence was censored and nobody was allowed to visit us. A special law had to be passed to legalize this unconstitutional internment of refugees who had broken no Norwegian laws.

'"The first days of our internment," Leon Davidovich wrote, "were a welcome respite after the terrible upheaval of the Moscow trial. It was good to be alone without news, telegrams, letters or telephone calls. But as soon as the first newspapers from Russia reached us, internment became a torture ... " All the protests, countercharges and messages Leon Davidovich sent were held back by the censor. When he started an action against the Norwegian fascists who had broken into our home and had libelled us in their newspapers, a special law was passed on October 20th authorizing the Minister of Justice to prevent interned foreigners from resorting to the courts.

'Leon Davidovich then wrote to our friends abroad instructing them to take action against his slanderers in Paris, Prague and London, and against the Stalinists in particular ... The Minister of Justice informed him that he must not engage in litigation anywhere in the world while he remained in Norway. It seemed that he had no more rights at all. We began to fear that, though we had "forfeited" Soviet nationality, the Norwegians might hand us over to the G.P.U. ...

'Still, the authorities themselves tried the young fascists who had broken into our home. The trial was held in camera and, during it, Leon Davidovich was able to testify freely, talk about the Moscow tragedy, refute his slanderers, and mention a recent event in Paris [November 1936].

'A part of Leon Davidovich's archives was deposited in the Institute of Social History at 7, rue Michelet, in Paris, where it had been entrusted to the care of the Russian Social Democratic historian, Boris Nikolaevsky. One night professional burglars drove up outside, cut through the service door with a blowtorch and stole all Trotsky's private papers, but neglected to take a host of historical documents that might have been of some commercial value ... The theft bore all the marks of the G.P.U., which obviously intended to use Trotsky's papers to prepare a more plausible tissue of fresh lies ... In Paris, our son, Leon Sedov, felt that secret, but blundering, watchers were closing in on him ... '

v. *Asylum in Mexico. Life in Coyoacan*

'We simply had to leave Norway, once so hospitable but now our prison. But where could we go? It was raining and growing colder under a grey sky; the policemen were playing cards and we were alone, as never before, alone with the ravings in the newspapers from Moscow. There the massacres were evidently continuing, as crushed men abased themselves shamefully and inexplicably – inexplicably because, after all, it is not so difficult to die without besmirching one's name ... In *Pravda* and *Izvestia*, Karl Radek demanded the blood of "that super-bandit Trotsky"; while Rakovsky, our old friend and once an upright and fearless comrade, now wrote: " ... No pity for the Trotskyist Gestapo agents! Let them be shot!" One must overcome a feeling of disgust and horror to quote at greater length from an article by Pyatakov: "The fresh, clean air of our magnificent and prosperous socialist country," he wrote, "has suddenly been filled with the disgusting stench of the political mortuary ... In the last stage of decomposition, [these Trotskyist criminals] do not only stink ... but must be destroyed like decaying carcasses ... " All of them were full of expressions of praise for "our beloved Leader Stalin", but as soon as they had signed their various slanders and eulogies, the G.P.U. would round them up like thousands of others; they, too, were merely "dead men on furlough" ... And yet they had all been enthusiastic, courageous and intelligent socialists, deeply committed men. How can one begin to understand or accept what they did?

'On the other side of the world, American and Mexican sympathizers were trying desperately to help us, and some, including the writer Antonio Hidalgo and the painter Diego Rivera, approached the Mexican President, General Lazaro Cardenas, on our behalf. We knew neither of them in person. President Cardenas, who had earned renown by his stand in support of the Spanish Republic, now decided to grant us asylum. In December 1936, we boarded the Norwegian tanker *Ruth*, and sailed under the escort of Mr Jonas Lie, a Norwegian police officer. There were four of us at the captain's table, and no other passengers. We never saw our friends the Knudsens, Walter Held and several others, again ... The sea was rough, and the ship pitched and rolled as it carried us into the unknown. Leon Davidovich calmly wrote up his notes. On January 1st, 1937, the *Ruth* sounded two blasts of her siren over the lonely sea to salute the New Year ... there was no answering echo. We were not allowed to listen to the wireless, and our nerves were all the better for it. The tanker steered an irregular course for eighteen days. It became hotter and we were sailing under tropical skies. On January 9th, we entered the port of Tampico. Leon Davidovich warned Mr Jonas Lie that he would refuse to disembark unless friends came to meet us – the G.P.U. had its agents in Mexico, as everywhere else. Then a launch drew up and all our fears evaporated. We were greeted by honest and smiling faces: our American friend, Max Schachtman; George

Novak, who introduced himself as the secretary of the Trotsky Defence Committee in the United States; the painter Frida Kahlo de Rivera, wife of the artist Diego Rivera; journalists, Mexican officials and comrades, all friendly, warm, open and welcoming. There was a great deal of encouraging news from New York; the whole New World seemed to have been incensed by the Moscow crimes. We gulped in the air of freedom.

'A train provided by the Mexican government took us through sun-baked country, scattered with palm-trees and cacti. The mountains blazed with splendour. At a small station, Antonio Hidalgo and Fritz Bach, a socialist of Swiss origin and one of Zapata's comrades-in-arms, were waiting to greet us ... All security precautions broke down when a crowd of unknown friends swarmed round us, and I tried not to lose sight of the only face I knew – Frida Kahlo's. We were shown a car which we were expected to share with policemen and strangers. Suddenly we felt afraid once again – were they, in spite of everything, taking us to prison? We arrived in a suburb of Mexico City, at a low house painted blue; it had a patio filled with plants, fresh, airy rooms, a collection of pre-Columbian objets d'art and a vast number of pictures ... We had come to a different world, the house of Frida Kahlo and Diego Rivera.

'It was there that we learned many things that our Norwegian captors had kept from us. The trial of the Thirteen had taken the West completely by surprise. That statesmen and old revolutionaries should conspire with an unscrupulous public prosecutor, that they should vie with one another in producing blatantly false self-accusations only to be shot after having given such extravagant proof of their loyalty to the Party – all this defied Western psychology. Frederic Adler rightly called it "a witch-hunt". For Leon Davidovich, myself and a small number of initiates, there was no longer any mystery about the confessions. Ever since 1927, Zinoviev, Kamenev and quite a few more had chosen capitulation, lulling their consciences with the hope that one day they might be allowed to speak out freely again. They had reached the age of fifty, broken by persecution, imprisonment and continued threats against their families, only to discover that their betrayals of principle had been in vain, that they were still considered potential enemies of the totalitarian state, in the running of which they no longer played any part. Then Stalin demanded a further sacrifice from them in the name of the Party. Cover yourselves with filth as a permanent pledge of your loyalty to me, and discredit Trotsky! They agreed, for they knew full well that the only alternative to this slender and miserable chance of survival was to share the fate of all those who had refused to lend themselves to Stalin's farce: to be taken away and shot.'

VI. *The Second Moscow Trial. Trotsky accused again. Pyatakov's lie. Sabotage. Mass executions*

'A second trial ended in Moscow on January 30th, 1937; this was the "Trial of the Seventeen". The nightmare continued and grew; the murder of the Seventeen was the prelude to others ... We listened to the radio, opened the mail and the Moscow newspapers, and we felt that insanity, absurdity, outrage, fraud and blood were flooding us from all sides, here in Mexico, as in Norway ... With pencil in hand, Leon Davidovich, over-tense, overworked, often feverish, yet tireless, made a note of all the forgeries and lies, much too numerous now to be refuted one by one. The vast Stalinist crime-manufacturing machine was working at full steam, and seemed to have grown completely indifferent to the credibility of its products. As soon as one lie was publicly exposed – and that meant much research into documents and checking a great many dates – ten or twenty new ones sprang up. The abridged and edited account of the trial of the Seventeen – needless to say, again no verbatim report was ever published – filled six hundred pages!

'The next cartload Stalin proposed to send to the executioner included Yury Pyatakov, Deputy People's Commissar for Heavy Industry; Karl Radek, who, not so long before, had been notorious in Moscow for his intimate friendship with Stalin; Sokolnikov, the economist, diplomat and financial expert; Serebriakov, the former secretary of the Central Committee and a member of several economic missions to the United States, where he was highly regarded; Muralov, fearless member of the Opposition; such heroes of the Civil War as Drobnis and Boguslavsky (who had been secretary of the Special Council of People's Commissars); Livshitz, a Deputy People's Commissar of Transport, who had recently been decorated for services to industry; some leading figures in the chemical industry and several less well-known people. The prosecution was obviously relying on a method perfected by Fouquier-Tinville during the French Revolution: that of filling the dock with an assorted mixture of leading politicians, spies, double agents, informers and genuine criminals, the better to tar them all with the same brush. Trotsky and Leon Sedov were once again the chief defendants in absentia. Except for Muralov, all the other defendants had broken with Trotsky in 1927 or 1928 and he had often slated their political conduct.'

From the very first hearing it was obvious that a new theme was being developed: 'Trotskyist sabotage'. It was blamed for the badly bungled policy of industrialization, the parlous state of the transport system and the terrifying number of industrial accidents. It mattered little that Trotsky, in writings naturally unavailable in Russia, had constantly called for an end to the chaotic, arbitrary and ruthless production methods – if 50,000 witnesses should be needed to incriminate him, Vyshinsky could truthfully claim that that number had already been arrested. A cry of dismay and disgust went up when the former Deputy People's Commissar for Transport, Livshitz, stammering and stuttering with shame, confessed that he had organized derailments acting under 'Trotskyist orders'; or when Knyazev, the Chairman of the South Ural Railways, confessed that with the help of accomplices he had organized some 15 major accidents and 1,600 breakdowns in 1934. The Paris *Temps* reported that the same Knyazev had blamed 3,500 railway accidents on Trotskyist activities, a figure that was not quoted in the official report of the trials.

As for the real causes of the wave of sabotage, they presented no problem at all to anyone who lived in Russia at the time of Stalin's Five-year Plans. Various defendants admitted to sabotage by 'squandering funds by building up secondary industries'; by 'failing to render plant operational on the dates stipulated by the government'; by 'slowing down factory construction'; by 'prematurely withdrawing old railway engines, sabotaging train timetables, creating bottlenecks at stations and sending poorly repaired engines back into service ... ' Now, as everyone knew, an engineer who sent anything but a completely broken-down engine back to the workshops, or who refused to run an engine that was not in perfect repair, was laying himself open to charges of sabotage. Everybody knew equally well that because of the shortage of materials, equipment and rolling stock, all construction work was behind-hand, which did not stop Stalin from ordering the completion of the first Five Year Plan in four years – 'the mad gallop of industrialization,' as Trotsky had called it. Everybody in Russia knew that an engineer who refused to build machinery with faulty materials would be accused of sabotaging the Plan; conversely, if he agreed to use such materials, he might be accused of disobeying orders on quality control; and if he tried to protect himself by sending memoranda to his superiors, he might be accused of 'sabotage by red-tape' (which is what happened in the engineers' trial). Everybody knew that during the terror most of the statistics were bogus and that the planners, afraid of incurring the displeasure of the Politbureau, tried to buy time by one piece of improvisation after the other. The resultant confusion was borne heroically by the workers and faced intelligently and loyally by the great majority of engineers.

The director of the chemical industry agreed that his Trotskyist colleagues had staged numerous accidents causing the death of many workers. On one occasion, this man – Rataichak by name – had himself directed the demolition of a badly damaged and dangerous factory building. This operation had meant sacrificing the lives of fifteen workers to save two hundred, and Vyshinsky now blamed him for the deaths. From 1932 and 1933 onwards, the situation in Russia was so desperate that people began to talk of a vast sabotage campaign organized somewhere at the very top of the Government, and Old Bolsheviks whispered among themselves that the organizer was none other than their inspired Leader, Stalin. They had spelt this out in so many words during the Riutin affair of 1932. A wave of resistance to this type of government sabotage and the inhuman regime that went with it had swept spontaneously throughout the Soviet Union. If the Plan could not possibly be fulfulled within the time-limit set and if people were not allowed to say so, they at least did their best to alleviate the suffering that went with it, by reducing overwork, protecting machinery against misuse and workers against accidents. And that was called industrial sabotage.

It was during a hearing late on January 23rd, 1937, that Pyatakov – looking drawn and pale – suddenly produced a sensational statement and caused a gasp of astonishment throughout the court-room; foreign journalists could not believe their ears. He confessed that in the middle of December 1935, he had flown from Berlin to Oslo with a false passport, and that he had had a long interview with Trotsky, who had told him about secret negotiations with the Nazi deputy Führer, Rudolf Hess,[3] and had given him orders to begin a wave of terror and sabotage. The very next day the whole

[3] When Hess was in the dock at the Nuremberg Trials, it would have been quite possible for the Russian judge and prosecutor to question him about these 'negotia-

story was exploded: the director of Kjeller airport, near Oslo, declared that no foreign aircraft had landed there between September
19th, 1935 and May 1st, 1936, and Konrad Knudsen, his family,
Erwin Wolf and every member of Trotsky's entourage at Vexhall
stated that no foreign visitor had come to Trotsky's house that
December, and that Trotsky himself had not left the place. Leon
Davidovich cabled the Tribunal a series of questions he wished to
be put to Pyatakov. Pyatakov had said that the journey from the
airport to Vexhall had taken half an hour, when in fact it would have
taken two hours in winter. Who had driven him there? By what
route? What was the exact date? Who had received him in the house?
Where did he spend the night before leaving? Members of the Soviet
missions abroad were watched and guarded day and night by the
G.P.U. and a daily log kept of their activities. Although Trotsky's
various cables reached Moscow in time, no mention whatever was
made of them during the hearings. The press ignored them as well,
and the Tribunal prudently refrained from asking the accused any
embarrassing questions about dates, facts or names. Not that the
military tribunal of the Supreme Court, under its President V. V.
Ulrich, could have done anything else; it was acting on orders issued
by the Politbureau, that is by the 'Leader of genius', Stalin himself.
It was a type of justice quite unlike any practised in civilized countries, imperfect though that may be. The judges and the prosecutor
were trembling with terror lest they might be thought to have fallen
down on the job they had been ordered to do. They were only too
aware that the man who had staged the trial of the Thirteen, Yagoda,
had been relieved of his post as People's Commissar for the Interior
and Chief of the Secret Police, and that the whole of Moscow was
expecting his arrest at any moment.

Vladimir Romm, the Paris correspondent of *Izvestia*, who
appeared as a witness only (one wonders why he was not among
the accused), testified that he had met Trotsky in the Bois de Boulogne at the end of July 1933, and that Trotsky had given him a letter
for Radek, with further 'directives for terrorism'. This letter, like all
the others mentioned before and after, had been neither preserved
nor copied so that no trace of it remained. Although the prosecutor

tions'. American and British writers had petitioned the President and members of
the Tribunal and the prosecutors to do just that, but this was a challenge the Russians
were careful not to take up. Like Delegorgue, who had presided over Zola's trial,
they refused to burden the court with embarrassing questions.

did not ask Romm for any more details than he had demanded of Pyatakov, the errors in Romm's testimony were no less glaring. Trotsky had arrived in France on July 24th, 1933. He had disembarked at dawn in Cassis near Marseilles and had travelled, accompanied by friends and a French police official, not to Paris but to Saint-Palais in the Charente-Maritime, a good distance from the capital, where he had stayed surrounded by friends and watched over by the police until October 9th. There were twenty-eight witnesses to vouch for this.

'Terrorist groups' had apparently been discovered in every nook and cranny of Russia, all of them directed by Old Bolsheviks. In spite of their numbers, however, they had failed to carry out a single assassination. In that case, how did the authorities learn of their existence? The answer was that the accused never stopped arguing among themselves about 'Trotsky's directives' and assassinations. To lend colour to all these fabrications, the court spent hours examining an alleged plan to kill Molotov in Siberia; his chauffeur was to let the car run over a cliff but lost his nerve at the last moment. That was all the 'terror' the authorities could dredge up – in a country that had developed revolutionary terrorism into a fine art under the old regime! An order must have been issued to label as a 'Trotskyist terrorist' every malcontent, every member of the Party, young and old, who had voiced the least criticism. I myself knew quite a few of the 'terrorists' mentioned at the trial who were shot later without benefit of trials themselves. They included Sachs-Gladnev and Tivel (who was executed with Zinoviev). Sachs-Gladnev was an erudite old Marxist, a man most at home surrounded by books, a brilliant editor, who had led an extremely sheltered life and who, though he had firm convictions, was quite incapable of taking any kind of practical action. Tivel, a young journalist, practised theosophy and studied Hinduism. Another group of 'terrorists' included the young Marxist historians Seidel, Friedland, Vanag and Pentkovsky, authors of works not without merit, and all of them zealous Stalinists. Pentkovsky, in particular, had rewritten his textbooks on the October Revolution after Trotsky's fall so as to boost Stalin's role.

Karl Radek saved this trial from degenerating into a complete farce and, in doing so, brought out the absence of any concrete proof. 'Everything rests on my confession and Pyatakov's.' He explained that his confession was not so much motivated by a concern for the truth as for its 'usefulness'. In short, he stressed the value of his services. He warned 'Trotskyists in Spain, France and other countries that they will pay with their heads unless they learn from our example'. These words are worth recalling because they were soon afterwards sealed in blood, in Barcelona and Paris. Radek also let slip what had been going on behind the scenes. He had denied everything for months, but when his interrogators had shown him fifteen files containing the confessions of the other accused, he had 'realized that all further resistance was pointless'. Indeed.

Prosecutor Vyshinsky spent hours trying to prove that Trotsky had been Lenin's bitter opponent ever since 1904 and that he had sabotaged the Russian Revolution. He spoke with emotion about the victims of the recent wave of railway accidents and was moved to a fine show of indignation by the – admittedly disgusting – articles Radek and Pyatakov were made to write before being arrested. He read passages from the *Opposition Bulletin*, misquoting as he went along. During the night of February 1st, 1937, Pyatakov, Muralov and Serebriakov, Lenin's old companions, Drobnis and Boguslavsky, both fighters for the October Revolution, various government and industrial leaders, *agents provocateurs*, spies and victims, were shot – seventeen in all. Four were spared – two docile minor figures, and Sokolnikov and Karl Radek. Radek was soon afterwards to be killed in gaol.

Trotsky noted a psychological feature of the 'Trial of the Twenty-one' in the margin of his review of the proceedings. The prosecution had given blatant proof throughout of its total subservience to its 'Leader of genius'. In fact, even had they been guilty as charged, the so-called 'conspirators' would never even have dreamed of turning to Trotsky for 'directives'. Those amongst them who had known Trotsky personally before 1928, and had shared a great many of his views, had later taken issue with him at length, finally breaking off all relations with him. The left-wing Opposition included respected militants but it had no leader and it was opposed to the very idea of one. The real Trotskyists in Stalin's gaols, even though they might have accepted this label out of respect for the 'Old Man', nevertheless questioned every one of his ideas exhaustively. The very idea of authoritative 'directives' was the product of a perverted imagination.

Leon Davidovich was asked to make a speech on the trial, for transmission to New York by telephone. An audience of some 6,500 came to listen to it, but as someone had tampered with the transmitting equipment, the speech – the text of which had been sent to New

York against just that eventuality – was read out by someone else. In it, Trotsky declared that if a public and impartial Commission of Inquiry found him guilty in the slightest degree of the crimes which Stalin had imputed to him, he pledged in advance to place himself voluntarily into the hands of the G.P.U. executioners.

VII. *The murder of Trotsky's younger son, Sergey Sedov, at Krasnoyarsk*

The house in Coyoacan was haunted by the faces of the tortured, by the faces of those who had disappeared and who were disappearing each day, and of those who would inevitably follow them in time to come. Trotsky was, perhaps, the only man in the whole world able to grasp the real depths to which the Russian Revolution had sunk. He worked on, because it was imperative that truthfulness, steadfastness, intelligibility and Marxist integrity be seen to oppose Stalin's degradation of the socialist conscience; and because it was essential to rid revolutionary knowledge and thought of the monstrous nightmare that had descended upon them. Trotsky planned new books; he wrote articles for the *New York Times* almost daily for a time, worked on analyses and essays in the *Opposition Bulletin*, and brought out *Stalin's Crimes*, a work of 376 pages, published in Paris. It was hard and bitter work.

And while he worked, the nightmare continued. A few days after Pyatakov's execution his colleague, Sergo Ordjonikidze, People's Commissar for Heavy Industry, died suddenly of a heart attack after being taken ill at a Politbureau meeting. It was known that he had often protested against G.P.U. persecution of his experts, much as he had previously opposed unjustified attacks on the Opposition. The trial of the Twenty-one was bound, one way or another, to lead to his death.

'A brief communiqué announced the execution of eighty-three Trotskyists in the Far East. Our twenty-eight-year-old son, Sergey Sedov (our children bore my name), who had been deported to Krasnoyarsk in Central Siberia, was also shot ... The Moscow papers mentioned his name; there had been an accident in the factory where he worked and he was accused of having "organized the mass gassing of workers ... " Though the mental perversion of the executioners had ceased to surprise us, we looked at each other in stunned silence. Words no longer made sense and reason itself wavered when faced with so much criminal insanity. I wrote and sent to the press an appeal *To the Conscience of the World*, in which I tried to vindicate our son, now lost to us. His last letter, dated December 12th, 1934, now two years old, lay before me on the table. "My general situation is grave, extremely grave – graver than one could imagine..." he had written. What had he suffered since then? He had never been interested in politics. At school, he had refused to join the *Komsomol*, and we let him be. He loved literature, music and sport. We hoped that as he grew older, he might come to share our interests, but the only passionate interests he developed were mathematics and engineering ... We had heard that he had been arrested in 1935, had spent about eight months in gaol and was then sent to Krasnoyarsk, where the G.P.U. had allowed him to work as a factory engineer ... But could they be expected to spare the life of one of Trotsky's sons? Desperately, I protested his innocence and integrity; that he loved his country and the working man ... Would no one speak up in his defence? Apart from our friends, no one did. No trial was held, and the executioners were silent. Sergey Sedov would never have confessed to anything; he probably turned on his interrogators himself with the full force of his honest scorn. We never heard any more.

'Leon Davidovich was depressed beyond measure. "Perhaps my death would have saved Sergey," he said to me. And at moments I felt he was sorry to be alive.'

VIII. *The Dewey Commission questions Trotsky in Mexico*

It is typical of American society that all those major political trials which have ended in unjust verdicts have aroused energetic and tenacious protest movements in the United States. Altgeld, the Governor of Illinois, became the champion of the condemned anarchists who had survived the execution of the 'Chicago martyrs'; Clarence Darrow wrote one of the most illustrious pages of his life when he defended Ettor and Giovanetti. The fight for the lives of Sacco and Vanzetti continued for seven years. The Moscow trials and the persecution of one of the old revolutionaries, now outlawed, aroused a wave of sympathy and protest throughout the world but nowhere more strongly and effectively than in the United States. The American Committee for the Defence of Leon Trotsky could boast hundreds of members, including such distinguished names as Franz

Boas, James Burnham, John Dewey, John Dos Passos, Max East-man, James T. Farrell, Sidney Hook, Dwight Macdonald, Reinhold Niebuhr, Norman Thomas and Carlo Tresca. The list also included such staunch opponents of Bolshevism as Max Nomad, many liberals and scholars, theologians like Niebuhr, and militants like Tresca.[4] A young woman from a famous family, Suzanne La Follette, assisted by a young left-wing lawyer, George Novak, watched indefa-tigably over the Committee's practical work.

The American Defence Committee was ably supported by the French Commission of Inquiry into the Moscow Trials, which was set up in Paris and included Magdeleine Paz, Alfred and Marguerite Rosmer, Marcel Martinet, Léon Werth, Gérard Rosenthal, Pierre Naville, Félicien Challaye, Maurice Wullens, André Philip, Victor Serge, André Breton, P. Monatte, J. and M. Alexandre, Lucie Col-liard, M. Dommanget and Daniel Guérin. A Rogatory Commission presided over by the Italian socialist G. E. Modigliani and assisted by Mme César Chabrun, President of the Committee for Aid to Political Prisoners, with M. Délépine, President of the Socialist Law-yers' Group, J. Galtier-Boissière, a writer and managing editor of *Crapouillot*, and J. Mathé, a former Secretary of the National Union of Postmen, carried out a preliminary investigation in Paris. It heard witnesses, including Leon Sedov, who supplemented his testimony by publishing a *Red Book*, a collection of facts and documents that demolished the gross inventions and forgeries of Vyshinsky and the G.P.U. A similar committee was set up in Prague under the chair-manship of the former Reichstag deputy, Anton Grilewicz. As a result of G.P.U. intrigue in which, as it turned out later, Stalin took a per-sonal interest, Grilewicz, a political refugee, was arrested soon after-wards and deported from Czechoslovakia as an undesirable alien.

The New York Committee thought it was essential to set up a special Commission charged with examining Trotsky's case in depth and then judging it in accordance with American judicial procedure. John Dewey agreed to preside over the preliminary investigation which, as there was not the slightest chance of Trotsky obtaining an American visa, had to be held in Mexico. When Suzanne La Fol-

[4] Carlo Tresca, the Italian-American freedom fighter whose life was one continuous struggle, conducted with courage, good humour and great ability, was murdered in mysterious circumstances in New York on January 11th, 1943. The crime was so care-fully planned that it must have been organized by a highly disciplined body – either Fascist or Stalinist. At the time of his death, Tresca was writing a book on the G.P.U.

lette told John Dewey that she feared the strain of travelling would be too much for him, he answered, 'But I am only seventy-nine.'

The Preliminary Commission began its work in Mexico on April 10th, 1937 and planned to finish there on the 17th. Those present were: Professor John Dewey, chairman; the writer Carleton Beals, member; Suzanne La Follette, secretary; Otto Rühle, former Social Democratic Reichstag deputy, member; the writer Benjamin Stolberg, member; John F. Finerty, former counsel for Tom Mooney and for Sacco and Vanzetti, legal adviser to the Commission; Albert Goldman, counsel for Trotsky; Albert Glotzer, recorder; Trotsky and his secretary, Jan Frankel, witnesses; the press and invited members of the public.

'The Commission met at Diego Rivera's house in Coyoacan, where we were still living under the watchful eye of the Mexican police. The Soviet Embassy in Washington, the Mexican and the American Communist Parties and the leading Mexican labour organizations had been invited to take part in the investigation, which meant, above all, cross-examining Trotsky. Ambassador Troyanovsky failed to reply to the invitation; Vincente Lombardo Toledano sent an offensive letter of refusal on behalf of the Mexican *Confederacion de los Trabajadores*, as did Hernan-Laborde on behalf of the Politbureau of the Mexican Communist Party. The Jewish Cultural League agreed to be represented by Jacopo Abrams, and Señor Luis Sanches Ponton, Mexican correspondent-member of the secretariat of the League of Nations, also accepted the invitation.

'There were rarely fewer than fifty people present at any one time. John Dewey, opening the first session, said, "The Commission ... believes that no man should be condemned without a chance to defend himself ... Our sole function is to ascertain the truth as far as is humanly possible ... If Leon Trotsky is guilty of the acts with which he is charged, no condemnation can be too severe." Speaking for himself, the old philosopher added, "I have given my life to the work of education, which I have conceived to be that of public enlightenment in the interests of society. If I finally accepted the responsible post I now occupy it was because I realized that to act otherwise would be to be false to my lifework."

'Leon Davidovich stressed that for a year he had been calling on the Soviet authorities to initiate extradition proceedings against him, which would have compelled them to submit to foreign courts what evidence they had to substantiate Vyshinsky's charges, and would have enabled Trotsky and Leon Sedov to prove their innocence before international opinion. Leon Davidovich's situation was quite extraordinary. Having been toppled from power at the end of 1923, subjected to close political surveillance by the secret police from 1927 to 1929, and forced to live abroad ever since 1929, he had suddenly been transformed into the leader of a vast conspiracy involving some of the very people who had persecuted him, the majority of Lenin's party and tens of thousands of intellectuals, technicians and Soviet workers of all kinds! A militant socialist since the age of seventeen, and a veteran of two revolutions, he was now accused of having betrayed his inmost convictions, of having organized the most monstrous crimes and of collaborating with the Nazi and Japanese secret services! He placed all his papers, archives, correspondence, accounts of income and expenditure, writings, in short everything he possessed, at the complete disposal of the Commission. He answered all questions that were put to him, and did so in English.

'As Vyshinsky had claimed that Trotsky had fought all his life against Bolshevism and the U.S.S.R. – from his polemics against Lenin in 1904 up to the derailments in Siberia – the Commission studied Leon Davidovich's curriculum vitae in considerable detail. His 1904 pamphlet *Our Political Aims*, in which he had opposed Lenin's "proletarian Jacobinism" with a socialist conception of revolutionary democracy, was duly filed, and so was Leon Davidovich's admission that, on organizational questions, Lenin had been right thirty-three years earlier, and he himself had erred ... Also into the files went an article in *Pravda* of March 14th, 1923, entitled "Leon Trotsky, the Organizer of Victory", and an anonymous article in the same paper published on March 8th, 1929, entitled "Mr Trotsky in the Service of the British Bourgeoisie", and a further thirty-one documents or series of documents. There was only one disagreeable incident, namely when Carleton Beals asked whether it was true that Trotsky had sent Borodin to Mexico in 1919 to found the Communist Party there. Leon Davidovich considered that this allegation – which he denied, in any case – was likely to compromise him in the eyes of his host country, and Mr Beals withdrew from the Commission.

'With the exception of Albert Goldman, the Commission was made up of intellectuals hostile to Bolshevism and *a fortiori* to Stalinism which they considered an inevitable consequence of Bolshevism. The only Marxist among them, Otto Rühle, one of the great militants of the 1918 German revolution, a biographer of Karl Marx, and the author of a large number of learned works, took much the same view, which Leon Davidovich did his best to refute with historical facts and arguments. The analysis of the two Moscow trials took up a great deal of time and during the proceedings Leon Davidovich clearly gained the Commission's sympathy.

'Two interesting details, which throw light on subsequent developments, should be noted here. Otto Rühle quoted an article in the *Prager Presse* on the growth of exports from the Third Reich to Russia, the secret journeys of members of Hitler's general staff to Moscow and a possible rapprochement between the U.S.S.R. and Nazi Germany. "This is a partial confirmation of my hypotheses," Leon Davidovich explained. "Perhaps it is all bluff but a bluff can become fact ... " The enquiry was being held in the middle of the Spanish Civil War and Leon Davidovich warned that Stalinist crimes must be expected in a country already so steeped in blood.

'The Preliminary Commission returned to New York and submitted its findings to the Commission of Inquiry for its verdict.'

IX. *A new wave of crimes. Execution of Marshal Tukhachevsky and of seven Red Army generals. Murder of Ignaz Reiss in Lausanne and of Erwin Wolf in Barcelona*

Trotsky felt very much better for having returned to the fray, for having recounted the story of his life, and for having demonstrated that the charges against him were false. Moreover, he had done so before a body that was something like a court of justice, made up of honest and scrupulously fair men, and presided over by the admirable John Dewey, 'the embodiment of American idealism', his serene face marked by more than half a century of intense intellectual effort. The nightmare was over – for a short time, at least.

Three weeks later, there was a flood of bad news. At the beginning of May 1937, the Stalinists had provoked a series of mutinies in Barcelona, and when Largo Caballero had refused to outlaw one of the revolutionary parties, the P.O.U.M. (Workers' Party of Marxist Unity), he had been forced to hand over to Dr Negrin. The P.O.U.M. was crushed and the Spanish Republic, with its back to the wall, was at once hideously defiled by a string of crimes.

G.P.U. squads, sent from Russia to Spain, had started to kidnap and murder the opponents of Stalinism. Mark Rhein, the socialist engineer who was the son of the Russian Menshevik leader, Rafael

Abramovich, disappeared after being seized in a hotel corridor, and was either killed or taken back to the U.S.S.R. in secret. The bullet-ridden bodies of the libertarian philosopher, Camillo Berneri, and of another well-known anarchist were found in an alley in Barcelona; both had just been arrested by Communist policemen – the Communist Party had its own secret police, as well as a large number of agents in the Catalonian *generalità* and in the Republican police force. Andrés Nin also disappeared. Trotsky had known him well in Moscow and had been a friend of his for years. As secretary of the Red Trade Union International, Nin had supported the left-wing Opposition; on his return to Spain in 1931, after the fall of the monarchy, he became one of the founders of the P.O.U.M. and had held the post of Minister of Justice in the Catalonian *generalità*. Trotsky had engaged in a heated discussion with him by correspondence, which had ended in a political break, but this had not stopped Trotsky from admiring Nin's integrity, intelligence and erudition. Republican ministers tried in vain to save Nin's life when they heard about his disappearance. He was taken from Barcelona to Valencia and then on to Madrid by Communist Party agents; he finally disappeared near a Soviet-held airfield in Alcala de Henarés and no further trace of him was ever found.

'On May 12th, 1937, a special communiqué announced that death sentences had been passed by a military tribunal on Marshal Tukhachevsky and seven of the most outstanding military leaders of the Revolution, and that they had been duly executed. "The Red Army has been decapitated," was the verdict of Trotsky, who knew the worth of these men – decapitated at the very moment that the international situation was deteriorating month by month and that Hitler and Mussolini were marching towards victory in Spain! The chief political commissar of the Red Army, Gamarnik, committed suicide. There were arrests, mysterious disappearances, and secret executions throughout the U.S.S.R. In July, Budu Mdivani, Okudjava, Eliava and several other old Georgian Bolsheviks, whom Lenin had promised "to support with all his soul", were shot. It was said that during their secret trial they hurled defiance at their lying accusers and executioners. Others, Kavtaradze among them, assassinated in the G.P.U. cellars, did not have even that last satisfaction ... The brothers Nestor and Mikhail Lakoba, whose guests we had been in Sukhumi, perished as well. Nestor Lakoba, Chairman of the Council of People's Commissars of the Abkhaz Autonomous Region, was shot in unknown circumstances. Mikhail, the weaker of the two, stood trial, confessed to imaginary crimes, denounced his brother, and was executed. Both of them had tried to alleviate the hardships of forced collectivization in their small, sunny land ... The faces of all these men – and those of innumerable others that went to the grave with them – were familiar to us, as were the stories of their brave lives ... We wandered about in our little tropical garden in Coyoacan, surrounded by distant ghosts, each with a hole in his forehead ...

'For eight years we had grown used to living with the spectre of an attempted assassination. In his indictment during the second Moscow trial, Vyshinsky, the public prosecutor, had exclaimed, "This is the end of Trotsky and of Trotskyism!" The policy of extermination had an inexorable logic.

'At the end of July 1937, our young friend, Erwin Wolf, who had acted as Leon Davidovich's secretary in Norway with such single-minded devotion, disappeared in Barcelona. Though of middle-class origin, he had a burning desire to serve the workers' cause. Victor Serge, who met him in Brussels as Wolf was preparing to leave for Spain, told him, "You must be mad! You are going to your certain death. You must realize that you are an essential witness of Trotsky's life and activities in Norway and that the G.P.U. will do everything they can get rid of you!" Nodding his young, high-domed head, Wolf said he would take every precaution ... Nevertheless he travelled to Spain under his real name and joined up with the Fourth International in Barcelona. He was arrested, but released when nothing could be proved against him. Three days later he was kidnapped in the street and disappeared. His wife, the courageous Jordis Knudsen, escaped a similar fate by a miracle: the Norwegian consul hid her away and helped to smuggle her to France ... Catalonia was in the grip of Stalinist terror. When the Czechoslovak government made strong representations to the Negrin government on Wolf's behalf, it was informed, on October 20th, 1937, that Erwin Wolf had been released on September 13th. In others words, the Spanish authorities admitted officially to his arrest and to the fact that there was no case against him. But, in the circumstances, he could only have been released with the approval of the Russian and Communist secret services, who must have seized him the moment he emerged from gaol ... He was never seen again.

'On September 4th, Ignaz Reiss was assassinated in Lausanne ...

He had been one of the chief Soviet secret agents abroad, but having wrestled with his conscience for a long time, he had broken with Moscow, protesting to the Central Committee against the massacre of the revolutionaries. Special execution squads had been formed from among the most dedicated servants of the G.P.U., and as a reward for their services all of them were decorated with the Order of the Red Banner (before being executed themselves). Reiss had sent back his own decoration ...

'The Swiss police pursued their investigations unsparingly, and so – thanks to the personal intervention of the socialist Minister of the Interior, Marx Dormoy – did the French. The threads of a bloody intrigue, involving the G.P.U. officials and running to Paris, were unravelled, the murderers were identified, and the informers arrested. A special envoy from Moscow called Spiegelglass had organized the crime. He had been assisted by Beletsky, Grozovsky and Lydia Grozovskaya, all members of the Soviet commercial mission in Paris. Those of the culprits who enjoyed diplomatic immunity were requested to leave France at once; Lydia Grozovskaya, who was released on bail set at a very high figure, disappeared. The French police also established that one of the G.P.U. agents, a man called Semirensky, had taken a room in the rue Lacretelle, with just a wall separating him from the room occupied by our son, Leon Sedov, in the house next door ... It was discovered that Leon Sedov was being shadowed and that there was a plan to kidnap him during a proposed visit to Mulhouse ... It also appeared that he had been surrounded by G.P.U. agents during a brief holiday in Antibes, where he had gone unbeknown to anyone but a close and reliable friend. A woman spy, who was afterwards implicated in the assassination of Reiss, had invited him to join her on a boat trip ...

'At the end of that September Kurt Landau, a young Marxist, known in Central Europe under the pseudonym of Wolf Bertram, was picked up in Barcelona by uniformed police, who were in fact Stalinist agents. He disappeared as if swallowed up by the ocean ... He had at one time been a member of the International Bureau of the left-wing Opposition, but had later grown sharply critical of some of Trotsky's ideas. As far as the G.P.U. was concerned this obviously made no difference ...'

X. *The Dewey Commission finds Trotsky not guilty. Suspicious death of Trotsky's elder son, Leon Sedov, in Paris.*

'On December 13th, 1937, the Commission of Inquiry into the charges made against Leon Trotsky in the Moscow Trials returned its verdict. Its deliberations covered two hundred and forty-seven points and ran to a four hundred-page volume published by Harper Brothers of New York under the title *Not Guilty*. Its conclusions, that "we therefore find the Moscow trials to be frame-ups" and "we therefore find Trotsky and Sedov not guilty", were signed by John Dewey as Chairman; Suzanne La Follette, writer, as secretary; John Chamberlain, writer and journalist; Alfred Rosmer, member of the Executive Committee of the Communist International 1920–1 and Chief Editor of *L'Humanité*, 1923–4; Edward Alsworth Ross, Professor of Sociology at the University of Wisconsin; Otto Rühle, former member of the Reichstag; Benjamin Stolberg, journalist; Carlo Tresca, editor of *Il Martello*; Francisco Zamora, journalist, former member of the National Committee of the Mexican Confederation of Labour; Wendelin Thomas, former member of the Reichstag; and John Finerty, lawyer and counsel for Tom Mooney.

'The verdict filled us with delight, if one can speak of delight in such circumstances. Six days later a communiqué from Moscow announced the summary execution of eight people: seven members of the Commissariat of Foreign Affairs and our former neighbour in the Kremlin, the Georgian Avelii Enukidze, for fifteen years Secretary of the Central Soviet Executive. We had been fond of this good-looking, fair, somewhat plump man, with his regular features, his air of benign earnestness, and his blue eyes. Conscientious and liberal by temperament, he had fought hard against abuses and had tried to blunt the edge of the persecutions. He had known Stalin since youth and the two of them had been like brothers ... That Stalin could have had him killed seemed, even in the midst of this slaughter, inconceivable to us. "That Cain!" Leon Davidovich said over and over. Another victim in this batch was Karakhan, who had been recalled from the Soviet Legation in Ankara ostensibly to be given the Embassy in Washington – the elegant Karakhan, who ever since the critical days of Brest-Litovsk [1918] had been one of the best Soviet diplomats, both in China and in Turkey ...

'After the deliberations of the Dewey Commission, Leon Davidovich felt completely exhausted. An American lecturer lent us his villa in Taxco, set amid some of the finest scenery in Mexico. We spent some time in peace and quiet, isolated from the nightmare outside. When we returned to Coyoacan, Leon Davidovich resumed his work. He was haunted by the Moscow trials and the executions; he continued to check dates, count up the victims and lived day and night with the destruction of a whole generation, whose worth he knew better than anyone else. Never in recorded history had any country been so bent on annihilating its entire elite ... We saw very few people and felt lonely.

'Meanwhile, Diego Rivera, who had a vivid imagination but was this time a most vigilant host, had begun to feel great anxiety for Leon Davidovich's safety. He had noticed suspicious comings and goings in a nearby house, and persuaded Leon Davidovich to spend a few days with our friend Antonio Hidalgo, an old Mexican revolutionary who lived in a quiet house near Chapultepec Park. Hidalgo would go off to work, his wife would be busy with her chores, and the whole house seemed to be dozing in the warm sunshine. Leon Davidovich could work without interruption.

'Then some journalists rang Diego up ... He went rushing over to Hidalgo's house, burst into Leon Davidovich's room and – either because he was carried away by emotion or else because he was singularly insensitive – said bluntly and point-blank: "Leon Sedov is dead!" – "What? What did you say?" Diego showed him the message. "Get out of here!" Leon Davidovich shouted at him. He had to be alone before he lost control and collapsed. He stayed for some time by himself, sunk in a numb despair.

'I was at Coyoacan, busy sorting out old photographs of our children. The bell rang and I was surprised to see Leon Davidovich. I went to meet him. He came in, more bent than he had ever been before, and his face ash-grey; he seemed to have turned into an old man overnight. "What is it?" I asked in alarm. "Are you ill?" He answered in a low voice, "Lyova is ill, our little Lyova ..." Then I began to understand. I had been so afraid for Leon Davidovich that the thought of something happening to Lyova had never occurred to me ...

'Lyova – Leon Sedov – had died in Paris on February 16th, 1937, in mysterious circumstances which gave rise to the strong suspicion that his death was not due to natural causes. Hard-working and overstretched, constantly short of money, suffering as intensely from the nightmare as we did and fighting against it as vigorously, he had for some time been running slight temperatures in the evenings.

Then acute appendicitis was diagnosed and he was taken to a clinic run by a Russian émigré, Dr Simkov, for an emergency operation. Lyova was registered as a French engineer by the name of Martin. The operation, simple enough in itself, was successful and there were no complications. Yet a few days later, after this routine and commonplace operation, Lyova became delirious and died. Some strange facts came to light. The patient had taken food at a time when eating should not have been allowed under any circumstances. Was this negligence or something worse? A doctor had spoken to him in Russian ... Had he been identified? A White Russian nurse, who worked at the clinic, was known to move in pro-Stalinist circles ... The public prosecutor ordered a post-mortem but our own friends, Leon Sedov's girlfriend, Jeanne, and even our lawyer disagreed with the findings ... Under her Popular Front government, which was honeycombed with Communist cells and allied with the U.S.S.R., France feared a scandal that might implicate certain secret service organizations. Crimes as notorious as the assassination of the Russian economist Navashin, in the Bois de Boulogne, and the seizure of General Miller by the G.P.U. in the middle of Paris, had never been cleared up. Similarly, the discreet inquest never discovered the true causes of our son's death. Had it been a tragic coincidence, or something more? Dr. Simkov, the director of the clinic, lost his two adolescent sons in a macabre accident a little later; they were buried alive while playing in a sand-pit. The papers reported that a car had been seen parked nearby ...

'Leon Sedov died at the age of 29. He had always shared Leon Davidovich's political views. He had grown up during the Revolution, victorious at first and then imperilled, and his personality had been moulded in the semi-underground Opposition Youth Movement. In Turkey, Germany and France he had worked as a publicist, shouldering the difficult task of publishing and distributing the *Opposition Bulletin*. His writings were always sound; we never saw his last article, which dealt with the execution of the Eight, because his papers had been impounded by the public prosecutor ... In Berlin, he had been an able student of mathematics. He led a more than frugal life in two tiny fifth-floor rooms. He knew he was being shadowed by the G.P.U., and the French police had proof that he was watched more closely than he ever realized. He matured early, and his character displayed a highly developed moral sense and the precise mind of a research scientist.

'When we heard of the tragedy, Leon Davidovich was finishing a small book called *Their Morals and Ours*.[5] He dedicated it to our son's memory.'

XI. *Third Moscow trial of Old Bolsheviks (Bukharin, Krestinsky, Rykov, Yagoda). New series of false charges against Trotsky: Bessonov's letter. The missing millions*

Fifteen days later – as if to fling a new challenge at world opinion, already deeply confused by the previous trials and alerted by the verdict of the Dewey Commission – an even more monstrous third trial was started in Moscow (March 2nd–13th, 1938). This time, the twenty-one accused included Nikolai Bukharin, the leading theoretical exponent of Communism; Alexey Rykov, Lenin's successor as Chairman of the Council of People's Commissars; Henryk Yagoda, ex-People's Commissar of the Interior, former chief of the secret police and stage director of the first Moscow trial; Christian Rakovsky and Nikolay Krestinsky, two former diplomats; Rosengoltz, the former Commissar for Foreign Trade; Chernov and Grinki, two former members of the Government; Khodyaev, one of the best-known political figures in Soviet Central Asia; several leading Russian physicians, and some minor figures – all accused of high treason, conspiracy, espionage, sabotage, terrorism and of having, in the words of Vyshinsky, formed 'an anti-Soviet bloc of Trotskyists and Rightists'. A totalitarian regime takes no heed of truth and lies, the probable and the improbable, of what is felt and suspected at home or proved and known with certainty abroad. The President of the Military Tribunal of the Supreme Court, his assistants and his indefatigable public prosecutor were not in the least troubled by the whole demonstrable fraud. Stalin's Politbureau had a guillotine with an exceedingly sharp blade and that was all that mattered.

Trotsky was once again the principal defendant. In the U.S.S.R., thousands of officials, the newspapers, radio, books, the theatre and the cinema kept up a stream of accusations against him, and he was presented to the submissive and downtrodden people – for the terror invaded every single home – as the very embodiment of evil, as the devil incarnate, to whom witches confessed when they sold their souls. Old Rakovsky, broken after his long and determined resistance, declared, 'I have known since 1926 that Trotsky is an agent of the

[5] Pioneer Publishers, New York, 1942.

British Intelligence Service; he told me so himself.' Others confessed
that Trotsky, their leader (or even 'Leader') had 'made agreements
with Nazi Germany and Japan' to dismember the U.S.S.R. and either
to restore capitalism or to introduce fascism in what was left of
Russia – they were not quite certain which. Trotsky's 'terrorist directives' were brought up once more. And again, the entire case was
quickly exposed as a tissue of brazen lies.

A man named Bessonov, a member of the Soviet trade mission
and later an embassy counsellor in Berlin, swore that he had been
Trotsky's and Leon Sedov's confidant and had carried messages from
them to the U.S.S.R. Naturally, none of these was produced, but
Bessonov went too far in mentioning a last letter from Trotsky,
allegedly written at the end of December 1936. From the beginning
of September 1936 until his departure from Norway, all Trotsky's
mail had been checked by the authorities. Moreover, Bessonov had
specifically stated that the letter was dated the end of December 1936,
but Trotsky had boarded the *Ruth* on December 18th, 1936, bound
for Mexico and in the company of Mr Jonas Lie of the Norwegian
police. Mr Lie assured the press that Trotsky had no way of sending
letters from the middle of the Atlantic. Nor could the letter have been
written earlier and post-dated, for it was supposed to have been
written in reply to one of Bessonov's, of which, incidentally, the
Norwegian authorities could find no trace.

Nor was that all. Krestinsky declared that he had met Trotsky
and Leon Sedov on about October 10th, 1933, at Merano in the
Italian Alps. Trotsky could easily have shown that, at the time, he
was living at Barbizon near Paris, surrounded by friends and visitors
and discreetly watched by the *Sûreté*. But what good would that have
done? The next day, Stalin's secretaries might announce they had
met him in China. Leon Sedov had just died; perhaps that was why
the number of people who claimed to have met Trotsky's son increased
so rapidly.

The lies rose to a crescendo when Rosengoltz spoke at length on
'the financial support extended to the Trotskyist movement by the
People's Commissariat of Foreign Trade' of which he had been chairman. People reading the Proceedings could not believe their eyes.
From 1931 or 1933 onwards (it was not quite clear which, as
Rosengoltz and Prosecutor Vyshinsky both mumbled), Trotsky was
supposed to have received $300,000, £27,000 and 20,000 German
marks from Soviet State funds held abroad. How were those vast

transfers effected? What middle-men were involved? What ruses were used to circumvent the extremely stringent checks to which all Soviet commercial operations were subjected? Vyshinsky asked for no details, and with good reason. Considerable sums had, in fact, been diverted from commercial channels for purposes unknown to Commissar Rosengoltz and his colleagues, but this was done on orders from the Politbureau and the funds had been used, as the Commissar rightly suspected, to subsidize the Comintern and certain secret operations. Next, Krestinsky confessed that for seven years from 1923 (that is, all the time he had been Soviet Ambassador in Germany), he had received 250,000 marks per annum for transfer to the Trotskyist movement, or a total of about two million marks, give or take a hundred thousand. The well-informed reader might recall that after the Treaty of Rapallo, the German Reichswehr was offered the use of training-grounds in Russia for which they had to pay in cash.

'Hundreds of people – it must have been over a thousand – knew the austere life Trotsky had led, how great his material difficulties had been, and how often friends and comrades had come to his financial aid; the Dewey Commission had scrutinized his accounts; hundreds had seen Leon Sedov live and die in a state of poverty that at times deserved to be called something worse... When we arrived in Mexico, we owned practically nothing and American friends saw to our basic needs ... And the Trotskyist Movement? In every country where it existed, first as the "Opposition" and later as the "Fourth International", the governments and anyone who had had anything to do with its groups knew how poor they were and at what great personal sacrifice their irregular publications were brought out ... But let us suppose that all these dollars had been devoted to pioneering a conspiracy within the U.S.S.R. How, then, were they converted into roubles in a country where the State Bank works hand-in-glove with the secret police and where a citizen who receives twenty dollars from relatives abroad is suspect? And what was supposed to have become of these roubles? Nothing was easier in Russia than to check on the income and expenditure of a citizen. Neither the Prosecutor nor the defendants threw any light on these questions; indeed, they never even raised them. Many people wondered why the prosecution had thought it necessary to include this transparent fabrication in the indictment. The only explanation was that it was needed to fill a logical gap – the idea of a vast network of penniless international

Trotskyists and conspirators throughout the Soviet Union would have lacked all credibility, assuming that this actually mattered to anyone involved. Moreover, it could do no harm to associate the name of Trotsky with fabulous wealth in the minds of the most wretched people on earth.'

All this clearly shows the prosecution's technique of using acknowledged facts to establish falsehoods, often by giving perfectly innocent events a criminal slant. Members of the government and senior officials could not deny that they had had such-and-such a business discussion on such-and-such a date; all they were then required to do was to confess that the subjects of such discussions were sabotage, treason, and so on. Chernov, as People's Commissar for Agriculture, had taken a keen interest in epizootic diseases; he was now made to confess that his interest stemmed from his desire to foment them. Grinko, the People's Commissar for Finance, had for years been forced to drive a zig-zag course between inflation and deflation, applying the brakes or accelerating according to the different orders the Politbureau had seen fit to hand down to him; he now confessed that he had deliberately sabotaged the country's finances even though the whole of Russia could see that the economy was suffering from the government's own appalling bungling. Forced collectivization had culminated in a number of popular insurrections in Uzbekistan, but this delicate topic was conveniently glossed over by the Tribunal. Instead Khodyaev, the most influential political figure in Central Asia, was made to confess that he had sabotaged official policy for the benefit of Germany, Japan and Great Britain. Rakovsky, for his part, confessed that on his official visits to Japan he had met double-dealing politicians and had sold himself to the Japanese espionage service. Rykov, Bukharin, the late Tomsky (he had committed suicide) and a hundred others had often discussed the threat of war and, like everyone else, had expressed the fear that the U.S.S.R., in the grip of famine, over-work and general discontent, might be beaten – and that stamped them as defeatists. Because, furthermore, they had examined the consequences of Russia's losing a war and had wondered how they could be mitigated, they had clearly been planning the dismemberment of the Soviet Union. This process of rationalization is known to every psychologist under the name of projection or blame-shifting.

The trial revealed new depths of insanity. Like madness, it was founded on real distress and mixed truth and folly, the probable and the unlikely. It was the insanity of a clique in temporary control: totalitarianism bent on destroying all that remained of the Revolution. It was as if the Russian Revolution had never been, as if Bolshevism had never existed, but that, instead, a gang of unscrupulous adventurers had played a gigantic political confidence trick from which, in the nick of time, a 'Leader of genius' had saved the U.S.S.R. single-handed and made her flourish. Vyshinsky hinted that Bukharin might have been a foreign spy even before he returned to Russia in 1917. To that end he had brought into court several Social Revolutionaries, who had been lingering in various gaols for the past nineteen years, to testify that, in 1918, Bukharin had helped them to plan an attempt on Lenin's life with Trotsky's blessing. There was no reason for totalitarian madness to respect history when it was doing everything it could to crush the men who had written it.

The shadowy backcloth of the previous trials lay for a moment illuminated by the spotlight, which was aimed everywhere at random. It revealed that the then People's Commissar of the Interior, Yagoda, the stage-manager of the trial of the Thirteen, had called on Ivan Smirnov in prison and that he had 'indoctrinated' him. This was but one of many indications that the defendants at the first big trial had been given secret instructions, further details of which can be found in Walter Krivitzky's book.

And in the cross-examination of Yagoda, we stumble upon a particularly squalid corner of the hell that was Stalin's police state. Old Kremlin doctors admitted that, on the orders of the head of the G.P.U., they had caused the deaths of Maxim Gorky, of his son, of Kuybishev and of Menzhinsky by applying 'contra-indicated drugs'. Yagoda himself had a poison cabinet! And why not? All things are possible and nothing is inconceivable. In 1933, when I was incarcerated in the G.P.U. prison in Moscow, I spent a whole night in extremely painful and quite inexplicable distress and, in November 1936, published an article on the subject in Paris entitled *Florentine Methods*. As for the elder Gorky, who had been tuberculous since youth and died at the age of sixty-seven, we know that towards the end of his life he fell out with Stalin, was refused a passport and had his correspondence with Romain Rolland subjected to strict censorship. His secretary, Kryuchkov, now confessed that Gorky had been murdered and that he himself had acted as an informer. All Moscow knew that Kryuchkov was a blackguard.

It appeared that the right-wing Bolsheviks (Bukharin, Rykov,

Tomsky, Rudzutak and a number of others), after ousting Trotsky and playing their part in the persecution of the left-wing Opposition, had ended up in despair at the growth of a monstrous anti-socialist regime, and that they had secretly held many anxious talks on the subject. Did this amount to a conspiracy? Quite possibly when the first two tumbrils had carried off so many old Bolsheviks, these men realized that they too were doomed, and began to consider the idea of a 'palace revolution', as they themselves called it. The old Red Army figures, led by Tukhachevsky and Gamarnik, who were more energetic than most and in the best position to do so, were said to have considered seizing the Kremlin. This, too, was quite possible and even likely. They would have had to have the souls of lambs going meekly to the slaughter if they had not entertained such thoughts.

This mad trial was evidently going to be the last – trials were becoming too grave a threat to the regime. Several times, judges and prosecution had trembled as the entire scaffolding they had so carefully erected threatened to collapse around them. The chief defendants had clearly lost patience and had grown desperate. During the first two hearings, Krestinsky had caused a furore when he calmly denied all charges. He was an intellectual, with a high forehead emphasized by his receding hairline, a chin lengthened by a pointed beard, and glittering spectacles – one of the most cultured men in the entire government. He was fifty-four years old, and had been a militant since 1902, and a Bolshevik since the foundation of the Party; he had been arrested time and again by the Tsarist police and had been Lenin's confidant, Commissar of Finance, Secretary to the Central Committee, and Ambassador to Berlin. Right at the beginning of the trial, when Ulrich, the President of the Tribunal, asked him whether he pleaded guilty, he replied, 'No, I am not guilty of any crime. I am a Party member ... ' Vyshinsky returned to the charge several times. 'I lied during the preliminary hearing,' Krestinsky said. 'Why?' asked the Prosecutor. 'Krestinsky remained silent,' the official report states – and the Public Prosecutor remained silent, too, not daring to press the question. An hour later, Krestinsky went on to say, 'My rupture with Trotsky took place in 1927. I insist that this fact be entered in the record.' Three times he repeated that he had made false confessions at the preliminary hearings. Again the Prosecutor did not press him, but he was evidently concerned about Krestinsky's change of attitude and returned to the matter at hourly intervals. Krestinsky told him, 'The deposition I made on June 5th–9th is a tissue of lies from beginning to end ... ' Vyshinsky then questioned the other defendants, relying on their promise to co-operate which had been extorted from them in the murky shadows of the G.P.U. dungeons and on which they no doubt felt their lives depended. 'Is Krestinsky a Trotskyist?' 'Yes,' they replied in chorus. Krestinsky himself merely said, 'I feel sick.' An hour later, he denied that he had met Trotsky in Merano. 'My statements were false.' Vyshinsky: 'Why did you want to mislead me?' (An unwise question!) Krestinsky: 'I thought that if I spoke the truth [at the preliminary hearing] the Party and government leaders would not be told ... I spoke under duress ... The other defendants are lying.' The whole trial was about to collapse, and Vyshinsky quickly slackened his pressure. The following dialogue came in the last minute of Krestinsky's cross-examination, and its implied threat must have appalled the judges:

Krestinsky: *I deny everything.*
Vyshinsky: *Absolutely?*
Krestinsky: *Yes, absolutely.*
Vyshinsky: *You're sure?*
Krestinsky: *I am positive.*

The second sitting (March 2nd, 1937) had come to an end. What happened later that night? Did they threaten Krestinsky, and with what? What menaces or promises could have had the slightest effect on a man who already considered himself as good as dead? Was it enough to point out to him that he was undermining the whole trial and hence dragging the good name of the U.S.S.R. through the mud? Whatever the reason, Krestinsky apologized next day for his previous denials, which he attributed to his nervous condition, and confessed in full. From that point on he agreed – and at length – to everything that was put to him.

Some of the other defendants also flirted with the idea of non-co-operation. One had the feeling that they might tear up the pact they had made with the prosecution if they were driven just a little too far. Suddenly even Yagoda came out with categorical denials. Why should he have bothered? What difference could one crime more or less have made? A man in a delirium does not weigh his words. 'Yes,' said the former head of the G.P.U., 'I said that in the preliminary hearing, but it is not true.' 'Why did you say it?' 'I don't know.' The Prosecutor, realizing that he had pushed the defendant almost to turning point, relented for a while but returned to the charge a little later.

Vyshinsky: *Why did you make false statements?*

Yagoda: *Allow me not to reply to that question.*

And Vyshinsky allowed it. Twice the defendant replied in the same terms and twice the Prosecutor accepted the answer.

Bukharin, too, showed what can only be called impudent bravado from time to time. The chorus of confessions was shot through with discordant notes.

Vyshinsky then called for a verdict against all those 'Rightists, Trotskyists, Mensheviks, Social Revolutionaries, bourgeois nationalists, this rabble of assassins, spies and saboteurs ... ', which meant that the indictment included not only the two oppositional factions within the Communist Party, but the other two traditional parties of the Russian Left, as well as various national movements – enough in itself to demonstrate the lunacy of the charges. These 'unprincipled' rogues were supposed to have heaped crime upon crime under the direction of Trotsky and the British, German, Polish, Japanese 'and other' intelligence services. (In the case of Germany, the indictment failed to distinguish between Weimar and Nazi spies.) Now that all the Nazi archives, and those of the German and Japanese High Commands, are in American and British hands, everybody knows what to think of Vyshinsky's odious fabrications. No doubt, even he could have foreseen this development, he would not have cared. As it was, he levelled his insane charges at old Russian Mensheviks who had been abroad since 1922,[6] Magdeleine Paz, Alfred Rosmer, the managing editor of the Paris *L'Ordre*, Emile Buré and the English philanthropist, Lady Paget. The trial was followed by a quite superfluous rain of protests and denials from all over the world.

With the exception of Rakovsky, of an old Kremlin doctor and of Bessonov, for whom the Prosecutor demanded a mere twenty-five-year sentence, all the accused were to be 'shot like mangy dogs, stamped out like poisonous vermin'. 'Our radiant sun will continue to shine upon our happy country,' as 'under the guidance of our beloved leader and teacher, Stalin, we march ... ever forward towards

---

[6] Notably the historian, Boris Nikolaevsky, and, in a particularly offensive way, Theodor Dan, who was alleged to be working for the police and for German intelligence. Suffice it to say that this upright old socialist died in New York in 1947, having devoted the last years of his life to editing a pro-Soviet review, the *New Road*.

Communism.' Before this peroration, Vyshinsky had spent some hours raking over the details of the indictment, showing particular venom towards Bukharin, whose criminal career was supposed to have started in 1909 when he had a difference of opinion with Lenin about the Imperial Duma. Nor was he a newcomer to sabotage of the Revolution – he had been a saboteur ever since 1915 when he wrote an article entitled 'The World Economy and Imperialism', which Lenin had castigated as being anarchist in tenor! So it went on. These insane outpourings would have been merely ludicrous had they not been accompanied by so much bloodshed, and had they not been final proof – if such were needed – of the criminal nature of a regime that was totally deaf to logic, common sense, historical facts, moral values, intelligence and truth.

At the end of the trial, most of the defendants asked to be sentenced in almost the same terms as the prosecution had used against them. They, too, were mere puppets of the regime, who all confessed in the hope that their lives would be spared, a hope that could only have been entertained if they had been given a promise. Krestinsky offered a very curious explanation of his denials during the first hearing. 'Subjectively, I was telling the truth but, objectively, I was wrong ...' Anyone familiar with Stalinist terminology can easily translate this piece of sophistry: I was telling the truth when I rejected the senseless charges against me, but was wrong for reasons of state, which I now consider more important than my own fate. The former head of the G.P.U., Yagoda, who ought to have realized better than anyone else that, since he knew too much, the regime was bound to get rid of him, begged leave to join one of the armies of forced labourers digging canals he himself had organized. Rakovsky spoke about his thirty-four years of friendship with Trotsky, 'a man who has openly fought against the Party' (what remarkable reticence!), admitted to being a British and Japanese spy and put it to the judges that, since he was sixty-five years old, a prison sentence of twenty-five years was perhaps a little excessive. Rosengoltz recalled his military service on several fronts, blamed Trotsky, and ended by crying out, 'Long live the Bolshevik Party with its traditions of enthusiasm, heroism and self-denial, the most wonderful in the world, under the leadership of Stalin!'

Bukharin's reaction was altogether different. He destroyed the charges against himself so effectively that the words with which he confessed to even worse crimes seemed merely conventional slogans, which indeed they were. He tried to explain the trial in his own lucid way; one could sense that he was ashamed – and not for himself alone. His dialectical arguments were both crystal-clear and tortuous at the same time: he blamed the 'degeneration of men' for 'carrying us to the brink of pretorian Fascism led by prosperous peasants ...' The 'us' in that sentence was deliberately ambiguous. In the face of death, he was staring into 'a pitch-black pit' and wondered for what cause he was dying. In the face of death, with all hope destroyed – not in the face of truth! – he had decided 'to go down on my knees before the Party ...' He admitted that Trotsky and the Second International had been his allies but that Stalin alone was 'the hope of the world'.

Sentences were passed at four in the morning of March 13th, 1938. All the defendants – with the exception of Rakovsky, Bessonov and an old doctor, who were given prison sentences ranging from fifteen to twenty years – were shot in G.P.U. dungeons within twenty-four hours.

In all three trials, the defendants had obviously assuaged their doubts and fears by the conviction that, despite the inhumanity of the Stalin regime, the U.S.S.R. had laid the foundations of a better society. The Stalins might come and go but the future was bound to be glorious. These sentiments were shared by many honest Communists outside the U.S.S.R.

Leon Davidovich himself declared that the achievements of the October Revolution had not been lost, that the collectivist and planned society of the U.S.S.R. was a great step forward in the history of man. At the same time, he believed that Stalinist totalitarianism was jeopardizing these achievements, and that revolutionary action against it was as necessary as it was legitimate. It was this view, and not merely his interpretation of Marxist ethics, that divided him profoundly from the trial victims. The most outspoken of them had hoped for no more than a 'palace revolution', that is, for a change of government followed by major or minor reforms imposed from the top. Trotsky, by contrast, had been calling for the democratization of the regime ever since 1923 and, as he told the Dewey Commission, it was not until 1933, when Hitler came to power, that 'under the pressure of irresistible facts' he arrived at the conclusion that the 'popular masses cannot overthrow the bureaucracy except by *revolutionary* violence ... In accordance with the fundamental principle of my activity I immediately expressed this conclusion publicly. Yes ... I think the system of Stalinist Bonapartism can be liquidated only by means of a new political revolution. However, revolutions are not made to order. They spring from the development of society. They cannot be evoked artificially. It is even less possible to replace revolution by the adventurism of terrorist acts ... '[7]

Remarkably enough, throughout this campaign to liquidate the victors of October and of the Civil War, no real Trotskyists, or, to give them their proper name, Bolshevik–Leninist Left-wing Oppositionists, were dragged into the dock or had their names mentioned, whether in the Soviet press or in the reports of the trial. There were several hundred intransigent Oppositionists who had been imprisoned or exiled for the last ten years (since 1928) and who courageously held to their convictions in the face of gruelling persecution. We know that despite the horrible atrocities committed in Soviet prisons, none of these men, steeled in battle, would have lent himself to the machinations of the G.P.U. It is unlikely that any of them has survived. Their names are to be found in the *Opposition Bulletin* and in the books of two men who managed to escape.[8]

One of the rare reports about the fate of these Trotskyists was published in Rome. It was written by Poles who had experienced the full horrors of Stalin's concentration camps in 1939–41. We quote it here, and though the authors do not mention precise dates, all the evidence suggests that they are referring to 1938–9 – their memories seemed to be fresh when their Polish lawyer interviewed them.

'Several dozen of the best known Trotskyists had been sent to the Vorkuta forced-labour camp [in the desolate region of the Pechora estuary on the Arctic coast facing Novaya Zemlya]. Once there together ... they decided to keep their names alive by a final demonstration of their inflexible will ... They demanded: (1) that the camp should be run by the political prisoners; (2) that they be given work fitting to their ... professions; (3) that they should be kept together at all times. They threatened to go on hunger strike until they had either won their demands or were dead. When their demands were rejected, the Trotskyists embarked on a hunger strike which lasted for a hundred and twenty days ... They were force-fed by the administration. Many of them perished all the same ... The Trot-

[7] *The Case of Leon Trotsky*, Proceedings of the Preliminary Enquiry Commission, Harper, New York, 1937, p. 574.

[8] Anton Ciliga, *Au Pays du Grand Mensonge*, Paris, 1938; Victor Serge, *Russia Twenty Years After*, New York, 1938–9.

skyists were kept apart from each other by vicious dogs, let loose in their huts ... In the end, the soldiers took the weak ones away ... After a short time, no one mentioned them any more. It is almost certain that they were shot because none of them was ever seen again.'[9]

XII. *The extermination of the revolutionary generation. The murder of Rudolf Klement in Paris*

The nightmare raged on. The Russian Revolution had been paralysed by a bloodthirsty police campaign of unprecedented magnitude, and replaced by totalitarianism. In Coyoacan, Leon Davidovich was inundated with messages confirming the massacre of men he had known, men whom he had led to victory, whom he had loved and who had loved him. Three of the 'invisible' defendants in the Bukharin–Rykov–Yagoda trial, constantly mentioned in the official report, simply disappeared. They had refused to make a deal with the G.P.U., could not therefore be put on trial, and had been shot out of hand without the benefit of this propaganda exercise. They were Karakhan, the young comrade who had come to meet Trotsky at the Russo-Finnish border in 1918, had accompanied Leon Davidovich to Brest-Litovsk and had later been appointed Ambassador to Peking and then to Ankara; Enukidze, Lenin's right-hand man in the Soviet administration; and Jan Rudzutak, a member of the Politbureau for eleven years, a simple Latvian metal-worker who had been sentenced to ten years' forced labour by the Tsarist courts. What was one to make of a system of justice, which certain foreign lawyers pretended to regard as entirely above-board, under which a former member of the highest institution in the Party and State could simply disappear without trace? In the eighteen months that followed the secret trial of Marshal Tukhachevsky and of the seven Red Army generals – a trial that would have seemed far-fetched even in a Hollywood extravaganza – most of the marshals, generals and admirals who had signed the communiqué announcing the execution of their colleagues, disappeared one by one. In January 1928 Pravda had published the names of the reshuffled Politbureau; Stalin, Molotov, Kaganovich, Voroshilov, Kalinin, Andreyev, Kossior, Mikoyan, Chubar, G. Petrovsky, Zhdanov, Eyche, Yezhov and Khrushchev. Of these, Kossior, Chubar, G. Petrovsky, Eyche and Yezhov

[9] Mora and Zviernak, *Soviet Justice*, Magi-Spinetti, Rome, 1945, p. 302.

subsequently disappeared in mysterious circumstances. During the third trial, some of the wretched defendants had confessed their plan to assassinate both Eyche, the man in charge of the forced collectivization of agriculture in northern Siberia and considered one of the most able Stalinist administrators, and Yezhov, the new People's Commissar of the Interior, Chief of the G.P.U. and stage-manager of that trial. And now the Politbureau itself had abducted or destroyed these very men!

The *Opposition Bulletin*, now published in New York, carried Trotsky's comments on the first Soviet elections under the 'Stalin Constitution', which Romain Rolland had described as the most democratic in the world, even though it provided for domination by a single party. Just before the votes were counted, fifty-four official candidates, selected by the Party machine, had disappeared. They included the Vice-Chairman of the Council of People's Commissars, Valery Mezhlauk, six other members of the government, General Alksnis, the Commander of the Air Force, and seven other generals, as well as Latis and Peters, who had served in the *Cheka* from the start of the Revolution.

A purge of the Comintern was held at the same time by means of bullets in the back of the head or the despatch of Communist refugees from abroad to secret 'isolators'. We are listing their names at some length, and hope the reader will bear with us. The following German Communists disappeared: Kupferstein (one of the leaders of the Ex-Servicemen's Red Front organization, who had killed two Nazi officers during a street fight) and his wife; the writers Ernst Ottwald and Günther; Heinz Neumann, Heckert and Remmele, all members of the Central Committee of the German Communist Party; ex-Reichstag Deputy Schubert; Werner Hirsch, formerly Thaelmann's secretary, who had escaped from a Nazi concentration camp; several journalists including Zisskind of the *Rote Fahne*, Kurt Sauerland of *Aufbau*, Gerber or Herber of *Die Internationale*, Borosz of the *International Press Correspondence*; the military historian Rudolf Hauss (Hausschild); Felix Halle, the lawyer and great friend of the U.S.S.R. With their retreat cut off by the Nazis, the German Communists who had fled to the Soviet Union were utterly defenceless victims of Stalin's power.

The Polish Communists were in a similar plight – their escape route was cut off by the Colonels' regime in Warsaw. Those who disappeared included Jarski and his wife; Sockocki, a member of the

Polish *Sejm*; Voevodski, Klonowicz, Chrostel, Inulski-Buchshorn; Anton Werner, a member of the Central Committee; the poet Vardurski, the novelist Bruno Jascinski; the former Party leader, Lenski; Henrikowski and Bronkowski; the old Party scholars Waletski and Lapinski; and Unschlicht and his sister. Unschlicht, an old member of the Russian Bolshevik Party, had held important posts in the *Cheka*, the Red Army, the Foreign Office and the Air Force.

Béla Kun, the head of the 1918 Hungarian Soviet government, a good Stalinist of long standing and no friend of Trotskyism, died after long torture in prison. The survivors of the 1918 Finnish Revolution disappeared as well, while members of the Bulgarian, Yugoslav, Chinese and other Central Committees lingered in a secret 'isolator' in Yaroslavl. Once all these men had gone, Stalin felt he could rely on the total subservience, ideological and otherwise, of the remaining Comintern members.

Antonov-Ovseenko, Leon Davidovich's old comrade-in-arms, the man who had been responsible for the seizure of the Winter Palace, was made to play a shameful part as Consul-General in Barcelona, and there was good reason to think that he was privy to many of the crimes the G.P.U. committed in Spain. This no doubt extinguished what spirit he had, but there was no one to whom his spirit still mattered. While he was in Spain he was appointed People's Commissar of Justice in the Russian Soviet Republic and boarded a Russian ship for home. When the author of this book read this news item in the papers, he made a note: 'That's the end of Antonov-Ovseenko!' And in fact the new People's Commissar of Justice did not disembark anywhere, unless it was at his place of execution. Thousands of other names would be needed to complete the lists – the government of every republic and autonomous region in the U.S.S.R. was 'reconstructed' at least twice by the secret police, and we can guess by what methods.

What became of the families of those who had been shot or had disappeared? Their number was countless, their grief aroused pity and indignation, and they became a daily problem in the lives of the lower ranks of the hierarchy. It was thought necessary to drive the wives, sons and daughters of these 'enemies of the people' out of their homes, their jobs, and their schools, and the G.P.U. set up a large concentration camp for them not far from Moscow. From figures collated later, it appears that several tens of thousands of the wives and children of executed political prisoners eked out their lives in unspeakable misery. The law also provided for the deportation of the families of 'traitors' (including, no doubt, the grandparents) to the 'most remote regions of the U.S.S.R.' I learned that Rakovsky's wife and their daughter, an extraordinarily graceful girl, were among those who suffered this ugly fate.

Rudolf Klement, one of Trotsky's former secretaries, who had spent some time with him in Turkey and later in France, had since become secretary to the Fourth International Bureau in Paris. He was a self-effacing, studious and hard-working young German refugee, tall, thin, and stooping, with a pale face and sharp eyes. Needless to say, he was penniless and his papers were not in order. He was kidnapped from his room during the morning of July 13th, 1938, just as he was having his breakfast, which remained untouched on the table. A decapitated body strongly resembling his was later fished out from the Seine. Trotsky then received a strange letter in which Klement declared that he was breaking with him. It was written in a hand resembling Klement's but one that was strained and tremulous; the style of the letter was completely out of character and it was signed with a pseudonym Klement had not used for years. The letter had either been forged or dictated at gunpoint. Trotsky had no doubt at all that the G.P.U. had liquidated Klement. While police investigations were still proceeding, the Paris Communist press was busy laying false trails. A witness – a Russian officer never heard of again after his first 'statement' – claimed to have seen a person resembling Klement near the Pyrenees. But that was all.

Seven · The Assassins

I. *Trotsky's last writings. Bolshevism and Stalinism. The end and the means. The problem of art. The coming war. Trotsky against the Hitler–Stalin pact*

Some of Trotsky's most polemical work was written during this period. Despite the bitterness of the struggle – he felt it keenly – his powers of concentration and his capacity for work were as great as they had been when he wrote in his armoured train, travelling behind the firing lines. His contribution was much too copious to be treated more than cursorily in a book of this scope; however, because, as we have said before, Trotsky the man cannot be divorced from Trotsky the thinker, we shall note the salient features of his last theoretical contributions. Trotsky consistently defended Bolshevism against Stalinism, which he considered a hideous distortion of the former. He was pained to note that John Dewey, and most of the American intellectuals who had shown moral courage and impartiality during the Moscow trials, considered Stalinism the logical outcome (and proof of the failure) of Bolshevism. He believed that this false interpretation reflected an inadequate grasp of Marxism, of Russian history and of the history of the Revolution. 'The state founded by the Bolsheviks was the expression not only of the thought and will of Bolshevism but of the cultural level of the country, its social composition and the weight of its barbaric past ... *without a victory of the proletariat in the developed countries, the Russian workers' state ... had to collapse or degenerate.*' True Bolshevism, as represented by the left-wing Opposition, had made a complete break with the bureaucracy and the Comintern, now under Stalin's thumb. The proscription of other socialist parties during the Revolution had been anything but a Bolshevik practice; it was a measure dictated

245

by the blockade and the Civil War. The same applied to the suppression of anarchism; Trotsky and Lenin had more than once discussed the possibility of granting the Ukrainian anarchists territorial autonomy, so as to enable them to pursue their social experiments without interference.[1]

He reverted to these ideas in a little book, *Their Morals and Ours*, which summed up his thoughts on the matter so faithfully that he dedicated it to the memory of his son, Leon Sedov. 'Stalinism is a product of the old society.' To accuse Marxist revolutionaries of having adopted the motto of the sixteenth-century Jesuits – that the end justified the means – was a slander of both the Jesuits and the Bolsheviks. The revolutionary recognized 'the dialectical interdependence of ends and means'. The means could be justified by the end but the latter required justification in its turn. 'From the Marxist point of view, which expresses the historical interests of the proletariat, the end is justified if it leads to an increase of man's power over nature and to the abolition of man's power over man ... Anything that effectively leads to the liberation of mankind is permissible. As this end can only be attained by revolution, the freedom-seeking morality of the proletariat of necessity has a revolutionary character ...' The means derive from historical circumstances. They are organically subordinate to the end. Only participation in historical evolution 'with his eyes open and his will strained can give a thinking man supreme moral fulfilment.'[2]

When he was asked by *Partisan Review* to give his views on the relationship between art and politics, Trotsky complied, but 'with some hesitation' and only so as 'to pose the problem correctly'. 'In art man expresses his need for harmony and full existence ... which class-society denies him.' Hence any genuine artistic creation implies a conscious or unconscious protest against reality. Art alone could not find a way out of this impasse because it was dependent on society, and society could only be saved by a revolution.[3] 'The struggle for revolutionary ideas in art begins with the struggle for artistic truth, conceived not as obedience to this or that school but

[1] *Stalinism and Bolshevism*, Pioneer Publishers, New York, September–October, 1937.

[2] *Their Morals and Ours*, February 16th, 1938.

[3] 'Art and Politics', June 18th, 1938. *Partisan Review*, August–September 1938.

as the artist's inflexible fidelity to his inner self. Do not lie! That is the formula for salvation.'[4]

The problems Trotsky dealt with most frequently and at greatest length were the next world war, which he thought was bound to come, and the nature of Soviet society. In a review of a French book by 'Bruno R.' on bureaucratic collectivism, Trotsky wrote that 'all these various systems (Stalinism, Fascism, Nazism and the American New Deal) undeniably have many characteristics in common, because all of them are moulded by the collectivist tendencies inherent in modern economic systems.' 'Because of the prostration of the working class, these tendencies assume the form of bureaucratic collectivism ...' As for Soviet bureaucracy, it was not an organ but a tumour of the social organism; it had performed a useful function during the importation and assimilation of foreign techniques but had later become an obstacle to the development of productive forces.[5] Nevertheless, the economic foundations of the U.S.S.R. – collective ownership and planning – represented an enormous advance over other economic systems and ought to be defended against all external threats, as Trotsky never tired of proclaiming to anyone who was prepared to listen.

He wrote a number of articles on the Spanish Civil War and predicted the defeat of the Spanish Revolution and of the bourgeois Republic. To achieve victory, the war must be given social significance, Soviets must be established, the Republican Army purged of counter-revolutionary elements and a strategy of class struggle adopted. The choice was between the victory of the revolution and the victory of fascism. 'The tragic experience of Spain serves as a grave warning, perhaps the last before events of even greater import are upon us.'[6] If a socialist revolution did not prevent it, a second world war was inevitable.

In August 1937 Trotsky wrote a carefully reasoned article about the coming war, which has since turned out to be prophetic in more than one respect and which began with a quotation from Spinoza: 'Neither laughter nor tears; what matters is understanding.' The various power groupings were unstable; Germany sought world

---

[4] Letter to André Breton and the revolutionary French artists and authors, dated December 22nd, 1938.

[5] *Bureaucratic Collectivism*, October 1939.

[6] 'The Lesson of Spain: A Last Warning', December 17th, 1937.

domination and, in order to achieve it, might try to reach an accommodation with Britain against the U.S.S.R. or, failing that, with the
U.S.S.R. against the Western Powers. 'The smaller countries are like
satellites uncertain of their sun.' 'The whole world wants peace ... yet
the whole world will shed rivers of blood.' The United States wanted
to keep aloof but that was impossible for the most powerful nation
in the world; its greatest threat came from the Far East. Germany
was winning the arms race, having smashed the chains of Versailles
with a sure instinct and 'maniacal fury'. The Second International
and the Stalinist Third International believed that the object of the
war would be to defend freedom and civilization against fascist
aggression, but, 'it will not be easy to tell the sheep from the wolves.'
Stalin's political system increasingly resembled Hitler's, and the
democracies were allowing the Spanish Republic to be strangled to
death. The backward countries, short of raw materials and of mar-
kets, were naturally the first to embrace Fascism and proved the most
aggressive. Totalitarian states were better equipped for total war, and
the democracies would be forced to copy their methods. When would
the conflagration start? Germany required at least another two years
of preparation, so that the first possible date for the outbreak of war
was August, 1939; and by 1940–1, war would be a certainty. The
combatants would have to raise the largest number of troops with
the best arms; small professional armies had had their day. No overwhelming victory would be expected; there was not enough strategic
air power for that. 'The possibility that some extraordinary technological secret might make it possible to overwhelm an enemy taken
by surprise is more serious,' but as the manufacture of new arms took
at least two years, this seemed to preclude the use of a real secret
weapon. The next war would continue where the last one had left
off, but a great many new techniques would be developed. England
would have to defend herself on the Continent, and the war would
be decided on land and not at sea. 'The spiral will inevitably embrace
the entire planet. Left to its own logic, and given the power of modern
technology, the war will be a process of slow, complex and costly
suicide for mankind.' 'Technology gives the United States a colossal
advantage ... it will dominate the world, though the world may be
devastated ... and reduced to barbarism ... this may spell the twilight
of American civilization.'

Everything would depend on political and social developments:
revolution might put a stop to war. There was little chance that the

working class would prevent its outbreak, but it was possible that the masses might react more promptly than during the First World War. The U.S.S.R. was weakened by its regime, whose overthrow would be hastened by the war. But its social foundations would withstand every onslaught and even emerge the stronger for it. As for the capitalist countries, those that had not resolved the agrarian problem – for example, Poland, Hungary and Rumania – would be the first to go under. Germany and Italy might achieve brilliant successes at first but they would be subjected to social convulsions long before their enemies. The international commitments of France imposed an intolerable strain on her inner resources, and she would be more dependent than any other country on her allies, Britain and the U.S.A.; France would become a second-rate power with an unstable social structure. The British Empire, too, was bound to be weakened and to decline. 'The collapse of imperialism will usher in an epoch of social upheaval ... The face of the world will change.'[7]

Thus Trotsky was not surprised by subsequent developments, not even by the Hitler–Stalin pact of August 1939. 'The task Germany has set herself is beyond her. Germany has arrived on the scene too late' to dominate the world. The only reason Stalin was supporting her was because at that moment she was the strongest power. 'Who knows whether the French government and the Allied governments it shelters will not soon have to seek asylum in England?' However painful it might be, Stalin would follow Hitler as long as Hitler remained strong. But 'if Stalin survives Hitler, it will not be for long. The twin star will disappear from the firmament.'[8]

He held that the occupation of half of Poland by the Red Army was a lesser evil than Nazi occupation, but that it was Stalin who had allowed the greater evil to take place. He denounced 'Stalin's imperialism' but took care to distinguish it from capitalist imperialism. 'We have never undertaken to defend all the actions of the Red Army, which is an instrument of Bonapartist bureaucracy ... All that we shall defend in the U.S.S.R. are the aspects of a workers' state that it retains ...' The social foundations of the U.S.S.R., its collective ownership and planned economy, deserved unconditional support. In Poland and Finland, the Red Army was still providing a revolutionary impetus. After its reverses in Finland, partly due to the

---

[7] We have faithfully, if too briefly, condensed Trotsky's article *In the Face of a New World War*, written in Coyoacan on August 9th, 1937.

[8] *The Twin Star: Hitler–Stalin*, January 1940.

stupidity of holding the campaign in winter, Trotsky pointed out that there was a tendency to underestimate the Red Army's defensive capacity, which was infinitely greater than its offensive strength.[9]

During his long examination by the Dewey Commission, Trotsky had expressed a number of ideas that are not found in his writings. Thus when John F. Finerty asked him whether he felt a revolutionary government had a right to resort to terror, he replied, 'It is not an abstract right. I hope that after one or two victories in other countries [than Russia] the revolutions will become absolutely friendly revolutions.' Finerty: 'Bloodless revolutions?' Trotsky: 'Bloodless revolutions, yes. But the pioneers were everywhere severe people. I believe the Americans know that better than myself ...'[10]

Finerty then asked him whether he thought that, after the socialist revolutions, countries would be able to live together in peace; Trotsky replied that he thought world planning to be 'absolutely possible'. '... The scientists, engineers and leaders of trade unions will in a conference, a world conference, establish what we have, what we need, the productive powers, the natural resources and the creative forces of humanity, of mankind ... They will begin cautiously ... by a plan, not by war ... It is absolutely possible, absolutely possible.'[11] 'Until today,' Trotsky went on to explain to Benjamin Stolberg, 'mankind has not succeeded in rationalizing its history. That is a fact. We human beings have not succeeded in rationalizing our bodies and minds... But the question is not if we can reach the absolute perfection of humanity. The question is, for me, whether we can make great steps forward ... because after every great step forward mankind makes a small detour, even a great step backwards. I regret it very much but I am not responsible for it. [Laughter.] After the ... world revolution, it is possible that mankind will become tired. For some, a part of them, a new religion can arise ...'[12]

In reply to Stolberg's question, whether he considered the ruling bureaucracy in the U.S.S.R. as a caste or a class, he defined it as an 'intermediate body'. Whether it would come to destroy the present basis of the regime and thus turn itself into a new ruling class would depend on national and international developments, but the tendency was certainly there.[13]

[9] Articles and interview published in January 1940.
[10] The Case of Leon Trotsky, Harpers, New York, 1938, p. 370.
[11] Ibid., p. 435.
[12] Ibid., p. 436.
[13] Ibid., p. 438.

11. *Trotsky's struggle against the nightmare. Waiting for the assassins.*
Walter Held's disappearance in Moscow. Life in Mexico

'On his sixtieth birthday, Leon Davidovich felt alone, the last sur-
vivor of an annihilated legion. He had become a symbol for many
people and he knew it. It fell to him to uphold faithfully a doctrine,
an historical truth, with unswerving resolve. Because of this, he was
condemned to death. The executions in Moscow, Siberia, Turkestan
and the Ukraine, the assassinations in Barcelona, Lausanne and
Paris, had all been directed against the outlaw in Mexico. He knew
it and so did we all. Ever since the first Moscow Trial, that is for
the past three years, we had been expecting the assassins with absolute certainty.

'We had rented a large, dilapidated house in Coyoacan, which had
been restored very simply and which was surrounded by a fair-sized
garden whose ancient trees were alive with bird-song every morning.
The place was very isolated; on one side there was a wide stream,
which was dry most of the time, and on the other a dusty road with
some Mexican adobe hovels. We had a wall built round the grounds.
Any visitor had to pass through a solid iron gate which a young comrade would only open if he had received explicit instructions and
after he had examined the visitor through a spy-hole. Outside, the
police had built a brick *casita* with a loophole, thirty paces from our
gate. From inside it, they watched over our safety ... On entering,
the visitor would cross a garden full of huge cacti and agaves, shaded
by high leafy boughs, and step into a large room arranged as a library
and office. It was furnished with filing cabinets, books, newspapers
and typing desks. Trotsky's assistants, who were also his bodyguards,
spent most of their time in there.

'A door gave on to the dining room: a large pine table, chairs
painted in Hispano-Indian style, a few posters and nothing else. Leon
Davidovich's study was off to the left. It was a square, high-ceilinged,
well lit and well ventilated room, furnished functionally. There was
a pinewood table, bookcases facing it, and a telephone. That was
all. Among the books were the works of Lenin bound in red
and blue cloth. The light came in through a balcony window to
which Leon Davidovich turned his back while working. The study
adjoined the bedroom, which was also simply furnished. Comrades
and friends were put up in outbuildings at the bottom of the
garden.

'Leon Davidovich used to get up early, while the air was still cool, and before the always brilliant sky began to blaze. He had a moment of relaxation at the beginning of each morning, when he went to feed the rabbits and chickens. He would have a look at the cacti newly brought from Pedregal, that lava wasteland, wild and scorching hot, where he had gone specially to choose them. These exotic plants, hardy and savage, delighted him. Then he would shut himself up in his study and emerge only for meals. Work was pressing and all his energy focused on it: letters, articles, books and drafts of future work. Most of the time he would dictate to a Russian secretary. He had signed a contract with Harpers for a biography of Stalin, and was deeply preoccupied with this project, though he told me many times that he would have preferred to write about almost anything else. A book he had been dreaming about for a long time was one on the friendship and fruitful life-long collaboration of Karl Marx and Friedrich Engels. The deep understanding that existed between these two great champions of the proletarian cause, their insights, the subtle differences between them, their unwavering affection for each other – this was what he wanted to recreate in the written word. But the publishers and the public were much more interested in the fearsome tyrant ... For his *Stalin*, Trotsky gathered innumerable documents and notes. Stalin's origins were obscure, the part he played in 1917 difficult to establish, and the reasons for the warmth Lenin had shown him before he came to know him better – much too late in the day – were hard to discover. Trotsky scribbled comments, often in great irritation, in the margin of Boris Souvarine's *Stalin;* he used to say that it was remarkably well researched but that Souvarine's approach was disagreeably commonplace.

'In his own work, he was meticulous to the point of pedantry. He never used a reference without checking it first, and he was a stickler for accurate punctuation. He weighed up the worth of each piece of testimony and made sure that every document he used appeared in its proper context. In dealing with his enemy, he tried to be totally objective, and if the resulting book appeared to be excessively academic, that was just too bad. He eschewed all passion, other than that for the truth, and revulsion against inhumanity. Many of the notes he jotted down were written in the heat of indignation, but the final text was always the result of cool meditation.

'He was rarely able to work in peace; indeed, the words "in peace" are strangely out of place when applied to him. The nightmare was always present; the army of Russian corpses was rarely forgotten, and the murderers, we had no doubt, were weaving their intrigue around the house. The Communist press, the fellow-travelling press, and the reactionary press all did their utmost to foment hatred against Trotsky. General Cedillo organized an uprising against President Lazaro Cardenas, and the press at once alleged that Trotsky was in the plot ... Leon Davidovich read about the national-ization of the Mexican oil industry in the newspapers. He was struck by the boldness of this unexpected step and had no doubt that it served the interests of the country well ... But the press said that it had all been planned by Trotsky. Denial after denial had to be issued, but what was the use of denials in this fog of dishonesty? We had never met President Lazaro Cardenas, whom we held in high esteem and who had sent us his condolences on the death of Leon Sedov.

'Leon Davidovich still bore himself as of old: his head was held high, his gait was sprightly and his gestures were animated. He seemed not to have aged, though his unruly locks had become grey. He would generally receive visitors at his desk, his head slightly bent forward in order to hear them better, and fix them with his alert blue eyes. He always spoke clearly, enunciating well and tried, even in English, French or German, to construct his sentences precisely and lucidly. He was courteous and careful not to say anything, even un-wittingly, that might unconsciously wound or cast a shadow over personal relations ... Despite his habit of judging people objectively, which could appear harsh, he was a fundamentally kind man; he tried not to say unpleasant things about people, and disliked hearing them. His enthusiasm for a person, a book, an article, or an idea was easily aroused, but as he always adhered to his rigorous way of thinking and refused to admit that thought could be divorced from action, he never hesitated to argue uncompromisingly with friends, comrades and those who were dearest to him, or, if need be, to break with them politically. To him, ideas were not pieces in some intellec-tual game; they were living things, engaging the entire personality and forcing it to steer the correct course. This explains his uncompro-mising defence of revolutionary consistency.

'It also explains the breaks between Leon Davidovich and men who understood him, loved him and continued to defend him after all the arguments and polemics. The disagreements with Max East-man and, later, with James Burnham, were concerned with Marxist philosophy in general, and dialectical materialism in particular. Leon Davidovich also had several sharp disagreements with Otto and Alice Rühle, our neighbours in Coyoacan. The old German Marxist was a man of strong character himself, with convictions that had evolved during a lifetime of study and struggle. Ever since 1917, he had turned against "Lenin's methods", and one day he accused Lenin of dishonesty. "Lenin a liar?" Leon Davidovich protested. He knew Vladimir Ilyich's fundamental rectitude better than anyone else and refused to listen to another word. He saw much less of the Rühles from then on, though their mutual affection remained unchanged. They collaborated on *The Living Thoughts of Karl Marx*, part of the "Living Thoughts" series, each contributing a special section.

'Diego Rivera had shown us the deepest devotion: he seemed a convinced and enthusiastic supporter of the Fourth International and spared neither effort, nor money in furthering the propaganda campaign of the Mexican group. Leon Davidovich, sometimes beguiled and often amused by his bubbling imagination, admired the artist in him, the man imbued with a passionate, though somewhat naive, feeling for the social struggle as it was expressed in Rivera's best work, but he felt that Rivera lacked the firmness or lucidity of mind that went with serious political activity. And, in fact, Rivera eventually strayed into General Almazan's Mexican Party, which launched a demagogic campaign and soon folded up ingloriously... Relations with the painter were broken off in 1938 and were never resumed. Of all our old friends and comrades, he was the only one who later made a noisy conversion to Stalinism ...

'We used to travel from time to time. In Veracruz, Leon Davidovich spent a great deal of time fishing in the dazzling light of the Gulf. The dramatic sun-baked Mexican mountain scenery seemed to soothe him. We visited the pleasantest parts of Patzcuaro. Usually our trips would last a day and we would often make for Pedegral, that extraordinary landscape of lava, or for the Taxco Sierra, where one day we gathered orchids, or take the road to Laredo or to the Desierto de los Leones ... Leon Davidovich would try for a day to shake off all his cares. He took an interest in the plants and scenery we saw, and our friends were delighted to hear his quiet laugh once again and to see an untroubled look in his clear blue eyes.

'After these excursions, he would resume his work with renewed vigour and try to unravel the tangled skein of the problems of the day. Clear and precise warnings had reached us. A few months before he was killed and while he was still a secret G.P.U. agent, Ignaz Reiss had warned our friends in Europe that the best known among them were all marked down for assassination. Walter Krivitsky, one of the top Soviet agents in the West, confirmed this news after his friend Reiss had been murdered and he began to have qualms of conscience ... Walter Held disappeared. This young German refugee, whom the Nazis had sentenced to death, had proved a staunch friend in Norway. The authorities had refused to allow him, a naturalized Norwegian, to sail to Mexico with us. When the Germans invaded Norway, he fled to Sweden, obtained an American visa and made the fatal mistake of allowing himself to be persuaded – as were some other Norwegian and non-Norwegian refugees – to travel to the United States via the U.S.S.R. The Soviet consulate issued him with a transit visa, and he left with his wife and child and several travelling companions. Somewhere on the Trans-Siberian railway line, the Helds were discreetly asked to step off the train – so discreetly that it did not occur to the other passengers to ask any questions until it was too late ... And that was the end of Walter Held, his wife and child. Some of the finest people had apparently dropped out of our lives like stones down a well. For a long time, we dared not mention Walter Held's name, hoping against hope ... Then, in September 1940, I received a letter of condolence from him, in which he mentioned that he had sent me an article on Leon Davidovich's death. The article never reached me.

'When Leon Davidovich was alone in his study, I sometimes heard him heave a deep sigh and say to himself, "I am tired, so tired. I can't take any more." He would never have admitted it openly. The senseless humiliation, the moral collapse of old revolutionaries who had loved him and yet had died covering him and themselves with obloquy, filled him with inconsolable anguish. A man like Rakovsky ending his noble life in prison battling with his conscience! How Leon Davidovich had loved him, even while reproaching him for his levity and sometimes rash courage! Ivan Nikitich Smirnov; the steadfast Sosnovsky; Muralov, who had once written that the waters of the Irtysh would have to flow from the sea back to their source before he would recant; Kamenev, a Bolshevik with the temperament of a liberal don and yet so loyal – they had all died a terrible death, betraying themselves and the conscience of the Revolution. When alone, Leon Davidovich sometimes spoke their names to himself ... Even the wide-open spaces of Mexico did little to relieve his pain.'

III. *The attack at Coyoacan led by the painter David Alfaro Siqueiros on May 24–5th, 1940. Murder of Robert Sheldon Harte*

'Leon Davidovich, who suffered from insomnia, took a sedative before retiring on May 24th, 1940, and fell into a deep sleep. In the middle of the night I was woken by the sound of fierce gunfire at close range. Leon Davidovich was awakened as well ... I whispered to him, "They're shooting, they're shooting into the room ..." We slid down on to the floor. Lights flashed through the bedroom, the garden, the whole house; the night was filled with the sound of machine-gun fire ... The door to the next room, where Seva, our grandson, was sleeping, suddenly gaped open; there was a fiery glow, and on the threshold, silhouetted against the flames, I caught a glimpse of a man in uniform doing something ... his helmet, his distorted face and the metal buttons on his coat shone red ... We stayed where we were, crouched down together in a corner of the bedroom. I tried to move up a little more so that I could protect Leon Davidovich because I felt that the bullets were getting closer to him all the time. Suddenly we heard Seva scream, "Grandfather!" in a voice at once one of warning and appeal ... "They've taken him," Leon Davidovich whispered ... The flashes, the flickering shadows and the machine-gun fire went on for what seemed a long time and then stopped, making way for a deathly, total silence, an unbearable silence that chilled us through. We felt certain that all our friends, Alfred and Marguerite Rosmer and our young American comrades, had just been mown down. Now, I thought, they will surely come to kill him; what can I do, where can I hide him? I was sick with despair ... And then we heard Seva's clear voice, quivering with joy, ring out: "Al-fred! Mar-gue-rite!" He was alive! They were all alive!

'But why didn't anyone come? We tried to open the study door but the murderers had turned the key ... Their bullets had riddled the door; through the holes I could see the papers and books looking immaculate in the calm glow of the shaded lamp on the desk ... Fire broke out in Seva's room on the other side, where the door was open. The floor began to smoulder and a wooden wardrobe crackled in the heat. I quickly smothered the fire with a few rugs and blankets ... Then we pounded on the study door, and Otto Schüssler came running up from the other side and opened it for us ... We walked through into the miraculously untouched room ...

'Our friends gathered together: the Rosmers, Charlie Cornell,

Jack, Walter, Harold – and Seva. Bob Sheldon Harte was missing ... They had been cut off from us by fire from a machine-gun placed behind the eucalyptus tree on the patio between the house and the outbuildings. When the gun had stopped firing they hesitated to rush into the bedroom, afraid that they would find all of us dead ... We marvelled at our unexpected survival.

'The great iron gate stood open. The police sentries in the hut outside had all been overpowered and tied up. Our two cars which were parked near the entrance had gone. A few articles of clothing belonging to Robert Sheldon Harte and his revolver were lying on the concrete. Bob had disappeared ... He had been on sentry duty at the gate. He was twenty-three, a fair-haired young man with fine features, an idealist who had lost his heart to Mexico. He had loved watching the brilliantly coloured birds in the aviary ... The attack had lasted no more than five minutes.

'We managed to put out the fire. We found two small and rather primitive incendiary bombs which had not gone off although the casings had caught fire. Seva's foot was grazed and bleeding. Having first smashed the door to his room, two uniformed assailants had rushed off again, but one of them had returned later to fire under the bed where the child was hiding, wounding his foot. Seva had not noticed his injury and had followed some shadowy figures through the garden, to the secretaries' office and to the dining room. They had fired into all the rooms as they went and then vanished through the trees into the night. Our bedroom had been riddled with bullets from all directions; it was a sheer miracle that we had escaped with our lives. Either our instinct for self-preservation or pure chance had led us to seek out the only safe corner. Several bullets, probably fired by the man I had caught a glimpse of, were lodged in the bolster and pillows, where our heads would have been. A trail of blood along the garden path, on the tiles and the rush matting, showed where Seva had gone.

'Sixty bullets had been fired into the bedroom from four different directions. The room had two doors facing each other, one leading into Seva's bedroom and the other to the study; the murderers had fired through these doors in the direction of the bed, which stood in the middle between a balcony window and a glass door leading to the bathroom. Thompson machine-guns had been set up opposite the balcony and the bathroom windows, and bullets had been pumped into the room. It was precisely this excess of machine-gun fire that saved us: the murderers were certain that they must have hit us with their combined fire-power and they were afraid of killing each other. They had obviously made a careful study of the layout of the house. And Robert Sheldon Harte, our young American comrade on sentry duty at the front gate, had disappeared. We were convinced from the start that, having no doubt heard a familiar voice, he had let the killers in, and had then been kidnapped.

'Even before dawn, the Mexican authorities, the police and the magistrates of Coyoacan, some journalists and our friend Antonio Hidalgo, had started an investigation. Hidalgo took us aside and said to us, "Be on your guard; I can recognize some Stalinists ..." These were minor officials, who could be distinguished by their bad-tempered expressions. How had the attackers got in? There was no proof that Bob Sheldon Harte had opened the gate to them ... An ordinary ladder and two rope-ladders were found outside against the twelve-foot wall. The investigating magistrates believed that they had not been used. The five or six men on duty at the nearby police post reported that a major and a lieutenant had appeared at the head of a group of policemen; and that they had been taken by surprise, disarmed and tied up before they could put up any resistance ...

'Leon Davidovich was nervous but calm when he was questioned about the possible identity of the attackers. He mentioned the name of the Mexican painter, David Alfaro Siqueiros, and added that he had been acting on G.P.U. orders. He knew a great deal about the activities of this adventurer in the International Brigade in Spain. This statement was temporarily turned against us some days later, as was our cool and self-controlled bearing during and after the attack – an attack we had been expecting for so long!

'Hundreds of spent cartridge cases, several detonators, seventy-five cartridges, an electric saw, twelve sticks of dynamite, electric fuse-wire for the explosives and the two incendiary bombs were taken away ... The enquiry, headed by the chief of the Presidential Police, Colonel Sanchez Salazar, and by the district chief of the Federal Police, General Manuel Nuñez, marked time for weeks and produced no results. A declaration by the Mexican Communist Party, while demanding a searching investigation, tried to inculpate reactionaries, the expropriated oil companies and American imperialism. The daily newspaper, El Popular, owned by the Mexican Confederation of Labour (C.T.M.) and run by Alejandro Carillo on clearly pro-Communist lines, went further still: the attack was a provocation aimed at Mexico, and Trotsky should be expelled! As no further clues were discovered, Communists and pro-Communists began to speak about a "put-up job" and did this so insistently that on May 3rd, three of the young men who lived with us, Charlie Cornell, Otto Schüssler and Jean Bazin, were arrested and questioned at length about the alleged attack which Trotsky himself had set up ... Leon Davidovich at once wrote a letter on their behalf to General Lazaro Cardenas, the President, and the young men were released. Leon Davidovich had no doubt that the attack had been mounted on orders from Moscow – so large an operation involving so many men could not possibly have been organized by irresponsible individuals. He knew that the time allowed for his assassination had been fixed and that the machinery had been set in motion against him; the attitude of the press, orchestrated by the Stalinist party, served to confirm this. On June 1st, he accused Stalin and the G.P.U. before a group of journalists, and added categorically that "another attempt on my life is inevitable". *El Popular* wrote: "Trotsky is waging a war of nerves against Mexico ... the so-called attack on him is an act of international blackmail." The Communist Party continued to call for Trotsky's expulsion and the general secretary of the Mexican Confederation of Labour, Vicente Lombardo Toledano, sent an official memorandum to the Minister of the Interior, insisting that the attack on Trotsky had been a put-up job, and that Trotsky was guilty of espionage for foreign powers and of circulating anti-Mexican propaganda (June 6th, 1940). The New York *Nation* published an article by Harry Block entitled *Mexico's Phantom Conspiracy*.

'A few days passed and then the police announced the arrest of some well-known Communists. *El Popular* protested strongly about these "arbitrary measures against honest Mexican workers". The enquiry showed that two women, Anita Martinez and Julia Barradas de Serrana, who had been living in our neighbourhood for a short time, had established amorous relations with several of the policemen detailed to guard our house. They had subsequently disappeared, but were traced and arrested; they admitted that they had been instructed to watch Trotsky and to seduce the policemen. They had been hired and paid by Antonio Pujol, secretary to the Communist painter, David Alfaro Siqueiros.[14] One of the women was the wife,

[14] David Alfaro Siqueiros (born Chihuahua, Mexico, 1898) was editor of *El Machete*, the first Communist paper to be published in Mexico; one of the founders of the Mexican Communist Party; and 'Lieutenant-Colonel in the Spanish Republican Army'

or, more accurately, one of the wives, of a former member of the Spanish International Brigade, Serrano. Several hours before the attack they had been advised to disappear from the scene, together with a child called Sovietina. Another of the arrested was Nestor Sanchez Hernandez, a Communist and a "Captain" in the International Brigade. He gave a detailed account of the preparations for the crime in which he had taken part. He spoke of two organizers: David Alfaro Siqueiros, whom he had known in Spain and who had described himself as a Colonel in the International Brigade – the Lister Battalion of sinister memory – and a foreigner speaking excellent French, possibly a Jew, who had made a brief appearance in a car during the attack.

'Twenty-seven people in all were arrested and their statements made clear what had actually happened. Siqueiros had procured the police uniforms, the arms and the cars, and had himself directed operations in the uniform of a police major, seconded by his secretary, Antonio Pujol, in a lieutenant's uniform. He had kept looking at his watch. The "French Jew", the G.P.U. man, had shown up only for a moment, to make sure the operation had been successful, of which he was apparently convinced when he left. One of the assassins, Nestor Sanchez Hernandez, said he had seen Robert Sheldon Harte speaking "in a nervous and friendly manner" with the "French Jew", who was never traced. Siqueiros and Pujol went into hiding, but Siqueiros sent a letter from his hide-out to the press, in which he made no secret of the part he had played. "The Communist Party," he announced, "in mounting this attack was merely trying to hasten Trotsky's expulsion from Mexico; all the enemies of the Communist Party can expect similar treatment ..." (This singular text was followed, one day later, by an official declaration published in *El Popular* of June 20th, 1940, on behalf of the Communist Party: none of those inculpated, it said, was a member of the Communist Party; Sheldon Harte was the real culprit; a gang of uncontrollable elements and *agents provocateurs* had been responsible; Trotsky's very pre-

---

(from an entry in *Twenty Centuries of Mexican Art*, published by the New York Museum of Modern Art in conjunction with the Mexican government, May 1940). On December 21st, 1939 *La Voz de Mexico*, the organ of the Communist Party, reporting a meeting in celebration of Stalin's sixtieth birthday ('the leader of genius and pride of the international working class'), mentioned that Siqueiros sat in the Presidium by the side of James Ford, the Communist candidate for the American vice-presidency.

sence in Mexico was an act of provocation directed against the Communist Party and against Mexico itself.)

'The minor accomplices were released on June 25th; nine in all were imprisoned. Most of the press tended to believe that Sheldon Harte, of whom no trace was found until June 25th, was implicated. On that day, Nestor Sanchez Hernandez led the police to a small isolated house in the hills near Tlalminalco, in the Desierto de los Leones. It had been rented by Siqueiros's brothers-in-law, Leopoldo and Luis Arenal. An old Indian woman and an Indian youngster told them they had heard that some artists were expected to come to paint pictures of the scenery. A stripped bed was found in the dilapidated house. The earth appeared to have been disturbed fairly recently. The police started to dig and discovered poor Bob Sheldon Harte's body covered with quicklime. He had been killed in his sleep, for his body was that of a peacefully sleeping figure. His murder seemed to clear him of any suspicion ...'

IV. *Trotsky at work*

'Leon Davidovich worked on. He had animated discussions with our American comrades about the role of the U.S.S.R. in the war. On June 18th, 1940, he wrote a note which was subsequently discovered among his papers.

The capitulation of France ... is a European catastrophe ... Hitler is the ultimate, most severe and most barbarous expression of imperialism leading civilization to its doom. But as well as the general causes of the catastrophe, which reside in imperialism, we must not forget the criminal part ... of the Kremlin and its Comintern. No one has helped Hitler as much as Stalin. No one has brought down so many dangers on the U.S.S.R. as Stalin ... In spite of his territorial conquests, the situation of the U.S.S.R. has deteriorated very badly. The Polish buffer-state has disappeared. Tomorrow the Rumanian buffer-state will follow. German power, looming over Europe, now has a common frontier with the U.S.S.R. ... The German victories in the West are merely a prelude to a formidable campaign in the East. In attacking Finland, the Red Army, decapitated and demoralized by Stalin, has revealed its weakness. In his coming campaign

against the U.S.S.R. Hitler will be able to count on the help of
Japan ... It is possible that Stalin, the deceiver deceived, may
be forced to make a new turnabout in his foreign policy. Woe
to the nations if they again put their trust in the faithless agents
of the Kremlin's master.

The note, no doubt the draft of an article, ended, "Soviet patriotism
and unrelenting struggle against Stalinism are inseparable."

'In other notes, he tried to clarify the position of France. "...
Marshal Pétain's regime is not Fascism in the full sense of the word
... but represents a senile form of Bonapartism marking the decline
of imperialism." (In Marxist terminology, "Bonapartism" is a more
or less popular form of dictatorship that arises in times of political
instability and attempts to turn the class struggle to the advantage
of the bourgeoisie.)

The present war is a continuation of the last ... not a repetition
... It poses the question of social change in infinitely more urgent
and imperious terms than did the First World War ... Never
before in the history of mankind has the force of reaction been
so strong. However, it would be an unforgivable error to see
nothing else. The historical process is contradictory. Under the
wing of the official reaction, the masses are being radically transformed, gathering experience and becoming receptive to new
political ideas. The old conservative tradition of the democratic
state, which was so powerful during the first imperialist war,
survives as an unstable vestige ... Will we succeed in forming
a (revolutionary) party strong enough to step in at the moment
of crisis? ... Will the Stalinists not be at the head of the next
revolutionary upsurge and will they not lead the revolution to
disaster as they have done in China and in Spain? We cannot
discount this possibility, especially in France ... (Unpublished
article of August 20th, 1940)

'He handed the press a detailed study called *The Comintern and
the G.P.U.*, full of quotations from the Stalinist and pro-Stalinist
press ... Nothing could have been more tiring than that labour, that
trudge through the choking fog of misinformation, that analysis of
incoherent lies, that attempt to probe the most shameless depths of
the totalitarian mind ... He showed, in particular, how the same Sta-

linist writers had successively described Sequeiros as a hero persecuted by the bourgeoisie, a "half-crazed madman", an "irresponsible
adventurer" and even – one can hardly believe one's eyes – as being
in Trotsky's pay! Yes, Trotsky was supposed to have paid him to
organize a fake attempt on our lives! This was the topsy-turvy
delirium of the Moscow trials all over again; it all smacked more
of psychiatry than of the world of normal human beings. In this connection, it is worth recalling the evidence of Walter Krivitsky, who
states quite unequivocally in his memoirs, *I Was Stalin's Agent*,[14]
that the Chief of Security in the People's Commissariat of the Interior
was in charge of terrorist activities abroad. To avoid diplomatic complications, his orders were handed on by the People's Commissar
with Stalin's approval. All operations were organized by qualified
foreign service officials; all the assassins were agents of the Security
Branch and proved Communists, though some of them were not
official Party members. Krivitsky himself had been one of the leaders
of the G.P.U. espionage service for twenty years.[15']

v. *'Jacson Mornard', G.P.U. agent, presents himself at Coyoacan*

'For some time, a young American militant of Russian origins, Ruth
Agelof, had been working as one of Leon Davidovich's secretaries
at Coyoacan. In June 1938, her sister, Sylvia, a member of a U.S.
Fourth International group, had travelled to Paris in the company
of Ruby Weill, a friend who worked on a paper with alleged Stalinist
sympathies. Ruby introduced Sylvia to Jacson Mornard, who
claimed to be the son of a Belgian diplomat and a rich and travelled
young man. He told her he hoped to go into journalism. He paid
court to Sylvia and eventually became her lover. She became very
deeply attached to him. In January 1940, Sylvia and Mornard, whom
she treated as her husband, arrived in Mexico, and met our old
friends and guests, the Rosmers. Mornard was pleasant and helpful,
rendered them a number of small services and never tried to find
anything out about Trotsky. He was in Mexico on business, and
seemed to be making a good living. On one occasion he gave his

---

[14] Hamish Hamilton, London, 1939.
[15] On February 11th, 1941, Krivitsky was discovered in a hotel room in Washington
with a bullet through his head. It is possible he committed suicide but assassination
is more likely. He had more than once only just eluded death at the hands of his
pursuers.

office address to Sylvia as 820 Edificio Ermita, and when he could
not be found there, he explained that he had made a mistake; the
number should have been 620. (It was later discovered that 820 was
an office kept for Siqueiros.) On several occasions Mornard brought
the Rosmers to Coyoacan in his Buick, and one day Leon Davidovich said it was discourteous to leave "Sylvia's husband" standing
at the gate; he ought to be asked in for a moment, at least into the
garden.

'Three days after the raid of May 24th, 1940, the Rosmers, who
were about to board a ship in Veracruz, accepted Mornard's offer
to drive them there; when he came to pick them up on May 28th,
we asked him in for the first time, for breakfast. From then on, our
comrades on sentry duty opened the gate freely to him. In June, he
travelled to New York, passing through New Orleans, and his "wife"
did not hear from him for three weeks. When he returned to Mexico
in August, he was in such a state of nervous exhaustion that he had
to spend several days in bed. Sylvia nursed him ... One day when
he visited us at Coyoacan, he saw Joe Hansen, Leon Davidovich's
secretary, supervising some workmen who were reinforcing the surrounding wall. "Why are you having this done?" Mornard asked.
"To be on the safe side," the American answered. Jacson Mornard
shook his head. "That won't stop the G.P.U.," he said.

'On another occasion, he took some of our American friends from
Minneapolis on a drive to Toluca. On the way back, he pretended
he was going to drive the car over a precipice. "Then it would all
be over!" he said to our friend Anna Konikova, who attached no
particular importance to his sudden fit of depression. His visit to
the States had completely changed him – the somewhat vulgar *bon
vivant*, who had been content to lead an easy and leisurely life, was
suddenly in a terrible state of nerves ... He called on us seven or
eight times and we would speak to him for a few minutes in the garden and on two occasions in the house. "Sylvia's husband" seemed
neither interested in politics nor particularly likeable as a person.
Leon Davidovich would see him out of politeness during breaks from
his work, while feeding the rabbits ... Mornard, who was extremely
discreet about his business affairs, even with Sylvia, kept speaking
to Leon Davidovich about his "boss", a "brilliant businessman"
whose speculations had apparently earned him a fortune. Knowing
of our financial difficulties, his employers had no doubt advised him
to hint how useful he could be to us in that sphere. Leon Davidovich,

who was utterly indifferent to all this talk, replied with vague remarks about commercial ability and similar things. These short conversations used to irritate me, and Leon Davidovich disliked them as well. "Who is this fabulously rich boss?" he asked me. "We should find out. After all, he might be some profiteer with Fascist tendencies and it might be best to stop seeing Sylvia's husband altogether ..." Mornard used to call on the most trifling pretexts; he would bring me a box of chocolates from Sylvia; he was leaving for New York and insisted on lending us his car; his boss was winding up some important business and he was going to leave Mexico with him ...

'When he returned from the States in about the middle of August, he looked awful. His complexion had gone pale and grey. "Are you ill?" I asked him. "What is the matter with you?" He said that he had been ill in Monterey. I mentioned a mountain walk I had taken with Leon Davidovich. I was struck by his sudden interest. How had we got there? Why had we not taken him up on his offer to drive us? ... At the time, I failed to understand why he was so anxious to accompany Leon Davidovich to the mountains ...

'During his breaks from work, Leon Davidovich avoided serious subjects – those who sought political discussions with him had to make a special appointment. Leon Davidovich would receive them in his study, listen attentively, his head slightly inclined, his hands often clasped on the table, while he carefully weighed his answers ... A week before the black day, Sylvia and her husband had tea with us for the first time; Sylvia passionately defended the minority standpoint in the [American Trotskyist] Party. Jacson Mornard said hardly anything; it appeared that the arguments ranged so widely as to exclude him altogether. But a few days later, he asked if he could show Leon Davidovich a draft of an article he had written.

'Leon Davidovich saw him in his study for ten minutes ... He seemed worried after the interview. "He showed me a paper devoid of any interest. It's confused and full of banal phrases. He says he can produce some interesting French statistics." Leon Davidovich looked uneasy. "I don't like him. What sort of a fellow is he? We ought to make a few enquiries ..." Jacson Mornard, instead of taking a chair, had sat down on a corner of the large table, wearing a hat and carrying his raincoat over his arm ... It had obviously been a sort of rehearsal of his crime. We were so far from suspecting the man who, for two years, had been the companion of an unaffected and agreeable young comrade, that when one of our American friends suggested we search him, Leon Davidovich exclaimed, "Come, come! What are you thinking of?" But he did not want to see him again. Despite his long and unhappy experience of people, Leon Davidovich was not in the least suspicious. On the contrary, having spent the best part of his life among the revolutionary masses, he had great confidence, both reasoned and emotional, in the average man in the street. There was so much ability, so much potential and idealism in a crowd at a meeting or in a small group of labourers. He had so often devoted long hours to discussions with American workers, or with Spanish refugees ...'

VI. *The last day*

'Steel shutters had been put on our bedroom windows. "The Siqueiros won't get to us so easily next time," Leon Davidovich said. Another attack was expected at any time. In the morning, when we woke up, Leon Davidovich would say, "There you are. We've slept through a whole night and nobody has killed us. And you're still not satisfied." One day, he added in a thoughtful tone of voice, "Yes, Natasha; we've been given a short reprieve."

'On the morning of August 20th, he rose in excellent spirits, having slept soundly after taking a double dose of sleeping pills. He had not felt so energetic for some time. "I'll do a good day's work," he said. From a quarter past seven until nine that morning he worked in the garden, seeing to the rabbits, chickens and plants while the day was still fresh and cool. In the afternoon he was going to dictate an article on mobilization in the United States; he was working on another about the war and he hoped to do a few pages of his *Stalin*. A lawyer came to see us; some of the attacks in the pro-Communist press had to be answered at once. After luncheon, I opened the door to his study and saw him in his usual position, bent over papers and magazines, pen in hand. I was glad he was looking so well because he had been suffering earlier from his distressing fainting attacks ... It occurred to me that he was living in a self-imposed prison, like a cloistered monk, but one dedicated to a great struggle ... At about five o'clock we had tea. Twenty minutes later, I saw Leon Davidovich at the bottom of the garden, near the rabbit hutches. He had a visitor with him but I did not recognize him until he came up to me and took off his hat. It was Jacson Mornard. Him again, I thought. Why does he come here so often? (He had been to see us two days before.) "I am terribly thirsty," he said, "could I have a glass of water?" "Wouldn't you like a cup of tea?" "No, I had a late lunch, and I'm full up to here." He pointed to his throat. His face looked green and he seemed singularly nervous. "Why are you wearing your hat and raincoat," I asked, "in such fine weather?" "Because it might rain," he replied absurdly. "And how is Sylvia?" I asked. I could see he had not heard; I had obviously disturbed him by talking about his raincoat. Then he pulled himself together. "Sylvia? Sylvia? She is always well." He drank a glass of water and told me that he had brought an article, typed this time, for Leon Davidovich to see. "That's better," I said. "Leon Davidovich does not like illegible manuscripts."

'A little later, Leon Davidovich and Mornard passed me on the way to the study. Leon Davidovich said to me, "Sylvia is coming, they are leaving for New York tomorrow." I told Leon Davidovich that I had offered the visitor tea but that, as he was not feeling well, he had only wanted a glass of water. Leon Davidovich looked at him closely. "You don't look well. That's not good," he said reproachfully. "Oh, well, are you going to show me your article?" He would much have preferred to stay with his rabbits, but took off his gardening gloves – he was very careful of his hands because the slightest scratch interfered with his writing. I accompanied them as far as the study door.

'Three or four minutes went by. I was in the room next door. There was a terrible piercing cry ... Leon Davidovich appeared, leaning against the door-frame. His face was covered with blood, his blue eyes glittered without his spectacles, and his arms hung limply by his side ... "What has happened," I cried, "what has happened?" I put my arms round him in utter confusion. He answered calmly. "Jacson," he said, as if he had wished to tell me: "Now it is done." I helped him, as he slumped down on the mat on the dining-room floor. "Natasha," he said, "I love you ..." He spoke with an effort and indistinctly, as if in a dream, while I mopped the blood from his face and put ice on the wound in his head. "Get Seva away ... You know ... in there (he pointed towards the study) I thought ... I understood what he wanted to do ... he wanted ... once more ... I didn't let him ..." Jacson Mornard had tried to strike him again but Leon Davidovich had flung himself upon him. There was a note of satisfaction in his low murmur of, "I didn't let him ..." "He must not ...

be ... killed ... he must ... talk," he said slowly, dragging out each word.

'Charlie Cornell, Joe Hansen and Harold Robins had fallen upon the assassin, who cried out, "They made me do it ... They've got my mother ... They have put my mother in prison ..."

'The assassin, who had been sitting on the edge of the table while Leon Davidovich bent over his manuscript, had suddenly pulled out an ice-pick from under his raincoat and had struck him with it ... The trepanning operation revealed a fracture of the right parietal bone, laceration of the meninges, and a wound several centimetres deep in the cerebral matter ...

'A doctor declared that the injury was not very serious. Leon Davidovich listened to him without emotion, as one would to a conventional message of comfort. Pointing to his heart, he said to Joe Hansen in English, "I feel ... here ... that this is the end ... This time ... they've ... succeeded."

'A Green Cross ambulance took us to the city, where the evening lights were already blazing. The siren wailed incessantly. Leon Davidovich's left arm lay immobile and paralysed; his right arm kept making circles in the air ... "How do you feel?" "Better ... better ..." he answered me. At the Green Cross Hospital, the stretcher bearers had to elbow their way through a crowd of curious onlookers. I shivered. They might try to strike at him again here ... A nurse started to cut his grey hair. Leon Davidovich smiled at me and whispered, "You see, here's the barber." We had spoken that day of sending for one ... He called Joe Hansen over and dictated a few words to him; Joe put them down in his notebook. "What did he dictate?" I asked our friend. "Something about French statistics," he said. I thought it very strange ...

'The nurses began to cut his clothes. Suddenly he said to me distinctly but very sadly and gravely, "I don't want them to undress me ... I want you to do it ..." These were his last words to me. I undressed him, and pressed my lips to his. He returned the kiss, once, twice and again. Then he lost consciousness. I spent the whole night by his bedside waiting for him to come round, to come back to life. His eyes were closed and his breathing was sometimes stertorous and sometimes calm. That night and the next day passed without any change. Towards the evening, after the trepanning, the doctors said there was an improvement, but then he started to pant and to gasp for air ... They lifted him up and his head slumped on to his shoulder but his features retained their pride. I was hoping against hope. So often, throughout his life, I had seen him ride out crises, come safely through dangers and hold on when it seemed impossible to do so, that I still believed he could do it again. He would suddenly regain his strength, open his eyes, and take charge of his life again ...

'I was exhausted and dozed off in an armchair. A premonition – or was it some movement? – awoke me. Two doctors in white stood before me. I understood ... Leon Davidovich had died peacefully a moment before, at 7.25 p.m. on August 21st, 1940. He was sixty years old.'

Leon Davidovich Trotsky had devoted a long life of toil, thought and unflinching struggle against inhumanity to the workers' cause. All who knew him realized that he thought of himself as no more than an instrument in the performance of a great historic task, a task he shared with all the socialist masses conscious of the dangers and the opportunities of our age. 'The times are harsh,' he wrote, 'but we have no other country.' His character was whole in the full sense of the word; to him belief and action were one, and he refused to accept that wider ideals, which alone lend meaning and purpose to life, can ever be sacrificed to ephemeral, personal, and pettily selfish ends. His integrity went hand-in-hand with an intelligence that was both objective and passionate and that was always deep, broad, creative and just. Above all, he was simple. In the margin of a book that spoke of his 'will to power', Leon Davidovich wrote the following note: '(Another) wanted power for power's sake. Such ambitions have *always* been alien to me ... I sought power over people's minds and will.' Though he was not unaware of the practical uses of authority he regarded himself as a teacher who showed men the way, not by pandering to their lower instincts, but by appealing to their resolve to create a better society.

Those who tracked him down and killed him, as they had killed the Russian Revolution and martyred the Soviet people, will one day meet their condign punishment. Already they have brought down on the U.S.S.R., weakened by the massacres which went under the name of Stalin's purges, one of the most devastating invasions in recent history. They are following their course to hell ... A few days after Leon Davidovich's death, I wrote the following passage, of which I do not wish to alter a single word: 'Throughout his heroic life, Leon Davidovich believed in the future and in the liberation of mankind. Far from weakening during the last sombre years of his life, his faith grew stronger in the test of experience. When man does away with oppression, he will also do away with violence. That is the faith he has taught me, as he has taught it to so many others.'

Coyoacan
June 1947

Further Details of Trotsky's Death

I. *The last moments*

The chief surgeon was Dr Ruben S. Lenero, working under the supervision of Dr Gustavo Baz, the Mexican Minister of Public Health. Leon Davidovich's powers of resistance were so great that for a short time there was hope that his life might be saved despite the head wound, almost three inches deep, and the rupture of parts of the brain substance.

Joseph Hansen, who scarcely left Trotsky's bedside, claims that Trotsky dictated the following last political message to him: 'Please tell my friends that I am sure of the victory of the Fourth International ... Go forward!'

Leon Davidovich's brain was found to weigh two pounds and thirteen ounces.

The Mexican government took charge of the funeral arrangements. The body, guarded by comrades, lay in state for five days in a hall in the Calle de Tacuba; a hundred thousand people filed past in silent homage.

II. *Trotsky's study after the crime*

Trotsky's study was in a state of chaos after the two hand-to-hand struggles – Leon Davidovich's with the assassin and the assassin's with the young American guards. Death had spread confusion there. The last article on which Trotsky seems to have worked was entitled 'Bonapartism, Fascism and War', from which we have quoted extracts. Several pages of this manuscript lay on the desk. Other pages, part of the Stalin biography, were heavily stained with blood, and a file on the G.P.U. was spattered with it.

271

III. '*Jacson Mornard*'

In addition to the ice-pick hidden under his raincoat, the murderer also carried a dagger and an automatic pistol. Before the attack, he had written – no doubt with his masters – a justification of his action, typed in French, signed simply 'Jac' and dated the day of the murder.

This document, written in typical G.P.U. style, would by itself be enough to prove the complicity of the Soviet secret police. Jacson Mornard wrote: '... I propose to explain to the public my motives in performing this act of retribution ... I am a member of an old Belgian family ... '

Let us dwell on this point for a moment. During the investigation, the murderer claimed that his name was Jacques Mornard Vandendrechd and that he was born in 1904 in Teheran, where his father was Belgian ambassador; that he had been educated at the St Ignatius Loyola College in Brussels and later at the Dixmude Military Academy until 1924. An affidavit by M. Loriden, the Belgian Minister in Mexico, showed that all these claims were false. It should be added that, when Trotsky was murdered, Belgium was under Nazi occupation and that the G.P.U. had every reason to believe that, what with the Molotov–Ribbentrop agreement, this state of affairs would continue indefinitely. The true identity of 'Mornard' was never established. He seemed to know Russian; perhaps he came from the Balkans or was the son of Russian émigrés.

He went on to say that he had studied at the Sorbonne, and that after he had become a Trotskyist in Paris, a leading member of the Fourth International had suggested he go to Mexico, and had supplied him with money and the necessary papers. All this was untrue.

His 'frequent discussions' with L. D. Trotsky (false), had, however, disillusioned him greatly; to his sorrow he had discovered that Trotsky 'was consumed with hatred and a thirst for vengeance' (this is the usual style of the Moscow indictments). Trotsky had urged him 'to go to Russia to organize a series (*sic!*) of attempts against various persons and, in particular, against Stalin ... ' (again the style of the Moscow indictments, but even more absurd). A 'foreign parliamentary committee and a Great Power' would assist him. (What parliamentary committee and which great power?)

Mexico was divided by the coming presidential elections. A party with a reactionary reputation, that of General Almazan, was opposing the Government of President Lazaro Cardenas and the Revolutionary

Mexican Party. In this context, 'Jacson Mornard' said that Trotsky's sympathies were completely on Almazan's side, and that he was likely to be a party to a plot to assassinate Lombardo Toledano and Avila Comacho. (This piece of fiction was obviously intended to sway Mexican opinion against Trotsky. Vicente Lombardo Toledano, the Secretary of the Mexican Federation of Labour, was one of the most active pro-Communists; General Manuel Avila Comacho was later elected President of the Republic.)

Further quotations from the document manufactured by the Soviet secret service were that Trotsky 'detests those members of his own party who do not share his views', that the Trotskyist party was very poor (Moscow must have forgotten its own indictment) and that only the 'consul of the Great Power who calls on Trotsky so often' could answer the question of where the money to fortify Trotsky's house had come from. (Since Jacson Mornard's 'justification' was written while the Hitler–Stalin pact was in force, the consul he had in mind was most likely to have been British or American. There is no need to add that no consul ever visited Trotsky and that this allegation was added for no better reason than that it was part of the usual Moscow line.)

Finally, for the sake of newspaper readers, the murderer-cum-perjurer declared that Trotsky had urged him to leave Sylvia Agelof, whom 'he loved with all his heart' because she was a member of the minority group in the American Trotskyist Party. The assassin's last sentence seems to have been copied straight from Vyshinsky: 'History will vindicate me for having removed the bitter enemy of the working class.'

The murderer, who was also treated at the Green Cross Hospital, though only for contusions, seemed at first to be depressed. According to journalists, he even expressed his regrets. Later, he never ceased to display the greatest composure. Sylvia Agelof, when taken into custody, suffered a nervous breakdown, refused to eat, and said she wanted to die when she learned for the first time that Trotsky was dead, that she herself had been an involuntary accomplice in the crime, and that for years she had been a mere tool in a scoundrel's hands.

'Jacson Mornard' had come to Mexico from the United States with a Canadian passport, once the property of a member of the International Brigade who had been posted missing during the Civil War. In other words, he was part of the same gang of Stalinist criminals as Siqueiros and his accomplices. It is well known that the passports of International Brigade volunteers were seized by the G.P.U. as a matter of course, and that one of these documents had been used by a Soviet spy in the United States. (Report by the Canadian Royal Commission on Soviet espionage, Ottawa, 1946)

It was also known that his masters had sent the murderer to Paris with instructions to worm his way into Trotskyist circles, for reasons he himself did not yet appreciate. Louis Budenz, who had been one of the leaders of the American Communist Party for ten years before he embraced the Catholic faith in 1946, tells us in *This is My Story* that the heads of the American Communist Party, Earl Browder and Jack Stachel, had talked of liquidating Trotsky since the end of 1936, ever since the announcement of Trotsky's impending arrival in Mexico. Budenz also admitted that he had worked for several Soviet secret agents in the U.S.A., one of whom had asked him to find a sympathiser who might be able to introduce another agent to American Trotskyists in Paris. Budenz suggested a Miss Y., probably the Ruby Weill who introduced 'Jacson Mornard' to Sylvia Agelof.

The police dossier bears us out. Under questioning, Sylvia Agelof recalled that she had received a letter from New York and was reading it while her 'husband' was looking over her shoulder. The letter mentioned the actual or supposed arrest of two spies, probably Soviet agents, one of whom was called Stachel. 'Jacson Mornard' gave a start and seemed extremely worried. 'What does it say? Does it mention Stachel?' he asked.

The precise source of the large funds at the assassin's disposal has not been established, but there are fairly reliable indications that he was in touch with Siqueiros.

His general behaviour, his sudden change of mood, his indispositions and his extreme nervousness suggest that his masters had summoned him to the United States soon after the failure of their first attempt on Trotsky's life, and that they had instructed him to make good the omission, probably within a specified period of time.

When he arrived at Coyoacan on August 20th, the murderer took care to park in such a way that, on leaving, he would not have to waste any time turning the car around. His choice of weapon indicated careful premeditation. The murderer hoped to strike his victim down without making a sound; he could then leave the study, tell Leon Davidovich's secretaries that the 'Old Man' did not wish to be disturbed on any account, and make his getaway. In that case, it would have been difficult to prove his guilt, and the Communist and fellow-travelling press would have claimed that the assassination was the work of one of Trotsky's associates.

On April 16th, 1943, 'Jacson Mornard' was found guilty of murder and sentenced to twenty years' imprisonment (Mexico has no capital punishment) by the Fourth Criminal Court of Mexico. The judges – Don Manuel Rivera Vasquez, Don Rafael Garcia de Leon and Don Jose-Maria de la Garza – found that the murder had been premeditated but was not treacherous since the accused had been neither a personal friend nor a political associate of the victim; the court also found that the crime was motivated by self-interest, inasmuch as the murderer had served the Communist cause purely for the sake of the good living it gave him and not for ideological reasons, with which he was not greatly concerned.

In the Penitenciaria de Mexico, the murderer openly and constantly enjoyed the attentions of Communist officials and even of intellectuals known for their attachment to the Party. When interviewed during the war, he regaled the journalists with eulogies of Stalin. He was still able to draw on considerable funds of unspecified origin. In November 1941 plans were laid for his escape, for which purpose, as we are reliably informed, a recent arrival in Cuba from Europe dispensed a very large sum. At the beginning of 1946, such well-informed American journals as *The New Leader* and *Time* stated that a Communist from New York, a woman, was involved in a new plan for the murderer's escape and that the American and Mexican police were taking the necessary precautions.

It seems certain that 'Jacson Mornard', the hireling of the G.P.U., had not the slightest wish to escape because he feared that, if he did, he would never be seen again. There was, of course, a strong possibility that the G.P.U. might try and kill him in gaol once they realized that all escape arrangements must fail – while he was alive the murderer might always decide to talk and hence remained a constant threat to them. In May 1947 the Mexican prison authorities suddenly took stringent security measures to protect and isolate the prisoner. According to the press, a woman doctor, an official of the public health service and a leading member of the Mexican Communist Party, tried to sabotage these measures by fomenting trouble among the prisoners. There were a number of unpleasant incidents and these continued for a week.

IV. *The Siqueiros Affair*

The successful crime overshadowed the crime that had failed but that had claimed the life of young Robert Sheldon Harte. The 'French Jew', the main organizer of the attack of May 24th, 1940, could not, of course, be found. The fact that Sheldon Harte was seen speaking to him, as one of the assailants testified and several others confirmed, suggests that there may have been collusion between the young American and the assassins. The affair has still not been cleared up completely. The known facts can be summed up as follows: (1) Sheldon Harte opened the gate when he heard a familiar voice, which might conceivably have been Jacson Mornard's; (2) he was kidnapped by the raiders or left with them of his own free will; (3) he was killed two days later. Those who knew him were inclined to believe that force was used against him. It is not impossible that a member of the Communist Party had been infiltrated into Trotsky's house, that he should have grown to like Leon Davidovich and that the attack had so obviously troubled him that the gang had to do away with him for their own safety. It was established that he was murdered on a bed purchased by David Alfaro Siqueiros's wife, Angelica Arenal, while accompanied by Antonio Pujol, Siqueiros's confidential secretary. Siqueiros later admitted that he had paid the caretaker of the house. The brothers Luis and Leopoldo Arenal, who were believed to be directly responsible for the crime, escaped arrest.

On October 4th, 1940, David Alfaro Siqueiros and Antonio Pujol were arrested by Colonel Sanchez Salazar at Hostotipaquilla, a village in the State of Jalisco, where the local authorities had protected them. The statements of their underlings bore this out. Siqueiros did not deny the facts; he stated that he no longer belonged to the Communist Party but was considered a sympathiser worthy of its full confidence. He maintained that he had given orders not to kill anybody – all he had wanted was to remove Trotsky's documents. The shooting, his counsel stated, was started purely for its 'psychological effect'. The fact that Leon Davidovich's papers were quite untouched and that some sixty bullets had been fired into the bedroom from all sides did not embarrass the defence in the slightest, since all of it was based on sheer absurdity. Several influential people pleaded for the 'great painter'. On February 14th, 1941, some fifty Mexican and Spanish intellectuals published a petition addressed to the President, General Manuel Avila Camacho, in *El Popular*. The reader might like to look at a few extracts from this piece of special pleading.

The title of the appeal was, 'Independent (*sic!*) intellectuals and artists demand ... justice for Siqueiros.' 'We warmly express our moral support of the great Mexican artist ... David Alfaro Siqueiros's paintings have enhanced Mexico's standing in the world ... We appeal to the court to take into account the transcendental qualities of this artist's work which – we are convinced – must be considered one of the most authentic expressions of our culture ... We admire David Alfaro Siqueiros and, as artists, we declare our solidarity with him ... Inasmuch as all civilized countries look upon artists and scientists as the bulwarks of culture and progress, we demand that David Alfaro Siqueiros be judged in this light.'

Among the documents testifying to the servility of Stalinist 'intellectuals', this diatribe must be one of the most nearly perfect examples. When art becomes a shield for hired thugs, then culture and civilization have indeed fallen to unprecedented depths. For the rest, we know that several of the signatories are now heartily ashamed of their association with this document. This is why we have refrained from mentioning any of them by name.

In April 1941, Siqueiros was released on bail. On May 5th, he and his wife flew to Havana and then moved on to Chile. During the war, he painted some frescoes in Chile and also in Cuba. When he reappeared in Mexico in 1944, the press called for his immediate arrest, but on August 14th, 1945 the evening *Ultima Noticias* explained that the case could not be reopened because the Siqueiros dossier had 'mysteriously disappeared'. A magistrate later told *Tiempo* that Siqueiros had taken advantage of the statute of limitations. On April 23rd, 1947 the daily *Excelsior* published an interview with Siqueiros in which he said, 'I have not denied nor will I ever deny my responsibility in the affair, but I stress that I was acting as an independent agent. I feel obliged to say that I consider my part [in the attack at Coyoacan] one of the most honourable acts of my life.' As far as we know, none of his accomplices was apprehended. The file has not yet been closed.

v. *The organization of the crime*

Leon Davidovich and Natalia Ivanovna had known ever since 1929 that they were living under the constant threat of assassination.

However, in 1929–32, when they stayed in Turkey, Stalin had not yet prepared the ground and Trotsky's murder would have caused an enormous outburst of feeling in the Soviet Union.

The difficulties became even greater in 1933–4 when the U.S.S.R. joined the League of Nations. The Politbureau had to avoid major scandals abroad at all costs, the more so as the Comintern had begun its great flirtation with Western intellectuals interested in the 'defence of culture'.

But once the Moscow trials were over, the assassination of Leon Trotsky became a political no less than a logical necessity. It would have been pointless to shoot scores of thousands of men if the leading light of the revolutionary generation, a man impossible to erase from the pages of history, remained alive and at liberty. No fate was bad enough for one who, in the eyes of those of his compatriots who had been mesmerized by the sham trials, was one of the most diabolical figures in history. The only thing that still stood in the way of Trotsky's immediate assassination was the outcry of foreign socialists and liberals, and the consequent weakening of the Popular Front.

All that changed in August 1939, with the signing of the Hitler–Stalin pact. The U.S.S.R., its 'Leader of genius' and the Comintern had forfeited their reputation in the democratic world, no matter what else they did. And when war was declared, the Politbureau realized that it must act quickly. The greatest and most popular military leader the U.S.S.R. had ever known, the man who had organized the Red Army, had come out strongly and implacably against the Hitler alliance. If Russia were to enter the war on the side of Nazi Germany, Trotskyism would become a grave revolutionary threat, and all those thousands whose consciences were troubled would rally to its defence. If, on the other hand, the U.S.S.R. should find herself at war with Germany, she would suffer enormous reverses, and these, too, might make it appear to the masses that Trotsky had been right all along.

The first attempt on Trotsky's life, though mounted on a large scale, was badly organized. It had all the signs of hasty improvisation but must nevertheless have been planned at least a month or two ahead. Hence the orders for it must have been brought, no doubt by special messenger, in March or April 1940.

When the attack was launched in May 1940 conditions were extremely favourable, for the West was reeling under a series of blows compared with which Trotsky's murder would have seemed a very minor affair. The Nazis were marching from one victory to the next in Europe: Norway, Holland and Belgium fell in quick succession. In June, the French bastion crumbled. There was a growing paralysis of the will. In August, Goering's Luftwaffe began its assault on London. In the U.S.S.R. itself, people felt crushed by the alliance with the Nazis, Hitler's victories and fear of war; nobody would turn a hair if one more crime were committed. The moment had come and must not be allowed to pass. Somebody in the United States received a coded signal. That somebody urgently summoned 'Jacson Mornard', who was probably enjoying his quiet life as an informer and his sinecure in a pleasant land, and told him that the time had come to prove his loyalty by killing before the month was out. 'Jacson Mornard' turned pale and fell ill, but all to no avail. Somebody knew that he had strong nerves; no doubt he had proved it on some other occasion. Vigilant shadows had dogged every footstep; should he falter, he himself would be struck down without fail, to make way for another. He ran a great risk even if he pleased his masters, but there was a chance that he might get off scot-free, since it was an inflexible rule that the apparatus never abandoned its agents, and the totalitarian machine was all-powerful ...

In this reconstruction of the crime, I have relied in no way on speculation but solely on the known facts.

VICTOR SERGE

INDEX